READING LESSONS IN SEEING

Reading Lessons in Seeing

Mirrors, Masks, and Mazes in the
Autobiographical Graphic Novel

Michael A. Chaney

University Press of Mississippi / Jackson

www.upress.state.ms.us

The University Press of Mississippi is a member
of the Association of American University Presses.

First printing 2016

∞

Library of Congress Cataloging-in-Publication Data

Names: Chaney, Michael A., author.
Title: Reading lessons in seeing : mirrors, masks, and mazes in the
autobiographical graphic novel / Michael A. Chaney.
Description: Jackson : University Press of Mississippi, 2017. | Includes
bibliographical references and index.
Identifiers: LCCN 2016034588 (print) | LCCN 2016057481 (ebook) | ISBN
9781496810250 (hardback) | ISBN 9781496810267 (epub single) | ISBN
9781496810274 (epub institutional) | ISBN 9781496810281 (pdf single) |
ISBN 9781496810298 (pdf institutional)
Subjects: LCSH: Graphic novels—History and criticism. | Biography as a
literary form. | Autobiography in literature. | Popular culture and
literature. | Comic books, strips, etc.—History and criticism. | BISAC:
LITERARY CRITICISM / Comics & Graphic Novels. | SOCIAL SCIENCE / Popular
Culture. | LITERARY CRITICISM / Semiotics & Theory.
Classification: LCC PN6714 .C43 2017 (print) | LCC PN6714 (ebook) | DDC
791.5/35—dc23
LC record available at https://lccn.loc.gov/2016034588

British Library Cataloging-in-Publication Data available

CONTENTS

LIST OF ILLUSTRATIONS

ACKNOWLEDGMENTS

I'd like to thank the participants of the Illustration, Comics, and Animation Conference at Dartmouth College and the Festival of Cartoon Art directed by Jared Gardner at the Ohio State University, where I enjoyed significant and generous feedback from Julia Watson, Frederik Byrn Køhlert, José Alaniz, Ian Gordon, Charles Hatfield, Rebecca Wanzo, Damian Duffy, Henry Jenkins, John Jennings, Barbara Postema, Isaac Cates, Andy Kunka, Qiana Whitted, Brian Cremins, Shane Denson, Daniel Stein, Christina Meyer, Christopher Lehman, and Matthias Harbeck. I'd also like to thank James Sturm and Steve Bissette and many of their students at the Center for Cartoon Studies in White River Junction, a hometown mecca for comics; special thanks to Nicole Georges and Nikolaus Gulacsik, who helped to make crossover pedagogies possible. I also want to thank the English Department of Dartmouth College for sponsoring a seminar that enabled me to present work next to Hillary Chute, whose influence on the present volume has been pervasive and salutary. Thanks to my dear and inspiring colleagues George Edmondson, Tommy O'Malley, Don Pease, Pat McKee, Barbara Will, Andrew McCann, Colleen Boggs, Aimee Bahng, Aden Evens, Jeff Sharlett, Soyica Colbert, Bed Giri, Shalene Vasquez, and Gretchen Gerzina, many of whom not only politely suffered my relentless catechizing about comics but also read through drafts and gave plentiful insights. And, finally, I have been so grateful for the decade-long opportunity of teaching this material to relentlessly curious students who know all too well the contours and cadences of the arguments at the heart of this book and the curricula whereof it speaks. This is for them and (as always) Sara and Heike.

READING LESSONS IN SEEING

INTRODUCTION

The Pupil as Pupil, Or the
Instructional Unconscious of Comics

> The denotation of the drawing is less pure than that of the photograph, for there is no
> drawing without style. Finally, like all codes, the drawing demands an apprenticeship.
> —Barthes "Rhetoric of the Image" (43)

I n *Understanding Comics* (1993), Scott McCloud's enduring primer, comics are given a history going all the way back to cave drawings and hieroglyphic scrolls. What connects sequential sketches from antiquity to the Sunday funnies for McCloud is their unparalleled capacity to instruct and edify. The thesis of the present book, that comics—autobiographical ones in particular—teach their viewers how they ought to be read, may seem inaudible next to McCloud's robust applause for the medium's abilities to educate and to lure us into the willing position of apprentice (to borrow from Barthes in the epigraph above). But in spite of all those how-to manuals in the comics form in print and online—like those found in boxes of mass-produced furniture, breaking down the assembly process step-by-step, or tucked away behind airline seats in case of emergency—popular sentiment lags behind McCloud in casting sequential narrative in the role of teacher. Take, for example, the recent hubbub over the Ph.D. student whose Education dissertation at Columbia's prestigious Teacher's College is illustrated as a comic book. It is the latest in a long history of denigrative sensationalism, stoking the public imaginary whenever attempts to elevate comics threaten their association with all things juvenile—a crucial aspect of the form's ethos as teacher, which receives its own chapter here.

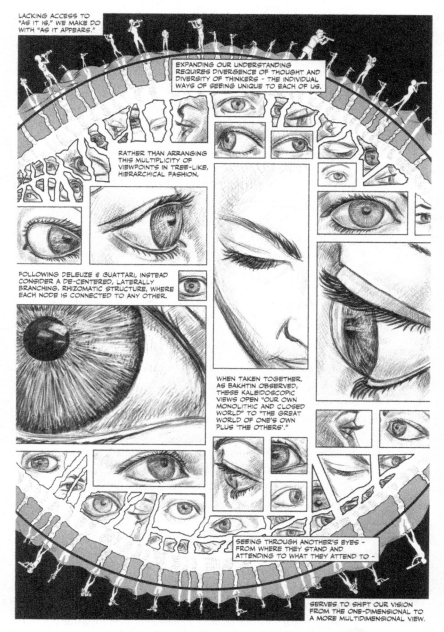

Intro.1 From the dissertation of Nick Sousanis.

Sydni Dunn's 2014 article on Nick Sousanis, "The Amazing Adventures of the Comic-Book Dissertator," appeared in the *Chronicle of Higher Education* and aroused considerable feedback in online comments. In addition to quoting former MLA president Sidonie Smith on expanding modes of academic communication and hailing the digital as the new frontier of scholarly exchange, Dunn's article goes on to bemoan the logistical snafu that unconventional dissertations entail, leaving aside (problematically) the conceptual challenge that Sousanis and his reflective work raises. "The visual system is really powerful," Sousanis is quoted as saying, "I don't think of this work as illustration. Rather than illustrating things, the images and the composition are the thinking."

More than an exposition, the page Sousanis creates *is* the thinking. No mere system of thought, in other words, comics are not just the direct object of cognition. For Sousanis and for my own approach to *autography*—Gillian Whitlock's term for autobiographical comics—the panels are the thinking.[1] Full stop. And yet it is with some difficulty that we grasp that bold equivalence. For if comics are the thinking and not merely a format or forum for thinking, what then becomes of writing—that *other* mediating system once championed for its nearly perfect simulation of cognitive interiority?

We need only to glance at Sousanis's panels to ascertain the ocularcentric root of the paradigm shift. Their theoretical captions about vision are as aware of the etymology of *theory* (a way of seeing) as are the many drawings of anatomical eyes. Thinking and seeing intermingle in Sousanis's panels, which become synecdochic reflections—we might surmise—of comics *tout court*. Such a conclusion would not be news to readers of Michel Foucault, theorist of the panopticon as a model for modernity's evolving dynamics of identity and power; or John Berger, the acclaimed author of *Ways of Seeing* (1977) who popularized a gendered understanding of gazing relations; or W. J. T. Mitchell, whose critical oeuvre helps us to see the cultural and theoretical pantomime of images, including their desires; or Kaja Silverman, who unveils through psychoanalysis the pervasive intrusions of culture and gender into the domain of the image.[2] Nor are those theories to be construed apart from the contexts that produce them. After all, the disembodied vocality of print no longer defines thought in action, in part due to the anti-Emersonian ascent of modernity's non-transparent eyeball and postmodernism's ecstasy of the utterly fragmented optic systems that both capture and get captured by subjects. Indeed, this optic engulfment of consciousness and cognition may be seen as one symptom of a larger condition—of post-late capitalism, the global centralization of the digital cloud, and the transformation of information into visual databits, gifs, and streams, not to mention the rise of object-oriented ontologies and economic network theories of relation. But it would be peremptory for us to dismiss the union of comics and cognition on the basis of its novelty or historical resonances—that it is, in other words, merely the shibboleth of the moment, a passing critical fad. Instead, I want to linger over this claim, saturating it in its historical moment while questioning its implications. What happens when we posit comics or its subgenre of autography as consonant with epistemology? What does it mean to study comics as the thinking?

For some, the epistemology of comics turns on the pivot of the form's braiding together of words and pictures—what many comics scholars describe as a formal hybridity. In this regard, Scott McCloud points out that while words and pictures function, on the one hand, like partners in a dance—"and each one takes turns leading" (156)—on the other hand, comics also work to unify symbol systems, eradicating the volatile détente of words and pictures to render irrelevant all such metaphors that hierarchize the word-image relationship in terms of leaders and followers.[3] More recently, celebrations of the dialectical, anti-dualistic affordances of comics convene under the banner of multimodal literacy, and comics have had no dearth of supporters carrying that standard. Gunther Kress has been outspoken in his push for scholars of social semiotics to adopt frameworks for addressing the combinatory nature of media, what he refers to as multimodality. With van Leeuwen, Kress defines multimodality as "the use of several semiotic modes in the design of a semiotic product or event, together with the particular way in which the modes are combined" (20). Throughout his prolific career, Kress has drawn attention to the social resources that fund meaning-making in an increasingly digital and visual age of communication. His critics, however, have noted Kress's insistence on the visual as a clue to the incompleteness of his notion of multimodality. Paul Prior, for instance, has complained of the rigidly binaric quality of Kress's treatment of words and images: "Words in his account are finite, sequential, vague, conventional, authored, narrative and/or causal, and open to critique. Images are infinite, spatial, specific, natural and transparent, viewed, and available only for design" (26).

Despite this tendency to compartmentalize media, Kress's semiotic theory of multimodality has achieved a relative degree of acceptance among comics scholars, who by virtue of the intersectional mediation of their objects of analysis have been working under a tacit theory of comics multimodality in the US since the first commentaries of the *Yellow Kid* at the dawn of the twentieth century. In *Graphic Encounters* (2013), Dale Jacobs relies on Kress and other New London school theorists to demonstrate the pitfalls of reading comics as a debased form of print literacy, rather than as a rich, multimodal environment for meaning: "[T]he key to reading the comic lies in going beyond the way we make meaning from the words alone and considering visual, gestural, and spatial elements" (14). Doing so, according to Jacobs, ultimately emphasizes the reader's agency in helping to complete the thinking that comics might be doing: "Every act of creating meaning from a multimodal text, happening as it does at the intersection of structure and agency, thus contributes to the ongoing process of becoming a multimodally literate person" (17).

Interestingly, even when comics matriculate from the status of degraded print forms of textuality to occupy a valorized site of the multimodal, they continue to produce exactly what nineteenth-century advocates of literary education espoused for the novel—a subject cultivated by reading to participate in the then-novel forms of bourgeois humanism, commodity culture, and democratic citizenship. So, it would seem, that although we have renamed the school and the curriculum, we continue to graduate the same types of pupils. From one angle, the new multimodal literacy operates just as the old one did to form and reform the human. More significantly, the singular object of either view posits an inherently pedagogical comics form.

It is the purpose of *Reading Lessons in Seeing* to analyze that pedagogy in graphic memoir's recurring tropes or lessons about mirrors, the child, the puzzle, artisanal labor, and history. These are but the usual modules in a curricula standard to the form. By *form*, I want to insist on the method rather than the content of the comics, and so I shall sometimes make claims not strictly limited to autobiography.[4] Nevertheless, the autobiographical dimension of comics has had an astonishing cultural reception, jettisoning several now-canonized texts by Art Speigelman, Marjane Satrapi, Alison Bechdel, and others to international approbation and causing no small amount of critical ink to be spilled as well. It is largely because of the firm ground established by so many critics and scholars on the nature of the medium when used as a means of life writing that I am able to build this critical study in the way that I have, relying, for example, on the foundational work of Joseph Witek's *Comic Books as History* (1989) and Charles Hatfield's *Alternative Comics* (2005), as well as special issues of *Modern Fiction Studies* (2006) and *Biography Studies* (2008). All of these pre-texts liberate the study of comics from the drudgeries of legitimization that burdened comics scholarship in the '80s and '90s. And thanks to the prodigious scholarly efforts of Hillary Chute in *Graphic Women* (2010) and Elisabeth El Refaie in *Autobiographic Comics* (2012), along with recent critical collections devoted to autobiography—Jane Tolmie's *Drawing from Life* (2013) and my own *Graphic Subjects* (2010)—the need for remedial discussions of the conjunction of autobiography and the comics form diminishes, allowing, I hope, for the extra critical slack required to re-theorize that conjunction.

In *How Our Lives Become Stories* (1999), Paul John Eakin reminds us that the authorial subject of autobiography is already a relational complexity, defying normative presumptions about it being singular: "We tend to think of autobiography as a literature of the first person, but the subject of autobiography to which the pronoun 'I' refers is neither singular nor first, and we do well to demystify its claims" (43). Further demystifications come in the prolific and pioneering work of Sidonie Smith and Julia Watson, who in their introduction to *Interfaces: Women, Autobiography, Image, Performance* (2003) scrutinize women's *künstlerroman* (artists' life writing) to enumerate the various ways autobiographical subjects become visual presences in their texts:

> four primary ways in which artists may texture the interface to mobilize visual and textual regimes: (1) *relationally*, through parallel or interrogatory juxtaposition of word and image; (2) *contextually*, through documentary or ethnographic juxtaposition of word and image; (3) *spatially*, through palimpsestic or paratextual juxtaposition of word and image; and (4) *temporally*, through telescoped or serial juxtaposition of word and image. (21)

Smith and Watson's regimes locate the contours of my own elaboration of the comics' ubiquitous "mirror moment" (as explained in Chapter One), in which drawn avatars of autobiographers become generically and—given autobiography's contractual pact with readers—juridically coextensive with the "I" of comics' captions.

These and other adjustments to Philippe Lejeune's famous contract, stipulating that the authorial voice of autobiography be the fusion of author, protagonist, and narrator, also impact the scholarship of Timothy Dow Adams and Linda Haverty Rugg.[5] In their different but equally path-finding insights, Adams and Rugg theorize the convergence of photographs and autobiography. The comics' emphasis on drawing rather than photography inversely orients us to the feeble analogy Adams intends to break in *Light Writing and Life Writing* (1999): "The relationship between the two media could be expressed in an analogy: painting is to fiction as photography is to nonfiction" (11). The impossibility of such a scandal of realism or "truth" in comics does not necessarily free the medium from similar hang-ups of representation, as shown in the I-conicization of drawn subjects during mirror scenes. The one that opens Lynda Barry's *One Hundred Demons* (2004) features a taxonomic blurring of autobiography and fiction in the caption that reads: "Is it autobiography if parts of it are not true?/Is it fiction if parts of it are?" However, that enunciation is perhaps less crucial than the visual one being expressed in the panel's depiction of *mise en abyme* (a picture-within-the-picture), which Hillary Chute in *Graphic Women* also notices: "In pointing to this act of physical creation across the gutter, the sequence highlights the meaning of 'fiction'—and also autobiography, too, she here implies—as the material process of making" (109). *Reading Lessons in Seeing* shall demonstrate that the meaning of autography and the comics form are also at stake in such moments. Part of the lesson has to do with the visually instantiated autobiographical subject, which Linda Rugg describes in *Picturing Ourselves* (1997) as "a visualization of the decentered, culturally constructed self; and it asserts the presence of a living body through the power of photographic referentiality" (19). Tweaking the statement to match the comics medium raises questions which the ensuing chapters pursue regarding the oddly comparable power of referentiality of non-realistic drawing as opposed to photographs. Readers of comics memoir must therefore overlay Lejeune's autobiographical contract onto fiction's willing suspensions of disbelief.

Moreover, *Reading Lessons in Seeing* coincides with Susanna Egan's response to the inherently refractive nature of autobiographical authority in *Mirror Talk* (1999) by starting with the same ubiquitous correspondence of subjectivity and the trope of the mirror that causes Egan to speculate how "autobiographers have always wrestled with the split between subject and object, between writing and written selves, seeing the very act of autobiography as present 'reflection' on the past" (11). The result is a specular subject of autobiography that becomes many orders more specular when illustrated as the narrating "I" of autography. These generic instabilities are the perfect textual laboratories for conducting experiments in trauma representation and exhibiting fragmented identity as crises of perception and psyche. And few scholarly works are as enduringly cogent on the interrelation of trauma and autobiography as Leigh Gilmore's *The Limits of Autobiography* (2001), which contends: "Texts that are concerned with self-representation and trauma offer a strong case for seeing that in the very condition of autobiography (and not the obstacles it offers for us to overcome) there is no transparent language of identity despite the demand to produce one" (24). Indeed, Gilmore's reasoning explains why artists who have suffered trauma would be drawn to such a medium in the first place: "[P]art of what we must call healing lies in the assertion of creativity" (24).

While the study of autography benefits from the findings of these eminent scholars of autobiography, one may readily see how aspects specific to the form complicate any such thing as autobiographical authority and enable productive variations on the theme of the split or fragmented subject. These variations have not gone unnoticed by comics scholars attentive to the iconic multiplicity of autographic authority whose implications are succinctly described by Elisabeth El Refaie: "[T]he requirements to produce multiple drawn versions of one's self necessarily involves an intense engagement with embodied aspects of identity, as well as with the sociocultural models under-pinning body image" (4). Nor has the thinking that comics do gone unclas-sified. Forceful recapitulations of the cognitive emphases comics place on simultaneity and the tensions between single image decoding and narrative processes of closure, sequence, and causation occur in a number of critical sources (by Will Eisner, Scott McCloud, Roger Sabin, Thierry Groensteen, Jared Gardner, and others). Exactly how autobiographical comics press these lessons upon readers as part of their ontology of visual didacticism, however, has received less attention.

As an introductory poster session on the reading lessons that comics make possible, let us turn to a patently non-autobiographical example, David Maz-zucchelli's *Asterios Polyp* (2009). Mazzucchelli's graphic narrative is driven by the same question that animates *Reading Lessons in Seeing*: How does the way one sees the world affect the world that one sees? And, tangential to that palindrome, how is it possible to transmit interiority visually, or symbolically, in the presence of conflicting, often contradictory points of view? The answer, as we shall see, lies in the text's formalistic tutorials in seeing.

The main character, Asterios, is a twin obsessed with duality who, as we learn, has videotaped portions of his life to artificially replicate his doubling. If that were not enough to convince even the most inattentive reader of Maz-zucchelli's pedagogical agenda, there are further depths to the character and story—postmodern, mythological, and self-consciously literary depths—and it is the reader's burden as well as her prerogative (with all implications of play and desire intended) to plumb them. Within just a few pages, the graphic novel offers us a plunger: Asterios's monograph, *Modernism with a Human Face*, a tome so heavy the winged cherubs lofting it up to the clouds are vis-ibly wincing and sweating under its heft. An overlapping triptych beneath the book on the same page positions the viewer among the sleepy generations of Asterios's students. The only speech visible from the most contemporary version of our soporific pontificator invites us to apply the dualities between the Apollonian and the Dionysian tendencies in Asterios's lecture and book to the graphic novel through which Mazzucchelli mediates them: "Thus, we see the Apollonian—as opposed to the Dionysian—tendencies expressed via . . ." Much hangs in the balance of those ellipses, much more than merely the effect of our drifting beyond a dull talk that drones on in its own empaneled past time. On a formal level, that page is like the students' flagging attention:

it wants desperately to be turned. But there is still plumbing for us to do in the gutters of those ellipses, clogging forward momentum.

A moment like this takes on inflated pedagogical meaning after repeated exposure. In it, we are cautioned about the philosophical vantages of our seeing. Verbal evidence for the ostensible dominance of one visual aesthetic over its supposed counterpart gets lost in the ellipses—"tendencies expressed via . . ." Just how and where the Apollonian supersedes the Dionysian eludes comprehension, so long as we search for clarity in the alphabetic. Weary perhaps of not finding it there, we might turn the page in order to escape sleepy identification with Asterios's students, but we would miss a more intriguing plot that develops were we to do so. At this moment of reading and seeing instruction, the lecturing text plays a favorite trump card of the comics. Our assumed reliance upon printed language fails us, deliberately so. For it is not in words but in pictures, and better yet, in their frequently antagonistic resonance, where we must go for semiotic plenitude, the whole picture. Although such thinking has become nearly formulaic for understanding the word-image relations in comics, the *thinking* that these relations *do* goes unexamined. We seem to lack a language for talking about this meta-layer of comics thinking.

Asterios Polyp, on the other hand, has no difficulty articulating the ineffable. Mazzucchelli's text exhibits fluency with abstraction, paradox, and the palpable significance of omission. In the final pages of the graphic novel, Asterios loses his wife, his vehicle, and an eye, but perseveres in his odyssey through a snowstorm to rediscover Hana, his estranged beloved. Whereas earlier panels of the couple stress their dichotomy, these panels highlight their resolution even at the atmospheric or stylistic level of color. Gone are the stiff cyan pencil lines that compose Asterios and his unyielding sense of the cold geometry of the world. Gone are the crimson hues that sketch Hannah's emotionality, her warm uncertainty. In their place is a chromatic plenitude of brown, green, and orange. These richer colors tell a story, a journey from primary separation to tertiary wholeness. The same story imbues the narrative with its heavy-handed references to Platonic ideals in Hana's sculpture or in the subplot of Asterios's twin Ignazio.

With one eye overlarge and blank, Asterios embodies the sudden liberation from a binocular view of the world to a monocular one. Instead of eliminating depth, this change announces his release from a crippling philosophical orientation towards duality as a psycho-cognitive fixation. Thus ridded of his physiognomic capacity for a parallax view, Asterios seems able to achieve with Hana the very human depth that binocularity was supposed to afford. Only here, at the end, can Asterios come to her, like Noguchi the dead cat that Hana eulogizes for going to her while it was dying "like he was trying

Intro.2 Meteoric ending of *Asterios Polyp*. Illustrations from *Asterios Polyp* by David Mazzucchelli. Copyright © 2009 by David Mazzucchelli. Used by permission of Pantheon Books, an imprint of the Knopf Doubleday Publishing Group, a division of Random House LLS. All rights reserved.

to comfort *me*" (emphasis in original). These final intimacies are heightened by Mazzucchelli's composition of the entangling tails of their speech bubbles (formerly another instantaneously recognizable difference between them). With their hands nearly touching on the couch, the two enjoy the tranquility of a self-conscious ending. The graphic novel is so anxious about the end that it includes a scene of their two faces, speaking the words "rest in peace" in a conjoined speech balloon that is doubly framed: it is rectangular (as are all of Asterios's balloons) as well as circular (as are all of Hana's). But while the framing of the balloon fuses the two distinct styles, the lettering of "rest in peace" is in an altogether new style, a *tertium quid* of script not seen before in the text.

All omens presage the doom that comes after a few more pages and a series of three exterior shots of the cabin in the woods, pictured farther away with each iteration. In the first of the three panels, we know by virtue of the balloon shape and font style that Hana says "this is nice" followed by Asterios's rectangular reply of "what's that noise?" One more page-turn reveals a two-page spread of a fiery meteor on a crash course for our couple's serene cabin.

That two-page spread conveys one ending of *Asterios Polyp*. It is an apocalypse that has been heralded by the symbolic crater at the middle of the book, which is both a literal and symbolic *aporia* calling attention to all the other gaps in the text. One earlier breach that this one recalls punctuates Asterios's encounter with Spotty Drizzle, or Steven, at the diner, in which the doomsday prognosticator informs the group of an asteroid "a few years ago, one about the size of a house [that] whipped past us—just sixty thousand miles from Earth—and nobody saw it till the day before!" As if to ensure that readers will not miss this cue of instruction, Mazzucchelli brings us in close on the oracle's perspiring face: "Somebody's gotta be prepared. Somebody's gotta be on the lookout." As readers of this narrative, we ought to be that "somebody." To be satisfactory pupils of Mazzucchelli's lesson, we must become lookouts, cautious watchers of the stars.

Of course, we are never without embedded models in these reading lessons. The two-page meteorite spread is only the penultimate ending. The actual conclusion comes after a chapter heading of a tree house illuminated in yellow and purple, colors used throughout for significant subplots. In a mere eight panels, this ultimate ending shows Jackson, a young boy, witnessing a shooting star. His father, Stiff, and mother, Ursula, instruct him to "make a wish," while cuddling in the background. The final images move the viewer farther and farther into space, until the last stand-alone panel of a distant shooting star. The heuristic questions posed by the sequence are: Is this shooting star that the boy sees sequentially and therefore ironically related to the flaming mass glimpsed a few pages before? Or is it less chronologically specific, of another time? Is young Jackson glimpsing the faint beginnings of what will become the catastrophic fireball? Or does the shooting star have far less to do with the fireball diegetically? Whatever our path to resolution, we must cede textual ground to the narrative emphasis on finality (the chromatic fusion) and death ("rest in peace" and Noguchi), mandating apocalypse.

Beyond the narrative proper, however, these endings are like final exams in duality. A likely essay question might take up the conundrum of parallax vision with which this and many other graphic novels—most notably, *Watchmen* (1987) and *American Born Chinese* (2006)—seek to educate and perplex their reader-viewers. In a parallax view, the ball on fire is no meteorite but an asteroid, passing very close to the Earth, perhaps, but far enough away to be seen as a shooting star from other vantages. The inexplicable remainder of this interpretation is the reason for Asterios's question: "What's that noise?" We only retrospectively assume that sound to be the atmosphere-ripping descent of the fireball. It could be a red herring of unknowability, little more than Mazzucchelli's version of muttering "Rosebud." The sound could be the novelty of silence between the couple, perceived suddenly as its opposite. It could be just one more question of the many that this more conversational

Asterios asks of Hana—How come you're still single? Is this yours? Where's Noguchi? Here, he asks more questions than he does anywhere else in the novel. Another interpretation is supernatural, mythological. It could be that he is hearing the asteroid that little Jackson sees as a shooting star, a power he may have acquired now that he and Hana have ascended to the Shamanic level Ursula mentions of the four sexes, the female men and the masculine women who trouble the familiar dichotomous gendering that results not only in "a lot of misery in the world" but in the "kind of simplistic thinking that creates fanatics."

The point in all of this sequentializing of the fireball's impact is that it is difficult not to read the scene through a predictable set of closures. It is hard not to see the fireball as a meteorite about to kill Hana and Asterios. Yet it is still harder to make such an ending compatible with the actual one we get of Jackson's shooting star. And, what is more, the parallax view of the end of all things is not just visual. In the graphic novel's generic metonymy of sight and thought, precept and concept, these two views are also divided worldviews. Whether asteroid or meteor or, most complexly, their unsteady coalescence, opposing philosophies come to occupy the same uncertain space of possibility in the text, rubbing shoulders nervously during the text's perilous heat re-entry into meaning. As with *Jimmy Corrigan the Smartest Kid on Earth* (2000), *Persepolis* (2003), and *Fun Home* (2006), by the end of this graphic novel, the only certainty able to withstand the text's relentless flicker is a lesson of visual pedagogy so essential to the form: to make *seeing* relativity and *being toward* it the same thing.

Although there are phenomenological as well as other theoretical implications to this idea, as I hope my language suggests, the lesson of being the same as one's seeing is not always complicated in the comics. Indeed, comics require that readers become viewers and that the transformation be as automatic as possible. What is unique to autography, however, is the linkage of image and sequentiality to iconic identity, for which reader-viewers, as will be shown, receive the most rigorous instruction.

The parallax relay of meaning in *Asterios Polyp* allegorizes a preoccupation of *Reading Lessons in Seeing* with the duplicities that comics perpetrate. The two opposed views, a pure ambivalence, appear in the first two panels of *Persepolis*, not only in the dichotomous author "I"-con imaged there, but also in the sequential logic of identity correspondingly established. As with the opening lynching scene of *Incognegro* (2008)—or the plethora of mirror scenes where avatars look at themselves at the start of a graphic narrative or even on covers, such as the image of Julie Doucet at her desk from *My New York Diary* (1999)—all are lessons in seeing, in part, because they occur so early on. These scenes initiate us to the rules and physics of the visual worlds they permit us to enter. Coming early allows them to function axiomatically, allowing for applications of the lessons they foster. And yet this simple process of the early lesson followed by later applications also reinforces a complex principle of sequentiality elsewhere violated in the same texts. Though etiological and concatenative, this sequential model of visual reading and learning is no prescription for linearity, which the comics break with all the time. Rather, it is another way of thinking sequence.

In other words, it is neither the fireball nor the shooting star that the structure forces us to choose between but instead their flicker. Irreducibility itself is the apocalyptic point. Comics harbor word-image tensions that facilitate and perhaps demand concomitant ambivalences of theme and trope. It is for this reason that the most celebrated examples of the medium (mostly autographic) are so prodigiously appointed with mirrors, masks, and the trope of *mise en abyme*. These optic doublings compel reader-viewers to think twice about the drawings and their suspicious claims to representational authority (as opposed to, say, photographs). In autography, the divergence from realism that every recognizable drawing communicates is harnessed persistently to mirror scenes as well as to other manifestly "primal scenes," to borrow a term from psychoanalysis. A destabilizing capacity for caricature and the grotesque is thus accorded to visualizations of autobiographical identity, "I"-cons, whether drawn as cartoons, elves, or the child that once was. It is for the same reason that comics simultaneously extol and exile their affinities with children and childishness. In both cases, formal instabilities get expressed at the tropological level, twinning the structural and the metaphorical, binding form to content. The same could be said of the iconic identities that proliferate in autographic texts—the many mirrored selves, picaros, picture-puzzlers, *künstlerromanic* laborers, and biographers of trauma at the center of the present investigation. All are ciphers of an essential split, like the picture puzzle of yin-yang examined below, that autography not only wants but has to tell us about in order for our reading to become seeing in the metaphysical sense, the precondition for objects of illustration and spectacle to achieve any precious semblance of being.

But, while *Reading Lessons in Seeing* shall seek to realize that idyll of interpretive integration, where the meteor and asteroid of comics instability collide, it also proceeds critically and dialogically in conversation with psychoanalysis, political theory, visual cultural studies, narratology, and philosophy. The aim throughout is to show how comics make abstractions of identity visible. In fact, they make them material. By instructing us in "reading" its tropes, the comics form carries out major and minor acts of hypostatization.

In rebellion against the evanescence of verisimilitude, comics want to be tangible and so they teach us at every turn how to see and think that they are.

The first chapter, "Mirror, Mask, and *Mise en Abyme* in Autobiographical Graphic Novels," theorizes the form of autobiographical graphic novels as well as their formal unconscious. Scanning a number of mirror moments that predominate autography, this chapter argues that mirrors in the comics mark "failed encounters with the real." Graphic novels like Laurie Sandell's *Imposter's Daughter* (2009), James Kochalka's *American Elf* (2004), and Marjane Satrapi's *Persepolis* hinge on tensions between the cartoonish and the cathartic. They propose graphic memoir to be epistemologically moored to anxieties that plague not just authorial self-portraiture (what this chapter theorizes as the I-con) but also representations of ontology (separating the drawn from that which is drawn from life). Apart from precipitating catharsis and cathexis, the comics' mirror also does reflective work outside of diegetic stories (as do masks), forcing reader-viewers to revise their assumptions about any text's capacity to reflect reality. What autography trains readers to recognize, then, is the comics' superior capacity to hint at what Jacques Lacan has called the Real as perhaps no other medium can by normalizing its ruptures of visibility. This chapter begins by arguing that the gutter separating the first two panels of *Persepolis* is a mirror and a *mise en abyme*. This initiatory gutter urges readers to apprehend a central fantasy underwriting *Persepolis*—that Marji's split identity is a marker not solely of individuality but of the Real, which from a Lacanian perspective encompasses Marji's terror of being identified by her separation from origins, ideals, and others. The focus on the mirror is developed as the chapter turns to analyze *American Elf* and the way Kochalka's I-con acquires the symbolic potential to express an impossible relation to itself. Once again, the mirror is shown to be autography's metonym for a spatial fantasy of an enclosed self-referentiality. There, whatever Kochalka's elf is meant to represent undergoes narcissistic multiplication and amplification. The chapter closes somewhat as it begins, by doggedly tracing the significance of mirrors to autographic subjects—in Sandell's *Imposter's Daughter* and David B.'s *Epileptic* (2005).

Having surveyed the deep structure of autographic identity formation in the first chapter, Chapter Two, "The Child in and as the Comics," interrogates one of the comics' most prevalent masks—the child, the default face of American comics. This chapter historicizes a range of comics children to argue that, regardless of the graphic novel's recent cultural pretensions, the child is a resilient emblem of the comics and its mediation. This is not to say that the medium is *essentially* juvenile, only that it signifies as such (regardless of content) due to formalistic, historical, and even phenomenological liaisons with *imaginary* children. This chapter locates both the espousal and the denial of the child in (and as) the comics in the picaresque workings of Richard Outcault's early twentieth-century strip *Yellow Kid*, which today's iconic child extends. And, as my analysis of Joe Sacco's *Palestine* (1993) will demonstrate, the child in the comics points to a juvenile function in even the most serious of graphic novels. The primary forms of this function organize later sections on the prophetic child in Kyle Baker's *Nat Turner* (2008), the queer child in Ariel Schrag's *Awkward* (1995), and the melancholic child in Chris Ware's *Jimmy Corrigan*. The purpose is to track the ways that childhood engages the form—that is to say, appearing before us as an effect of our successful training in dialogical reading and seeing, the curriculum inherent to every comic.

Chapter Three, "Picture Games in Story Frames and the Play Spaces of Autography," explores puzzles and other ludic devices in *Epileptic, Cancer Vixen* (2006), and *Fun Home*. The investigation builds upon the preceding analyses of I-cons and formal juvenility to understand the tendency in some autography for picture puzzles, labyrinths, and matching exercises. Offering more of a case study than previous chapters, this chapter worries over a single, arresting moment of narrative rupture in David B.'s *Epileptic*, in which a caption bids readers to play: "Here's a little game, dear reader. In the drawing below, can you tell the Yin elements from the Yang ones?" (49). The image attached to the caption is thereby transformed into a visual puzzle. Narrative space cedes authority to what I shall call the *ludic* spaces of play that overtake mimesis, reading, and narrative. As the story disintegrates, so too must the reader change, becoming a player or user according to new protocols of interactivity. This chapter measures such ludic intermissions for their revealing interference and for the ways that they expose the narrative logics of autographical identity by suspending them. It is my contention that temporary shifts in textual authority give rise to deeper shifts in the constitutive epistemological terms of our reading and seeing. As we shall see, these shifts to the ludic give rise to tactile "reading" experiences that lay bare graphic memoir's investments in embodiment and materiality.

Moving directly from the realization at the end of Chapter Three, that the labor of the artisan is partly what the puzzle conceals and articulates by turns, Chapter Four investigates "The Work Behind the Work of Graphic *Künstlerroman*." In particular, it probes self-portraiture in contemporary graphic novels to find them opposing the standard theoretical skepticism regarding the viability of cognitive mapping, or the ability to plot oneself in a social order defined by the dizzying phenomenal arrangements of late capitalism. Autobiographical comics proclaim artists to be self-mappable in tableaus of artists hard at work, reclaiming the labor that ought to be alienated from them according to a Marxist perspective. Drawing performs peculiar reclamatory labor in Julie Doucet's cover image of *My New York Diary* (1999), resembling two types of the medieval colophon: one showing scribes and illuminators busy at work, making the very text we hold in our hands, and the other showing them transfixed in spiritual rapture. Doucet's colophonic cover, with its object world run amok, invests in a fantasy of artistic self-representation that is replicated in David Small's *Stitches* (2009). Indeed, Small's traumatic experiences at the hands of his sadistic father (not to mention his traumatic reaction to the hidden sexuality of his mother) become the Oedipal fodder spinning the engine of his drive to become an artist, a figure who seems able to process psychic disturbance even while escaping it. That Small becomes a triumphant artist also aligns *Stitches* with the tradition of the *künstlerroman*, or narratives of the artist's development. This chapter closes by analyzing the ways that artistic escape and expressivity produce narrative stitches for artistic labor to cover over. As a result, holes of unnarrated experience are left to measure through elision the unrecoverable meanings of artistic labor.

Hence, the last chapter seeks to understand how history operates in certain autographic texts as a domain of lost experience and community. "Visual Pedagogies of Impossible Community in *Incognegro* and *March*" returns to questions of identity as form in the comics. Both texts are graphic histories that seek to restore to view history's losses, its formative diasporic traumas, while, paradoxically, translating the tribulations of a people into the triumphal story of an exceptional individual. Both texts also constitute an educable reader-viewer who must learn to see the national shame of racism in ornate metaphors of invisibility (in the case of *March*'s fascination with illegible words) or of violation (in the case of *Incognegro*'s lynched body). More particularly, in *Incognegro* a politics of space governs scenes of lynching, which afford scopic mastery by seeming to shelter viewers, placing them at a safe remove from a lynched body that is never easy to see in Warren Pleece's monochromatic illustrations. Thus distanced from a vaguely occluded figure of trauma, the viewer of *Incognegro* must negotiate a degree of ambivalence towards violence that viewers of John Lewis's *March* (2013) are spared. Whereas *Incognegro* seeks impossible communion with violated subjects of race history, *March* proposes unexpected unions with animal subjects that invoke the slave past. Both operate under an assumption pertinent to all of the autographic texts examined in *Reading Lessons in Seeing*: that readers pledge so much more than mere attention, yielding transformations that are never merely aesthetic, but which herald a new compact of twenty-first-century textual engagement.

Mirror, Mask, and *Mise en Abyme*
in Autobiographical Graphic Novels

Civilization's first gesture is to hold up a mirror to the Object, but the Object is only
seemingly reflected therein; in fact, it is the Object itself which is the mirror.
—Jean Baudrillard, *The Transparency of Evil* (172–73)

Why are there so many mirrors in graphic novels? Characters in comics are constantly playing Narcissus, particularly in the autobiographies. They look at themselves in mirrors ritually. Where actual mirrors do not appear, the gutters impersonate them and take on their properties. In such instances, gutters are neither empty nor simply connective but refractive. They reflect the panels between them while preserving a sovereign space of difference that allows panels to be read sequentially.[1] Given their provocative abundance, mirrors both actual and symbolic in comics prod us to wonder about matters of illustration and fidelity, those inevitable departures from the Real that any drawing conveys and which become all the more telling in the case of a supposedly autobiographical text.

Lynda Barry's *One Hundred Demons* (2002) opens by wondering the same thing. It begins with a mirror scene of Barry painting herself in a miniature self-portrait. She appears in the little picture exactly as she does in the larger one, the panel. A visual pun is created as a result of this arrangement. The smaller image may be seen as either a painting or a mirror. It is either an approximation or a faithful depiction of the painted world around it. Fortifying the conundrum, the accompanying captions raise questions of mediation and veracity as part of the memoir's obligatory pact to tell the truth. Philippe

Lejeune explains how the truth claims made at the start of any autobiography—what he calls the "autobiographical pact" (3)—help to establish an autobiographer's authority according to subjective rather than verifiable truths. Although the autobiographical pact usually takes the form of a proposition, it comes as a series of questions in *One Hundred Demons*. Sitting at her drawing table in the first panel, Barry muses, "Is it autobiography if parts of it are not true?" In the second panel, she inverts the question: "Is it fiction if parts of it are?" (7). Her posture in the second panel mirrors the self-portrait on the table before her and plunges the whole scene into the abyss of the comics' mirror.

The word "abyss" is apt as this scene exemplifies the classic trope of a reflection within a reflection, or *mise en abyme*, meaning "to place into the abyss." For Barry, authorial introspection conjures a space outside of and prior to narrative, in which vexations peculiar to autobiography suspend the story before it officially begins. By calling attention to the same homology of content and structure that Jean Baudrillard's epigraph describes above, Barry's figure of the mirror-within-a-mirror seeks to assuage those anxieties of self-consciousness.[2] The very act of holding up a mirror to behold the terrors it reveals about the self is shown to be essential to the game of misdirection played by both psyches and forms of representation like the comics.

In a way, Barry's outspokenness about the ineluctable fictions of life writing seems intended not solely to confess but also to bypass the paradoxes of her project. As Hillary Chute puts it in *Graphic Women*, "Barry embraces the discursive and generic fault lines of her work as productive, making that instability [. . .] the basis upon which we approach her work" (109). By bridging the gulf between fact and fiction, Barry implicitly forces her audience to lend credibility even to the most fanciful elements of her paintings, such as the unruly parade of demons in the margins. Moreover, Barry's collage-based aesthetic and scrapbookish sense of kitsch thicken the reading process, according to Chute, representing memory as a material construct, a "ruffling . . . [of] the visual surface of the text" (111). Eccentric, colorful, and surprisingly physical, Barry's pictorial style divulges as it veils.

This familiar paradox of art being the lie—to paraphrase Picasso—"that helps us realize the truth" is not unique to Barry (qtd. in Cummings 98). Tensions between the cartoonish and the cathartic typify autography (or graphic novel memoir), as authorial anxiety compulsively regards itself in mirrors in a range of texts.[3] Take, as another example, the climax of Harvey Pekar and Joyce Brabner's collaborative autobiography, *Our Cancer Year* (1994). In the devastating wake of chemotherapy, the atrophied protagonist ponders his role as the writer of the long-running autobiographical comic *American Splendor*

(1976–1993). In a triptych drawn by Frank Stack on the last page of Chapter Nine (the text is not paginated), Harvey looks at himself in a mirror wretchedly. The middle panel shows him asking Joyce, "Tell me the truth, am I some guy who writes about himself in a comic book called *American Splendor*?" A circular inset within that panel encloses his debilitated body like a filmic iris shot as he continues, "Or am I just a character in that book?" Determining where the self as a construct within a public text ends and the pained and private realities of existence begin is prerequisite to Pekar's overcoming of cancer. Once again, meta-pictorial commentary calls forth doublings. Harvey is not just the character of *Our Cancer Year* at this moment of utterance, but also the protagonist of *American Splendor*. Here, Pekar is taking a metaphorical snapshot of himself in *Our Cancer Year*, suffering the same conflation of self and subject that unfolds slowly and episodically in the *American Splendor* series. Charles Hatfield diagnoses this conflation as a crisis of self-ownership: "Pekar has succeeded in mythologizing himself, transforming 'Harvey' into a property that belongs to him (or he to it?) but which nonetheless exceeds him" (109). And perhaps it is this *excess* of identity that visual narratives manage so efficiently, while obscuring distinctions between psyche and soma, agent and object—blurring them in the refractory representations of the *mise en abyme*.

As a final prefatory example, Gene Luen Yang's semiautobiographical allegory of racial identity crisis, *American Born Chinese* (2006), includes a scene where Danny, a white teenager, discovers that he is the long-lost relative of Chin-Kee, who is little more than a montage of racist Chinese stereotypes. For much of the story, Danny exists in a state of constant embarrassment over the antics of Chin-Kee. Only near the end do we learn that white-bread Danny is really Jin Wang, a third character who struggles to accept his Asian difference. All is revealed when we witness how Jin awoke to see in a mirror that he had become Danny, the Anglo ideal he had so longed to embody. Simultaneous to these abrupt visual shifts is the demand that reader-viewers amend our understanding of the narrative logics of identity retroactively. Only through belated recognition do we comprehend the graphic novel's ethnic hyperbole as nothing more than internalized distortions projected as optic truths before the mirror.

All of these uses of the mirror reinforce an iconographic shorthand widespread in pop culture. The trope of the mirror as the screen on which the interior is projected derives from the same cultural clichés that equate happiness to a hearty appetite for looking contentedly at oneself. For evidence of this, we need look no further than pharmaceutical television commercials. How often do they portray people feeling good about themselves (presumably after taking the advertised pill) by showing them catch satisfying glimpses of their reflections, preferably in the rearview mirror of a sports car—and all this despite an obligatory tirade of morbid side effects?

But, in addition to being the barometer of a character's ego, the mirror in *American Born Chinese* and other graphic novels resonates with Oscar Wilde's pronouncement from the poem that opens *The Picture of Dorian Gray*: "It is the spectator, and not life, that art really mirrors." For at the end of the graphic novel, Yang grants readers fairy-tale closure through another pop cultural misrepresentation of Asian American identity: Jin Wang and Wei-Chen wearing Yao Ming jumpsuits sing together on a digital video. This single panel of the last page parodies a parody. While its outer shape mirrors that of a YouTube window, the shapes within the panel resemble the two Chinese art students whose YouTube skit of themselves lip-syncing to a Backstreet Boys song went viral in 2005. It is fitting that Yang's sometimes uncomfortably funny graphic novel of Chinese stereotypes bids readers farewell with one last provocation geared to make us self-conscious about racial spectatorship and laughter. For how many viewers laughed with, instead of at, the Asian performers who seemed to be laughing at their parodic targets—the Backstreet Boys or themselves acting like the Backstreet Boys or both? *American Born Chinese* ends, therefore, by figuratively putting resolution in scare quotes; it does so through sophisticated citations of racist visual humor that turns, like Wilde's mirror of art, more on the spectator than the "real" it supposedly reflects.

Mirror Moments and the Real

But why must these epiphanies of characters, interiorities, and spectators play out before the mirror? What do mirror scenes accomplish for pictorial autobiography? Posed in this way, the question assumes the reciprocity of form and content. Following David Carrier's insight that "the form of comics places very real constraints on its content" (5), this chapter analyzes not simply the form of autobiographical graphic novels but their formal unconscious. Drawing on comics scholarship, autobiography studies, and psychoanalysis, this chapter investigates the significance of mirror scenes of subject formation and fragmentation in Marjane Satrapi's *Persepolis* (2003), James Kochalka's *American Elf: The Collected Sketchbook Diaries* (1998–2004), David B.'s *Epileptic* (1996–2003; 2005), and Laurie Sandell's *The Imposter's Daughter* (2009). In frequency and function, all of these mirrorings mark "failed encounters with the real."[4]

The *real* in this formulation is a construct that only becomes legible in partnership with fabular devices like mirrors, exhibiting it sometimes by failing to do so. And yet, the skeptical reader will notice that few of the examples discussed so far can be categorized strictly as mirror moments. They do not all portray characters gazing into mirrors like the queen from *Snow White*. Expecting them to, however, confirms the enduring power of the mirror in Western storytelling. Enshrined as an archetype, the mirror is never quite sufficient as a metaphor or when hinted at merely. It must be seen and is in itself an iconic mandate of the visual as an organ of self-knowledge.

For the purposes of this chapter, however, the specificity of the mirror is less consequential than what it spawns. As the opening examples show, mirrors make use of the same dualities of revelation and fictionalization that subtend the comics. They X-ray the medium, catching it in the act, as it were, in literal mirrors, panels acting like mirrors, or panels seeming to contain mirrors within them as with the picture-in-picture mechanics of the *mise en abyme*. Apart from precipitating catharsis for characters, the mirror forces reader-viewers to confront assumptions about the text's capacity to convey reality.

Of course, to wonder if anything in an illustrated story may be said to be "really" happening at all is to pursue the very line of inquiry that the mirror activates. Questions of truth return us to the ground rules we bring to the stories we read, rules we adjust as we go. As the opening chapter of a book about the reading lessons in graphic novels, it makes sense to start with the comic form's obsessive instruction in mirrors, masks, and the *mise en abyme*. In these lessons, reader-viewers are trained to exercise a recursive process not unlike the symptomology of OCD, whereby we return again and again to the premise underlying and undermining every image: that it be itself as well as the sign of something else, its counterpart in the real.

As demonstrated by Pekar, the relationship between the real and the masquerade of images approximating it in comics is complicated by the slippery nature of autobiographical authority. The iconic authors of *Maus* (1986), *Blankets* (2003), *Fun Home* (2006), and so many other autobiographical graphic novels function both as symbols of consciousness and as visual figures scarcely different from any other represented object. All perform authorial identity in the third person and do so with two important implications. First, the form creatively invites and depends upon the reader's ability to playfully detach image from text. Divorced from first-person captions, iconic avatars of author-protagonists—what we shall call I-cons—remain objects of consumption. Reading a drawn life story we cannot so easily objectify a mental picture of the "real" person lurking behind the lexical abstractions of "I" or "me." Rather, the I-con of visual narrative tells us in a flash that the story is an approximation, its protagonist a caricature never entirely of our own mental creation.[5] What Linda Hutcheon ascribes specifically to *Maus*, that "it always reminds us of the *lack* of transparency of both its verbal and visual media" (306), may be asserted as a generic principle of the I-con.

Secondly, while these I-cons are the visual equivalent of the narrated "I" of written autobiography, they are always on view, being viewed rather than revealing the view.[6] Instead of telling the author's life story by depicting all that the author may have seen—which need not include the author, of course—these texts always keep the author in the foreground. The nearly universal absence of what film criticism refers to as the camera-I perspective in autobiographical comics has less to do with aesthetic paucity or blind adherence to convention than to the medium-wide investment in the primary conception of the I-con as an actor of memory and of temporality as a fluid construct. Flipping through the pages of some of the most celebrated autobiographical graphic novels, one finds plentiful evidence of the ubiquity of the I-con as an actor of narration. In its most exclusively linguistic form, narration occurs in such texts through first-person captions. These ordinarily create a retrospective temporality, making comments from the present about the past. Never separable from the words around it, the visual I-icon achieves greater complexity when tethered to writing, signifying beyond the spatiotemporalities that attend it as illustration.

One of the most compelling effects of the juxtaposition of writing (e.g., captions, speech balloons) and images for autographers is the I-con's visual fictionality. By implication, such fictions contemplate how an actor so obviously unreal may index real life.[7] When autobiographical protagonists are also comic images, they raise troubling questions, according to Ann Miller and Murray Pratt, "about the possibility of 'being' both in comics and in life, of simultaneously occupying ontologies with such divergent 'rules.'"[8] The trope of the mirror underscores these ontological boundary crossings. As Mieke Bal contends, "[t]he mirror is . . . an icon, an allegory, and a *mise en abyme* of this invisible boundary, in which culture touches nature" (228).[9]

The mirror also references ghostly structures of meaning lying beneath the visible surface, which in turn solicits a psychoanalytic approach to comics texts. Although it is outlandish to presuppose psychoanalysis either to be unitary as a body of scholarship or successful in precisely anatomizing the human psyche, as philosophy psychoanalysis is useful for our purposes in theorizing the tangled relationships that bind perceptual phenomenon and meaning to the unconscious. Rather than depending upon observable, ostensible drives and desires, psychoanalysis (along with materialist theories of culture, media, and language) equips us with tools for dealing with the invisible, subjective forces that impact the world subversively in states of latency or fantasy, as when the estranged twin (which all I-cons are) meets its double in the mirror. And as comics assume a flexible hold on such things as visual reality, time, and memory, while making truth claims about them nevertheless, we might avail ourselves of the fund of psychoanalytic interpretive structures that seek to understand, if not the real, then its double in representation: the exaggerated dream-work of human experience.

In what follows, the formal operations of the medium, as well as its formal unconscious, shall concern us as we consider not just the subjects talked about in graphic novels but the models of subjectivity that do the talking. These contradictory models of autobiographical authorship collaborate with the intermedial possibilities of the comics in order to reconcile memory to something we might call the Real. The result is a set of self-reflexive, visual statements uttering life and inner life in brazenly non-realistic tones. And to better articulate so mystifying a construct as selfhood or reality, this study draws from an evolving lexicon of psychoanalysis that, if nothing else, provides windows through which we may decipher subjective significance taking shape in key panels that contain or perform the mirror.

Whatever form the I-con takes, as the master-signifier of identity in the comics it reifies the psychosocial coordinates of the Imaginary and the Symbolic. It also puts pressure on the Real to show itself by and by. Though none of these capitalized terms can be understood independently of the other, for the sake of preliminary classification, we might define the Symbolic, following Fredric Jameson, as "the dimension of language and the function of speech" and "the Imaginary [. . .] as the place of the insertion of my unique individuality" (35). One way of thinking about the Imaginary, therefore, is as the dimension of reality that is constantly being fabricated by our own subjective experience of it. The third category of subject formation, the Real, "is the most problematical of the three—since it can never be experienced immediately, but only by way of the mediation of the other two" (349). With these definitions in mind, the I-con appears to serve as the symbolic mask of the Imaginary. It merges with captions and other conventions of sequential art and storytelling (the Symbolic) to produce an individual (the Imaginary). However, by fixating on the ways that the Imaginary submits to the urgencies of symbolization, autobiographical graphic novels—as the present chapter will show—voluptuously convert the unfinished business of identity into a terror of the Real.[10]

Never simply the cold hard facts perceived in the "here and now," the Real is compound, contradictory, and collaborative. It traffics in social fantasies and ego ideals, myth and misperception. Our grasp of it is always a fleeting compromise. And the argument that comics make about this ineffable Real is that it is best apprehended like Emily Dickinson's notion of truth in

"Tell all the Truth, but tell it slant"—delivered to us circuitously, masked, and mirror-distorted. And, as we shall see, graphic memoir represents the Real as perhaps no other medium can by normalizing its ruptures of visibility and verisimilitude.

The Gutter is the Mirror in the First Panels of *Persepolis*

Marjane Satrapi's two-volume autobiography *Persepolis* wastes no time initiating formative ruptures between the I-con and those whom the young Iranian Marji is called upon to represent. As with the interrogations of autobiography's truth claims that begin Lynda Barry's *One Hundred Demons*, Satrapi's opening panels construe a pact that flickers. Here, too, even the promise to tell the truth is slant—and appropriately so, since the power of the story rests on the quirkily precocious Marji, a visually young girl alloyed to a verbally adult consciousness.

The character of Marji has magnetic appeal, doubtless a chief reason for the book's commercial triumph. She is funny, occasionally cutesy, a mystic, a historian, and a revolutionary. When she reports on the terrifying changes happening in Iran, we are prone to accept this history as the personal reminiscences of an unguarded confidant. And what are the ideological effects of heaping so much familiarity onto the I-con of *Persepolis*? Indeed, Marji's charm is not altogether free of political tendentiousness. If the Middle East were such a fertile, character-building region of so many democracy-loving Marjis, then what is there for the post-9/11, presumptively Western reader to fear? With a friend like Marji, who needs a Middle Eastern enemy? And we could go on expounding the sentimental rhetoric that surrounds her character. But what is more interesting and less obvious is the way that Satrapi manages Marji's proximity and distance from an audience at times presumed as addressees, and at others, as viewers of a primarily visual record of truth told in all of its slanted glory.

Marji's mode of address is not exclusively testimonial, as is the case to a greater extent in *Persepolis II*; here, little Marji is at her best when playing autoethnographer or family chronicler. In its ten chapter-stories, *Persepolis* ranges from first-person accounts of the imposition of the veil to overheard stories of the imprisonment and torture of political resisters. While coming to grips with the epic changes sweeping across her country, Marji also awakens to her family's privilege; her great-grandfather, it turns out, was one of the last rightful emperors of Persia. From her portrayal of Iranian boys duped by ideology into blowing themselves up to the veiled troop of officious matrons

1.1 Opening panels of Satrapi's *Persepolis*. "Opening Panels" from *Persepolis: The Story of a Childhood* by Marjane Satrapi. Translation copyright © 2003 by L'Association, Paris, France. Used by permission of Pantheon Books, an imprint of the Knopf Doubleday Publishing Group, a division of Random House LLS. All rights reserved.

who accost the young Marji for wearing emblems of Western teen culture, Satrapi cleaves to an aesthetic of juxtaposition that charms even as it shocks. It does so by relying on the stock reversals that child protagonists have brought to narratives from *Huckleberry Finn* to *Harry Potter*, and by blending Western and Arabic approaches to art. As one reviewer puts it, the style "deploys all the paranoid Expressionism latent in the comic strip's juxtapositions of scale— the child dwarfed by looming parents, would-be rescuers dwarfed by giant policemen guarding the locked doors to a movie theatre that's been set on fire—but when Satrapi depicts a schoolyard brawl, it's straight from Persian miniature" (Eberstadt 2003).

Instead of proceeding now to interpret the plot and themes of Satrapi's graphic novel in their totality, I want to linger over the intricacies of the book's first set of panels (Fig. 1.1). For it is in view of these opening panels that we may interpret the text in the microcosmic genesis of its word-image relationships. All of the primary lessons of the text appear in these panels that figuratively ask us to see and to un-see. We are hereby cautioned against unexamined or extreme forms of identification; instead, we are encouraged to cultivate a simpatico that preserves boundaries of difference, however transitory.

One reason why Western readers would want to identify with Satrapi's autobiographical persona is that she incarnates a besieged and beleaguered individuality. That she is suspended in a state of exception in her own panel at the start aligns her, at least spatially, more with her Western readers than with those Iranian girls in the following panel, whom she not only resembles but visually replicates. The second panel shows Marji to be nearly the mirror image of these other Iranian girls and provides an early occasion for the viewer to marvel at Satrapi's acumen as a minimalist—what one reviewer describes as her "amazing way of conveying sanctimony, fury or desolation in the spare lines of her characters' faces" (Goldberg 2003).

The binaric arrangement of the first two panels divides Marji from her peer group. Minor facial differences may hint at small differences between the girls in the group, but the chasm of the gutter amplifies Marji's dissimilarity. It is as if these panels were trying to teach us a basic lesson of categorical analysis, forcing us to distinguish between the superficialities of content and the less apparent yet still pressing implications of form. No matter how similar the girls may look (content), Marji has been formatted to appear singularly alone and as the first in a series (form). Thanks to the implications of the panel arrangement, in league with an assumed Western priority of a left-to-right reading order, the girls' faces of the second panel signify as deviations, variations, or copies of the original face in the first panel that Marji alone bears.

The first two panels of *Persepolis* dramatize a conflict between individuality and universality that recurs throughout the narrative.[11] The first one verbally situates the young author-protagonist in a particular time and place—Iran in 1980—at a time when the cultural and political revolution of fundamentalism made the veil a compulsory article of female dress. The second panel then contextualizes the author in relation to her peers who come to embody that history. The second panel thus emphasizes Marji's struggle to achieve independence amidst an overwhelming tide of conformity and mass replication. The relationship between the deictic words ("this," "I," "me") and the image of the first panel is coordinative. The words petition us to receive the concomitant icon of the veiled girl as continuous with the captionary voice of enunciation. The phrase "This is me" also gives rise to two domains, each complexly multilayered and each layer the antithesis of the other: object (this) and subject (me), vision and voice, past and present, Iran and (in light of the original French edition) the West. Even though words and image conjoin to found that property of the comics Linda Hutcheon dubs "a fictive heterocosm, a complete visual and verbal universe" (301), they also bring this universe into being along the *axis mundi* of a fundamental division.

To elaborate, we might translate the words of the first panel of *Persepolis* as saying: "This girl you see in the panel is not just a fair likeness of the girl I was at 10 in 1980, but this illustration is the Me of enunciation, then and now." Such a paraphrase asserts that the author function (both the writer Marjane Satrapi and the I-con of little Marji in panel one) is an unequivocally seamless identity that coheres over time. This seamlessness is why Rocío Davis alerts us to "approach contemporary graphic autobiographies as increasingly sophisticated forms of inscribing the past" (269). In this way, the author function that spans decades assumes visibility in the shape of the little girl, who in later panels speaks to us (in speech balloons) in the present. Although our next chapter will investigate childhood as a theme and structure of American comics, it suffices to mention here that adolescence is elevated in *Persepolis* to the status of an iconic language. The young girl facing out from the panel alone to meet the reader-viewer's gaze, typically with one finger upraised, is Satrapi's archetypical storyteller, her version of the quintessential prophet.

Because of the complications of their word-picture relationships, autographics lay claim to an author that is utterly, yet never merely, the represented protagonist. An exclusively verbal autobiographical narrative could include passages where the author writes, "I was 10 in 1980" or even "this is me in 1980," but the picture Satrapi provides turns the referent that the word "this" summons into an object: the caricature on the page. One reason to belabor the verbal *deixis* of the first panel has to do with the shift in meaning in the "this" of the second panel. The pronominal "this" of the first panel equates to the author; that of the next, to the class photo. Reference focuses on the represented in the first panel and the means of representation in the second. Whereas the first is associated with self-portraiture, singular identity, and a one-to-one correspondence between the icon and that which the icon symbolizes, the second traffics in the dislocatory, de-individuating force of the collective. If comics allow for an unmediated form of self-presentation, photography is shown here to allegedly obliterate the author through referential elision: "I'm sitting on the far left so you don't see me."

Curiously, however, there are two spaces that answer to this location of being "far left" and in both *we do see her*. One is the left margin of the second panel where, undoubtedly, we can glimpse the cut-off portion of Marji's left arm and right hand. If we do not at first notice Marji as margin, the eyes of Golnaz, the fully visible girl on the left, leads us here. Or perhaps Golnaz too sees into this other space where we see Marji across the gutter. Jumping over the gutter, we see Marji intact and analogous with her classmates. Now that the comic has trained us first to entertain and then to reject the demands of its words and the conventional gutter space separating its images, the classmates seem more than ever to embody not different, specifically named girls of a class photo, but versions of Marji—studies in seriality.

The gutter therefore sutures in at least two ways simultaneously. On one level, it bears out Thierry Groensteen's argument that through their "coexistence, through their diegetic connections, and their panoptic display" (9) comic images create an "iconic solidarity" (19) that is foundational to the medium and makes adjoining panels "predisposed to speak to each other" (35).[12] On another level, Satrapi's initial gutter sutures the cut verbally inflicted by the caption of the second panel. It is on this level that the opening gutter in *Persepolis* teaches readers to obey and obliterate the spaces between panels, with or without the consent of the verbal.[13] More than suggesting Marji's inclusion in the group, this first gutter materializes that inclusion. This type of hypostasis—taking shape across the gap rather than imaginatively within it—comes closest to supporting Marc Singer's claim that comics "have proven effective at embodying the real through hypostasis, the somatization of abstract concepts and desires into human figures" (275). In these two panels, Marji hypostasizes isolation despite identicality.

In Satrapi's opening, the gutter reminds us that the two panels may be worlds apart despite the resemblance of the girls and other indicators of continuity, such as the dark, table-like space upon which the girls' hands uniformly rest.[14] The similarity of pose, dress, size, and contrast might invite us to see the panel-to-panel relationship presented here as one of moment-to-moment—the transition Scott McCloud says requires the least amount of closure or narrative synthesis.[15] At first glance, no great effort of closure is needed to make the first two panels relate. Indeed, they cohere explicitly, like portions of the same set occupying the same space and time.

But visual positivism has many detractors in the comics, making it difficult for us to see these images as wholly innocent in representing what they seem to represent. In *Persepolis*, for example, the stark chiaroscuro of Satrapi's minimalistic drawings are always on hand to amplify those qualities of ambivalence and disruption for which so many critics praise comics—their "utter non-objectivity" (Hutcheon 1997, 306); "their refusal, or inability, to instantaneously and unproblematically offer a face to the readers" (Miller and Pratt 2004); their way of allowing readers "to recognize the norms that govern which lives will be regarded as human and the frames through which discourse and visual representation proceed" (Whitlock 2006, 976); in short, the universally acclaimed manner by which a comic's pictoriality disrupts verbal reference such that "the very pictoriality of the . . . comic is significantly disrupted as well" (Huyssen 2003, 134).

Ultimately, the gutter that separates the first two panels of *Persepolis* is a mirror in the vein of the *mise en abyme*. The mask that is Marji projects the individual that Satrapi nostalgically re-members herself to be as well as the gendered collective which that individuality both sees and refuses to see itself in. In *Alternative Comics*, Charles Hatfield explains how self-caricature precedes the creation of the autobiographical self as an object, arguing that the resulting mask is only partly estranging, since it yields greater image-control over the authorial self (114–15). Similarly, Rocío Davis notes that the third-person perspective sustains metacritical consciousness in *Persepolis*, claiming that Satrapi has "fuller control of her subject—herself—as her life writing act involves actual, though stylized, self-portraiture" (271).[16] Consequently, the I-con or mask "mirrors an internalized abstract self-concept—a self-consciousness prerequisite to personal narrative" (Hatfield 117). What Satrapi's opening teaches us, then, is that as successful comics readers and viewers we must be aware of the way the I-con mediates ideologically loaded impressions originating from an external social order and how it turns them into an individualized code of self-display and psychological misadventure, without which neither autobiographical acts nor pacts are possible.

My effort to unravel the conjuncture of theme and form in *Persepolis* may prove the reversibility of David Carrier's dictum that "to interpret a comic we need to identify the ways in which it reflects the fantasies of the public" (7). As this section has shown, the fantasy underwriting *Persepolis* is available even in its first two panels, proposing Marji's split identity to be a marker of individuality rather than a terror of the Real—the fear of being dependent upon the ruptures that separate her from origins, ideals, and others.

The Imaginary Is the Real in James Kochalka's
The Sketchbook Diaries

It is with great curiosity that we notice the sheer number of graphic autobiographies haunted by de-centering returns to that rupture, the Real. But why do so many graphic autobiographers interrupt their narratives to admit another self, an alternative or competing I-con, at once alien to the narrative yet crucial to its verisimilitude? It is as if in such mirror moments a swatch of patterns is delivered up to the reader as a kind of palette key to the visual style of the work, as seen in *Persepolis*, though the narrative proper clings only to one or two samples from this palette for the sake of consistency.

James Kochalka's *American Elf: The Sketchbook Diaries*—a comic diary of an angsty comic artist who appears as an elf—deliberately veils the author-protagonist's psychic terror of the Real through stylized distortions. The book grows out of a countercultural mode of comics autobiography that Hatfield and others locate in the late 1980s and 1990s and characterize as being

1.2 Opening scene from Kochalka's *American Elf: The Sketchbook Diaries.*

inspired by the humdrum, seedy realism of Harvey Pekar's *American Splendor*. These comics are "alternative" in that they forego the colorful superheroics of mainstream comics for the idiosyncrasies of quotidian antiheroes who eek out meaning from a sordid, neurotically abject existence.

Kochalka's iconic abstraction of the human and the comic's quartered panel composition aestheticize the diary and confer lyrical depth to the elf's random observations. Indeed, as Isaac Cates has ably shown, the sheer volume of *American Elf*'s entries of self-examination demand that we "see in the daily record of individual events the possibility of lyric autography [. . . . and] recognize those aspects of diary writing that work against narrative closure" ("The Diary Comic" 223). Vaguely rodent-like, Kochalka's elf literally sees itself transformed into a cartoon with horizontally elongated ears, extruding upper mandibles punctuated with protruding buck teeth, and two dots, mere commas, for eyes (Fig. 1.2). As both autobiographer and self-portraitist, Kochalka has claimed during interviews a special symbolic status for his illustration style: "It's not just that it's an elf, but the specific way the elf looks. Also, the relationship between the way the various characters look, it's all symbolic" (Garcia 2008). The last part of this statement is especially intriguing, for Kochalka's I-con acquires the symbolic potential to express an impossible relation to itself, multiplied in the panel structure's spatial fantasy of an enclosed self-referentiality. Is it not this preoccupation with the self and its

reflections that punningly justifies the use of the "elf"—for its lexical proximity to the word "self"? Regardless, the narrative urgency in graphic memoir to make the autobiographer visible risks not just the valorization of the author, but also the devaluation of other characters.

For example, female nudes in Kochalka's egocentric, existentialist musings are unsurprisingly available for erotic revelations. "I love drawing comics about her," he says of his wife in one entry, and though he admires her "cute little smile," the comic artist loves nothing more than pulling her shirt up over her face and drawing her breasts (Fig. 1.3). The wife's face is shown asleep in this set of four panels, rendering her oblivious to the nakedness the protagonist enjoys revealing to us and simultaneously taking from her. And why not, as the comic's logic would have it, for this nakedness is not really hers. The artist is essentially redistributing what already belongs to him—the comic he loves to draw about her. Authorial presence vocalized through captions contrasts the woman's reduction to pure image. Kochalka is represented by an I-con that conjoins with the symbolic order through captioned words that attempt to fix pictorial phenomena. In contrast to the author's grandiose embodiment of a war between symbol systems, the wife exists in these panels at the level of static picture and cited verbal object, the catalyst for his artistic and libidinal excitation.

Like the other girls Marji resembles, the wife here represents a subjective threat to the aggressive narcissism exercised at the level of the visual in autography: perhaps as a result of being rendered in the same potentially simplifying tonalities of illustration as the overly present autobiographical "I," other human subjects often seem to undergo a form of expulsion, distancing, or objectification in graphic memoir. Here, the wife's expulsion from the Symbolic is assured by her represented slumber, which redoubles her status as a spectatorial object suspended in the amber of the diarist's erotic gaze.

Aside from the elf's expostulations of love, the image serves as alibi against the charge of misogynistic violation. The first two panels may not be his view of her at all, but the products of that view *avant la lettre*, pictures of pictures all along. In another interview, Kochalka inadvertently certifies one of Paul de Man's reasons for refusing to sunder autobiography from fiction when he admits that his actions in life are "governed by the technical demands of self-portraiture" (de Man 920). He modifies his behavior with his wife and others in order to ensure sufficiently interesting memoiristic content. "There have been occasions," Kochalka admits in an interview, "where I've said things to people, just to get reactions from them, so I could draw a strip about it. I've done that to my wife before. It's kind of a mean trick" (Heater 2007). Other interviews, in fact, intimate a prior discord stemming from this "mean trick": "There's certain things that she doesn't really like me to draw, like sex stuff, so I try to limit the amount of sex stuff I draw or how graphic it is. But I don't leave it out entirely" (Mautner, 2007).

By analyzing this scene, I intend neither to incite nor defuse its potential to aggrieve. Rather, I want to track how disturbing ambiguities in the image—in this case, having to do with the ethics of the wife's exposure—encourage reader-viewers to invest the images and captions with affect. A ponderous literalism renders the scene innocent; the tautological drawing of the protagonist drawing (another *mise en abyme*) defiles insofar as the reader-viewer opens up an affective relation to what is, on one level, nothing more than an empty visual sign. However, images cannot remain so empty in comics, a point on which Kochalka's prickling irony depends. His aesthetic is therefore "haunted by the spectre of representation" that Miller and Pratt diagnose as the fear that "[t]he barrier between dream and reality may not be so permeable, and a gap between signifier and signified, enunciator and subject may still open up."[17] With its reference to the unconscious as a site for transgressions in the Imaginary, this scene informs a later one that seizes the I-con before the mirror of the Real.

The twin extremes of violation and veneration in the wife drawings find disquieting resonance in Kochalka's metacritical view of his own representation in the text. In an entry dated January 25, 1999, Kochalka's protagonist comments on the comic's distance from the Real. "I draw myself like this,"

1.4 From Kochalka's *American Elf: The Sketchbook Diaries.*

the caption in one panel announces; "not like this," says the following caption, presenting an image of a human-looking face. The character flees to "watch more television" in the fourth panel (Fig. 1.4). Whereas the disclosure of unconscious female flesh yields warped rapture, exposing his face one step closer to the Real exacerbates fear.

Profoundly self-alienated, Kochalka's elf epitomizes a preoccupation in autography with form and identity or with identity as form. By calling attention to these two styles of representation, the scene assumes abstraction to be measurable, as though the panels were able to perform a comparative weighing of two abstractions—like this and not like this. For readers who have grown accustomed to divining the authorial in the rodent-like mask, the "not like this" is as much a caricature as the "like this." In other words, the denied Real is just another embellishment, which gives it the ironic effect of imputing psychological verisimilitude to Kochalka's arch visual style. Kochalka thus suggests the elf to be truer than the human (as evidenced in the third panel) and more cozening than TV (as evidenced in the fourth).

Self-consciously making fun of the identity crisis that its form naturalizes, Kochalka's mirror scene records a paroxysm of characterization that affirms M. Thomas Inge's claim that "[r]ealism is incompatible with comic art, whose virtues reside in the distinctive and inimitable drawing styles and points of view of the individual comic artists" (14). There is little doubt that Kochalka is being facetious about the nature of realism in comic art in these panels. In them we may observe a parody of Scott McCloud's *Understanding Comics*, published some four years prior—particularly, McCloud's panel of himself drawn more realistically and saying, "Would you have listened to me if I looked like this?" (36). McCloud's famous point is that cartoonish images foster greater possibilities for identification than realistic ones, whose details remind us less of our own mental self-conceptions. Kochalka arrives at the same point from a playfully oblique angle. His elf adds self-effacing humor to McCloud's argument about the power of iconic abstraction. Never mind reader-viewers, Kochalka's comic seems to exclaim, this I-con cannot bear seeing itself in any other guise than the cartoonish.

The situation is funny in more ways than one. On top of its parody of McCloud, this diary entry also spoofs the idea of the mask as a source of humor. That notion, it turns out, is at least as old as Aristotle, who reasoned that the *prosopon*—or mask—"that excites laughter is something ugly and distorted without causing pain" (59). The comic upends this formula so that it is the ugly and distorted *prosopon* (the elf) whose tenuous membership among the familiar is threatened by contact with a less distorted *prosopon*. And it is this ugly mask that is made to feel pain as a result of their uncanny rendezvous. More than a reversal of opposites, whereby the distorted becomes the non-distorted, the comic duplicates opposites, in the fashion of the *mise en abyme*—Kochalka's elf is a drawing that shows itself drawing. To be sure, there is a game afoot with verisimilitude in all of this *prosoponic* play.[18] We are never meant to see Kochalka's elven I-con as anything other than reality's substitute, just one mask among many.

The encounter between the chosen mask and the un-chosen one, the mask by which one is seized, posits at least two implications about authorial subjectivity in *American Elf*. The first, as mentioned, is that the I-con of Kochalka the elf is the mask (or prosopon) of Kochalka the author.[19] The second is that the chosen drawing style that confronts and then denies the scabrous truths of the Real (whatever these may be) resists literary realism. Such a choice is not just a matter of style. On the contrary, it proceeds from a politics of opposition that pokes fun of the spectatorial passivity of conventional visual arts. Unlike TV, and presumably other mass visual media such as cinema, comics banish the psychic pressures of visual realism, flouting pressures of likeness and sometimes even of legibility. Where such legibility is repudiated, as here, trauma supplants realism's affective and aesthetic protocols of escape, entertainment, and enlightenment. In terms of how we might feel about comics, then, Kochalka insinuates that there is nothing therapeutic about them that is not also potentially terrifying or absurd.

Graphic Affect and the Real

Among the many roles the human in the mirror performs in Kochalka's text, it also operates as a *punctum*—Barthes's term in *Camera Lucida* for the wounding detail witnessed in a photograph.[20] Like *puncta* that simultaneously puncture photographic objectivity as they sew the image to viewer desire and dread, the revelations in this quartered unit of narrative weave anxieties of form and content into the very fabric of the reading experience. It is an occasion of unmasking manqué, a faux unveiling (because humorously staged as such) in which the iconic subject we have been invited to read as that triumvirate entity from the autobiographical pact—author-narrator-protagonist—turns out to be neither integrated nor accurate. Kochalka's *American Elf* creates genre trouble by showing its protagonist to be more problem than person, a betrayal of the myth of individuality that the novel has had in store for readers at least since Georg Lukács's observation that: ". . . because the novel can only comprise the individual in this way, he becomes a mere instrument, and his central position in the work means only that he is particularly well suited to reveal a certain problematic of life" (83). In sum, the elf is not a self after all; scandalously, it is but the means of disclosing selfhood as a problem.

Are we betrayed by this revelation? Surely not, for how could we have misapprehended grotesquerie for something akin to the author? And yet just such a betrayal is at stake, if not for the reader then for the protagonist, as the authorial voice of the captions prefers the grotesque over the Real. Here is where betrayal enters as misrecognition. Embedded in this diary entry are three successive propositions: 1) that the distortion mistook for authorial presence is not singular (as are most conceptions of authorship and authority) but one among many possible others; 2) that the realistic likeness of the author is not among these options; and 3) that the distortion with which we have identified (if we concede to a non-oppositional reading) has likewise been the one with which the author most identifies—in protest against the human. In consequence, the terms of our reading pact must be renegotiated, since a significant codicil of the prevailing contract has hinged upon our consenting to the visual equivalence of elf and self. If such a pact has been in effect, we are hereby disabused of it, at least provisionally, seeing, as we must, the author suddenly seeing himself—not in elf-face as he wants to be viewed, but in the anthropomorphic guise of average white masculinity (the one bugged-out eye notwithstanding). That the transaction appalls the elf-masked self-portraitist affords amusement in proportion to the intellectual expenditures necessary to revise the reading contract.

Aside from parodying an identity crisis, these panels disrupt any pleasure readers might find in a consistent representation of authorial identity.

But there are other pleasures besides consistency. Indeed, the surge of autobiographical comics of trauma and survivorship attests to this other kind of reading pleasure, strangely wedded to the form of the comic, which resists continuity in favor of a semiotics of selfhood grounded in caricature and the grotesque. Never solely the trigger for schism, authorial self-discontinuity becomes a structural homology in many autobiographical comics, as Kochalka's demonstrates.

To elaborate, let us return to the punning of scene, seen, and seeing that these panels visually present. The elf's discomfiture at seeing himself drawn realistically corroborates one of the negative reactions commonly ascribed to the gaze of psychoanalysis. According to one theorist, the disparity between the eye and the gaze—or the difference between personal, embodied forms of perception and externalized, disembodied forms—engenders so enormous a realization of lack that it gives rise to a plaguing sense of shame, betrayal, and threat scarcely able to be symbolized in language: "[T]he cut of the subject, introduced prior to any mention of the eye or the gaze . . . becomes evident through the . . . failed encounter of the subject with the Real, where . . . the former is dumbfounded, perplexed, disconcerted, that is, in a state of schizia" (Harari 106). In keeping with so many other autographic subjects, Kochalka's ludicrous epiphany is also a "failed encounter with the Real" that is constitutive of identity, wherein two of reality's most obscure masks collide: the Imaginary and the Symbolic.

Were we to attempt to plot these psychoanalytic categories onto Kochalka's diary entry, we could hardly ask for a clearer model to start with than Don Ault's:

> The comic page most directly invokes Lacan's "imaginary" order through its pictorial dimension (its visual images); the "symbolic" order through its linguistic dimensions (its letters, words, and syntax); and the "real" through the interruptions or cuts in the body-spaces of the page which leave blank spaces between the panels. (283)

Extrapolating from Ault, but opening up his grafting of the image-word dichotomy onto Lacan's Imaginary-Symbolic dyad, it follows that if the Imaginary corresponds to the function of the gaze, masking the symbolic structures that underlie it, then the first panel with the elf face belongs to the Imaginary. The second panel obtrudes upon the Imaginary, exposing the Symbolic field of Kochalka's realistic imago normally hidden by the veiling effects of fantasy. Hence, this second image belongs to the Symbolic.

At the same time, these terms are neither so simply nor so singularly attributable to representational phenomena as Ault's schematization would suggest. Our reading must not stop here. Nor can we ignore that other district of the unconscious, the Real, which, despite being conceptualized rhetorically through significant absences, eludes symbolization *even when it is routinely articulated in absences.* In short, gutters cannot be the home of the Real in the comics, for they are as natural to the form as paragraphs or punctuation are to prose. As McCloud's discussion of closure indicates, comic readers constantly and routinely transform gutters of interpanel whitespace into units of meaning (66–67). Because gutters are anything but disruptive to the grammar of the comics, they do not meet the criteria of the Real of psychoanalysis.

To consider how the panel of the "realistic" face may also operate as this more theoretical Real, we must first recapitulate the concept of the gaze. In Lacan's formulation of the scopic drive, subjects desire the voyeuristic omniscience to see all. But since no individual can transcend his or her located perspective, this desire for the gaze that surpasses embodied acts of looking forever evades the subject; it exists outside of individuals in the field of the other. What is important in all of this is that the gaze entails an externalized scopic totalization as well as the failure of it. The gaze of the "big other" is never complete. It too lacks.[21] And it is for this reason that the Symbolic regularly disrupts desire for scopic mastery. As with Lacan's interpretation of the skull in Hans Holbein's painting *The Ambassadors* (1533), the realistic face of Kochalka gives order to the visual field despite being alien to it.[22]

Moreover, the realistic face is no mere unveiling agent of the Symbolic that shatters the normative consistency of fantasy in the Imaginary. It has been seen by its other. And, in this reciprocal regard, its dependence upon the reader is acknowledged—perhaps formulaically so. As will become increasingly clear, all mirror moments implicate readers. Customarily, readers are configured in comics as agencies lying beyond the text whose necessary interventions precipitate completion and coherence. But there is another way that readers are implicated, as this case shows: as double agents annihilating the very world outside the text to which they belong and to which the text stands in opposition. Staging the choice of caricature over realism, Kochalka's comic draws readers into a polarizing fantasy of art vs. the world, which theorist Georg Lukács observed in nineteenth-century identifications with classical art as "an attempt to forget that art is only one sphere among many, and that the very disintegration and inadequacy of the world is the precondition for the existence of art and its becoming conscious" (38). The mirrors in autography insist on just such a relation as readers are encouraged to imagine themselves becoming apostates to the world they occupy outside of texts in order to identify with those subjects of caricature that exist within them.

And yet fidelity to the drawn world is an oxymoron in the comics. The idea that comics would harbor anxieties about systems of resemblance is ludicrous.

Those are the preoccupations of realism and its associated media. The anxiety expressed in this or any mirroring, then, is never exclusively in response to the rigors of mimesis, because comics do not labor under the expectation that its copies shall duplicate real-world models. Rather, the anxiety inherent to the comics is of having too much authorial noise or style preventing such resemblance, obscuring legibility with overcompensating structures of authorship, style, code, mimetic materiality, and so on. The result is a media-wide pictorial narcissism, one symptom of which may be noted in the conventional omnipresence of authorial I-cons in the panels of autobiographical graphic novels.[23]

Epileptic's Imbricative Mirrors and Striving Readers

Why must autobiographical graphic novels show their protagonists at all? Couldn't they be told in the first person, visually as well as verbally? For better or worse, self-consciousness is corporeal in the comics. And the medium's tendency to resurrect its authors is as insistent as it is naïve. When authorial protagonists are translated into drawings, a collapse of antinomies ensues, producing an imbrication of figure and ground, storyteller and story. And the figure of the mirror frequently serves to illuminate those ecstasies of indistinction.

David B.'s *Epileptic* opens with a mirror scene (Fig. 1.5) that situates the autobiographer in dangerous proximity to his older brother, Jean-Christophe, whose lifelong battles with epilepsy have rendered him monstrous. The first panel of the first page shows a young man swathed in shadow brushing his teeth in front of a bathroom sink. The perspective makes it seem as if we are perched in a far corner of the ceiling, looking down. The man's angular face is vaguely sketched on the surface of the mirror. A caption announces the time and place, but its more crucial task is to perform *deixis*—the rhetorical "this is me" that yokes I-cons to autobiographical utterance: "1994. I'm in the bathroom, at my parent's house in Olivet." Although the panel that follows can be seen as the scarred and bloated brother entering the room with his fingers still on the opening door, the fact that it comes unaccompanied by any explanatory caption permits it to be read another way—that is, as a visual analogue for the reader. Indeed, the close-up on the brother's face in spite of its scar-ravaged skin and hideously missing teeth mirrors our position before the comic panel, watching the author-protagonist brushing his teeth through the same bordering devices that lineate the panel of the brother's face.

1.5 Opening page of David B.'s *Epileptic*. Excerpt from *Epileptic* by David B. Copyright © 2005 by L'Association, Paris, France. Used by permission of Pantheon Books, an imprint of the Knopf Doubleday Publishing Group, a division of Random House LLS. All rights reserved.

Riffing off of the classical cinematic technique of shot-reverse shot, the comic induces us to see ourselves uncomfortably mirrored in the brother's entrance of the second panel. He seems transfixed there at the threshold where the lines that delineate the framing of the door are unnaturally multiplied, as if to emphasize the various frames of the medium that his visage is on the verge of passing through: from the door to the panel that contains that door to the page of the comic and so on into the domain of the reader on the other side of representation. The third panel, showing the brother looking down at a stunned David B. saying, "It's me," releases us from reflexivity. It redirects us, initiating the recursivity so common to comics reading, in which we retreat intermittently to correct earlier missteps in the reading order or to revise misconstrued images clarified later. Still, it is only in support of the narrowest understanding of narrative meaning that these earlier missteps are rectified. They are never erased nor seldom outweighed by parochial rereadings and secondary revisions.

Nevertheless, the image of the brother as he first appears to our author brings about a difficulty of closure that permeates the entire graphic novel: How are we to recognize the brother "without his public face on," as the author says in a later caption? Put differently, how are we to take the crudity of a drawing, with its raw and unsettling lines, as representative of the Real? Self-enclosed, the first page is a mirror scene that plays out between David B. and his brother—that is to say, between the author's mental image of his brother and this rawer form in actuality. And all of that is perhaps another way of understanding the contrast between the brother as a character and an allegory for all the emotional verities of life that go masked in art. Murray Pratt considers the same encounter "coupled with the poetic non-sequitur of self-identification as Jean-Christophe names himself as 'I,' [as] effect[ing] a threat of displacement, the menace that the (br)other might occupy the physical, if not psychological, space that should rightfully be David B's" (139). With Pratt, we may wonder whether we are in the brother's position or if our surveying of his difference from a superior limit of the visible world is not already a traumatic site of deferral for the author. All of these relations are imbricated, folded one into the other until their distinctions are obliterated, and there could hardly be a more poignant emblem of imbrication than the mirror at the beginning of the text.

Of course, ambiguities surrounding this opening ought to be placed within the larger context of the book's opening section. Technically, while the mirror dominates the first panels, it does not express the book's first words. In Pantheon's 2005 edition of *Epileptic*, which compiles the six issues of the original French-language comic book series *L'Ascension du Haut Mal* (1996–2003), the first words of the book belong to the sister. In her epistolary forward, Florence helps to solidify an autobiographical pact based on accuracy and truthfulness by corroborating the general facts of the story. She writes about the "shadows of our childhood," as she puts it, which David B. captures, according to her, in a manner consistent with his lifelong concern for "the correct detail . . . [and] faithful reconstruction." Beyond these predictable gestures of authentication, however, the forward also offers a counter-representation to David B.'s strategy of depicting epilepsy as an ornately patterned dragon: "It's funny: For my part, I always pictured it as a powerful little kernel, lodged in the contours of his brain." This image would seem to be the feminine counterpart to her brother's style of visual memorial, juxtaposing his aggressive aesthetic of gargantuan and byzantine exteriorization with an image of miniature potentiality, a budding interior. But in spite of divergences in style, Florence's approach to the illness is not so different from David B.'s. Her metaphor of epilepsy as a kernel conforms to the mental picture of memory that she describes earlier in the letter as "a tiny little seed, dense and dark, which encircles one irreducible fact. . . . epilepsy." Interestingly, her conceptual alignment of the content and processes of traumatic memory parallels a related analogy that David B. employs throughout *Epileptic*.

Although it bears mention that Florence's clitoral counterpart to David B.'s phallic representation of epilepsy registers a gendered critique of his autobiographical project—a placeholder, perhaps, for a more extensive objection to erasures of the matrilineal and the feminine in the text—what concerns me here is the surprising correspondence between the siblings' method for comprehending their own interiorities. Both see themselves as split subjects vis-à-vis the memory of their brother's epilepsy. Florence's image of her brother's epilepsy (as a "kernel") mirrors her image for memory (as a "seed"). The entirety of David B.'s *Epileptic* is similarly organized around a supposedly external subject, the *corpus vile* that is both his brother and his brother's epilepsy. But this conglomeration is also a mirror. It also forms the self-regarding metaphor of the author's memory-work. Just as David B. comes into being along the traumatic fault line of his brother's illness, so too does the sister confess to being divided when faced by other people's lack of knowledge about her diseased brother and their excess knowledge about and interest in her authorial one:

Sometimes people ask me, "How's your brother doing?"—"Fine, he's fine . . ." and this is followed by dispatches about your current work, your projects, your loves. At that moment my spirit splits into two. In my head, I answer this question, which could have had to do with my other brother. But no one knows my two brothers, and my second voice chokes between my heart and my throat.

Thus, Jean-Christophe's illness is an object of consciousness not just for David B. but for the sister, whose "second voice" implies that she has one voice reserved for public discourse and another that cannot speak. The first voice is rooted in the symbolic order where her authorial brother reigns, while the muted second voice belongs to the imaginary where reference withers altogether in the ricochet from affect (*my heart*) to language (*my throat*). For both Florence and David B., then, grappling with naming the traumatic image or assigning it a face *is* the trauma. These acts of proper reference create a paradigm for memory as well as a mask for consciousness. As with Kochalka's protagonist, the struggle to name the trauma becomes the means by which Florence and David B. understand themselves to be split subjects. And nothing in *Epileptic* captures this predicament better than the literal mirror scene that immediately follows Florence's Forward.

When, at the beginning of an autobiographical narrative, as in *Epileptic* and *Persepolis*, the diegetic mirroring also reflects our entry into the text, it implicates reader-viewers as participants in the text's construction. What is at stake for the protagonist thus resembles our own meaning-making challenges. How are we to fuse and refuse ourselves in the other? David B. must learn to accept the physically altered person in the bathroom as his brother in the same way that any comics reader must learn to decode the drawn figure as a cipher of humanity, iconic of life's real joys and tragedies. So long as we strive for such identification, we remain open to interpreting disfiguration as transformation. Whether pictured as dragon-shadows or the seed of abstraction and memory, epilepsy takes on a vibrant life of its own in *Epileptic*, animated to haunt characters within the story as well as readers without. After all, we too must strive, like David B., to reconcile the unfamiliar and indecipherable details of an outward form to a private ideal. The reading lesson *Epileptic* poses at its multi-voiced and mirror-scene beginnings prompts us to make impossible connections. The visual narrative requires that we connect with the monstrous.

At the same time, connection is easier said than done in the comics. *Epileptic* skillfully uses ambiguity to usher readers towards the task of reading epileptically. One way that this is accomplished is by forcing readers to wade through dizzying details in search of interpretive stability. While the number and arrangement of panels per page are regularized, the contents of the panels are anything but regular. They teem with soldiering figures and mix "real-life" characters with the talking skeletons and anthropomorphic beasts that make up the young David's dream retinue. Is it coincidence that these onrushes of high-contrast minutiae cause many readers the same kind of disorienting search for order found within the story?

We shall explore the ludic implications of *Epileptic*'s predilection for such picture puzzles further in Chapter Three, but it suffices to say that our efforts at decoding the text have mimetic value in relation to the story. As we strain to distinguish weapon-brandishing warriors or the yin from the yang elements in various panels, so too must David and his parents strain to differentiate hoaxes from healing. Here again, the graphic novel is engineered to condition reader-viewers to cognitively (and, in some cases, physically) engage in practices that are idealized as themes within the narrative.

Like *Persepolis*, the opening page of *Epileptic* provides readers with a microcosm and a heuristic. Sprawling, intricate, and surreal, *Epileptic* makes its palette of black and white the ironic backdrop to its relentless focus on the existential gray areas of life—of dream and reality, of past and present, and most pressingly, of self and other. But even that urgent dyad is a gray area, for the brother is no ordinary other but a near or proximate one. Therefore, a more cogent synopsis of dyadic relationship presented in *Epileptic* is of the debilitated (br)other who anchors an object world and the ingenious self who authors and thereby releases them both. All of these conflations play out before the mirror in a present quite remote from the timescape of most of the graphic novel's nearly 400 pages, spanning the brothers' childhood, adolescence, and young adulthood. That the two brothers meet as adults on the first page, nearly as strangers, rehearses a familiar narrative gambit, piquing the reader's desire to know how this unusual present has come about.

In addition to building narrative desire, it is significant that this blip of the Real set in the super present, the temporal home of the reader, takes place in a bathroom. Like the mirror, the bathroom is a gray area of propriety, a zone where nature meets culture. Risking a scatological metaphor, which the style of *Epileptic* incidentally courts, it could be said that the bathroom is indeed a kind of Real in the Lacanian sense: a space apart, defining us on the one hand for the business we all do there, and on the other for denying that business and taking great collective pains to render it unrepresentable within the social order. Little wonder then that it is in this ultra-private sphere that David B. initiates both the mirror scene that forges a correspondence between his authorial voice and his I-con and the mirror scene that exacerbates those ruptures of visibility and verisimilitude for the reader ineluctably drawn into them.

Mirror Memento Mori: Embodiment and Instability in *The Imposter's Daughter*

We have seen how the mirror in comics marks the site of a threshold where nature meets culture and where stories intertwine with storytellers. More than a trope of consciousness or self-reflection, the mirror emblematizes the comics as a meaning-making system. But the mirror also plays harbinger to the demise of that process, a pictorial memento, if you will, of subjective death. Mirror scenes encapsulate how we come to be subjects in relation to other subjects, to ourselves, and to the tools that measure such relations. Because the mirror is often the receptacle into which we deposit that all too familiar discord between integrated and fragmented self-perception, its appearance in autography signals an attempt on the part of "the subject to reintegrate his or her alienated image" (353)—to borrow from Jameson.

Reintegration is a structural imperative in the comics as well as a thematic and emotional focus of several autobiographical graphic novels. Like Alison Bechdel's *Fun Home*, the author-protagonist of *The Imposter's Daughter* (2009) endeavors to obtain the truth about her father's clandestine life. Rather than poring over historical, pictorial, and memorial evidence to affirm her father's closeted sexuality as with Bechdel's story, Laurie Sandell's heroine conducts interviews with her pathologically lying father and covertly visits those who knew him during his hidden early life in Argentina. Similar to Bechdel's narrative, Sandell desires attachment with the estranged father, but her relationship to him is far less symmetrical than the psychological relation that tethers Bechdel to her father, in what Julia Watson refers to as a "genealogy of desire" ("Autographic" 27). While Bechdel achieves textual union with her father by narrating a shared homosexuality, Sandell is less forthright about the terms of paternal identification. If Bechdel's father is finally made to incarnate an ethic of confession in *Fun Home*, Sandell's father is the antithesis to the archetypical autobiographer. He is a contra-muse, whose alienated truths must either be reintegrated or else revisited traumatically in abusive relationships and recreational anesthetics.

Although Sandell's graphic novel has not met with even a fraction of the regard Bechdel's masterpiece has deservedly received, it manifests several of the same formal and topical predilections. While I do not wish to glaze over the differences between them, the similarities between Sandell's lesser known work and Bechdel's celebrated memoir nevertheless refocuses our attention on the peculiar functioning of mirror scenes—metaphorical ones (which abound in *Fun Home*) and literal ones (where an actual mirror appears), which recur throughout *The Imposter's Daughter*. Indeed, the mirror in *The Imposter's Daughter* dramatizes the reflective parameters of autobiographical subjectivity and, in particular, it highlights Sandell's intertextual aesthetic. In this way, Sandell complements Hillary Chute's assessment of women's autography in *Graphic Women*, which similarly "use the inbuilt duality of the form—its word and image cross-discursivity—to stage dialogues among versions of self, underscoring the importance of an ongoing, unclosed project of self-representation and self-narration" (5). Were it not for these mirror scenes, readers might be tempted to misjudge Sandell's efforts to stage these dialogues of self. Indeed, we might mistake Sandell's allusions to the masterworks of graphic novel autobiography that precede it for ineptitude or unoriginality, rather than "cross-discursivity"—to expand Chute's phrasing. We have already mentioned that the story echoes Bechdel's scenario, but we could go on to itemize Sandell's other similarities with now-canonical graphic novels, such as the coloring style of Barry's *One Hundred Demons* or the design for chapter titles from Satrapi's *Persepolis*. More resemblances emerge in Sandell's use of allusion, as when the author as a girl asks her irascible father about his suspicious guarding of the mail, to which he responds in a dialect rather like Vladek Spiegelman: "Ach, it's all junk mail, see?" One could find fault with so brazen a citation, especially since Sandell's father never speaks in this dialect again. But the validity of these criticisms would depend upon a standard of consistency that Sandell may be forsaking in lieu of other principles, aesthetic or otherwise. Of interest to us is not whether or not Sandell's actual father spoke like Vladek Spiegelman, but that Sandell seems perfectly willing to have his character speak like him once and, in so doing, highlight the correspondence between her father and his generic template.

It would be easy to chalk up Sandell's referentiality to a knee-jerk form of postmodernism, flattened of ideals and thus capricious towards an antiquated (paternalistic) value of artistic originality. We could just as well see it, however, as a reprise of modernist exhaustion whereby the burdens and Bloomian anxieties of trying to outdo Oedipal forefathers must be exorcized on the surface of the text.[24] With such a view in mind, we might wonder how Sandell could avoid characterizing her complaining and traumatically problematic father as another iteration of Vladek—the first of his type? And if she cannot avoid the connection (perhaps the logic goes), then why not overstate it, at least at first? The result is a graphic novel with a preponderance of allusions to type, which, along with a relatively unspectacular drawing style, may lead some to peremptorily dismiss the work, never noticing how its reflective capacities and relentless referencing of other graphic novels are key to understanding its structure and subjects.

The cover image (Fig. 1.6) introduces the theme of mirroring. It is essentially a portrait of the author's I-con, but where viewers expect to see Laurie's face, the I-con holds a Polaroid of the father proudly wearing his phony medals. Interestingly, this drawn photo bears a label that seconds as the subtitle of the graphic novel—*A True Memoir*—with the word "true" added with a diacritical carrot in blue. The amendment implies the phrase "a memoir" below the portrait of the father to be an insufficient promise of truthfulness. But what is perhaps more telling about the cover is that the image of the father

1.6   Cover image of Sandell's *The Imposter's Daughter*.

serves as the mask or public face of Laurie's I-con. As with David B.'s *Epileptic*, confusion over just who is at the center of the memoir elicits psychic ambiguity. Here, too, no clear determination is possible between the self and the proximate, intimate other whose intrusions form the intertext that catalyzes authorial selfhood.

The net effect of all this psychic intertextuality is a model of selfhood that is anything but coherent or consistent. Witness the cleverly embedded impostures represented on the cover image of *The Imposter's Daughter*. As with any photo, the Polaroid is a simulation, but this one is more precisely a drawing of a Polaroid and thus a copy of a copy. Moreover, insofar as any con artist is

1.7 Early mirror scene from Sandell's *The Imposter's Daughter*.

a fraudulent copy of an absent, authentic original, we could more accurately see this doubling of copies as a tripled relation—a drawing of a photo of an imposter. Nor does the simulacral chain end there, since the sum of this now tripled relation constitutes the author's mask. Indeed, Sandell's I-con is hereby defined for reader-viewers in terms of its ability to both comprise and compromise the author's public face by manipulating the father. Thus, the Polaroid announces Sandell's larger project of repurposing the archival inventory of the more realistic or actual photos that link her to her father, as Hillary Chute contends for Bechdel: "[T]he regeneration of archives is about asserting the power of comics as a form to include and also to fruitfully *repurpose* archives" (*Graphic Women* 200). It is therefore interesting to note how supposedly faithful reflections are repurposed in Sandell as unstable mirrorings.

Two mirror scenes in *The Imposter's Daughter* importantly link the I-con and authorial consciousness and both are punctuated by bodily anxiety. The first (Fig. 1.7) involves the author at seven years old, putting on her Brownie outfit. Officiously, her father is there to produce a set of random Girl Scouts badges that the young Laurie is to wear even though she has not earned them. In one stirring panel, we see father and daughter posing before a floor mirror with a caption that reads: "The awards gleamed on my chest. My father gazed at me proudly. In the mirror I saw a Brownie who had passed every test, accomplished every goal. Perhaps I *had* earned them" (17, emphasis in original). Similar to the cover image of the father, the daughter here sees in the mirror an unearned simulation of herself. The Brownie in the mirror both is and is not the one who stands before it. Yet in its illusory presentation of an accomplished self, the mirror articulates a bewitching ideal. And the author of that counterfeited ideal is less Laurie than her father. By giving her the badges the father inscribes an ego ideal directly onto his daughter's body, which is refashioned in the process as a malleable sign. Is it any surprise that the next panels relate the author's discovery of her early talent as a caricaturist, a talent she uses to please her cantankerous father, her first subject? "In each drawing," Sandell recalls, "his head was huge, outrageously out of proportion to the rest of his body" (18). Thus, the primal scene that founds creative writing and drawing for the author lays bare the over-admiring father, whose discourse works like a funhouse mirror, bulging, bending, and blurring the truth.

The second mirror scene (Fig. 1.8) involves the same kind of cheval mirror from the first scene with Laurie as a Brownie. It comes in a panel that emphasizes Laurie's negative body image in morbid contrast to her father's indiscriminate self-aggrandizement. In opposition to the father's aggressively optimistic fantasy of the ideal self transformed into a reality in the mirror, the panel exhibits the adult daughter's self-abjection. The scene occurs

1.8 Later mirror scene from Sandell's *The Imposter's Daughter*.

immediately after Laurie and a lover, Ben, have sex. Although Ben praises her body, Laurie examines herself in a mirror with dismay. Explanatory captions accompany the image to itemize the various pejoratives with which Laurie castigates herself, such as "flat chest" and "knobby knees" (110). Sandell typically uses panels like these with arrows and captions in the style of call-outs as a source of humor. She labels herself as a "nervous wreck" in one panel and in another names vaguely drawn items in a suitcase as "sexy thongs" and "condoms" (102). The caption for this latter announces that she "planned accordingly" for a meeting with Ben. Thus, the captions of these panels use humorous self-effacement and ironic labeling as alibis for their wounding details. Later, as Ben sleeps, Laurie turns from the self-diminishments she finds in her mirror to a pharmaceutical bottle. The move links her self-medicating practices to perceived deficiencies in the Imaginary. And this linkage has a defined origin, as we have been shown, in front of a mirror with a dissembling father and unearned Brownie awards.

If there is a psychodynamic unity to Sandell's plot, its center would no doubt be a dialectical, unrepresentable Real. Were we to trace its momentum, we would find it perpetuated by scenes of Laurie seeming to be other than what she sees herself to be. Of course, this is exactly the sort of psychic predicament that comics are adept at communicating as ruptures of visibility. The mirror scenes already discussed exemplify such ruptures, staging Laurie's split identity and proving just how efficient comics can be at representing egos in dialectical relation—in Laurie's case, vis-à-vis the father or one of his many substitutes in the Symbolic. And, as demonstrated in *Persepolis*, the mirror proves once again to be one of the form's archetypical devices for signaling story and structure, helping to bring the invisible relations at the center of any story into articulation.

Mirrors replay a principal reading lesson of the comics. They encourage us to close the distance between a mental self-ideal and a reflected image in order to discover the fiction of identity lying somewhere in between. The resulting construct of identity is no longer reducible to visual objects, bodies, or names, but based in practice, emerging from dialectic. Moreover, this lesson is applied by virtue of the same kind of seeing that every act of comics closure relies upon, as reader-viewers make one integrated narrative unit out of two or more. To be a successful closer of Sandell's narrative is to take up the same practice of integrative seeing and psychic well being that tragically eludes the protagonist. In other words, to read this book is to engage in corrective acts of closure, but this is just one way to interpret our relationship to the protagonist. From another angle, our successful reading always puts us in a space analogous to that of the father, in a state of ambitious desire—for the end, to control a world of tractable signs, to bypass psychic fixity, and to move on to the next set of panels.

As efficacious readers of *The Imposter's Daughter*, we are trained to dwell in the realm of the father. This is not to valorize Laurie's father specifically, but the "father-function" as an incarnation of the Symbolic order that aggressively imposes its meanings onto the Imaginary. In this way, we might say further that there is something phallic about Sandell's many satiric captions with arrows that literally pinion the Imaginary with the Symbolic and its attendant fixities. And are we any less assailed? We are partly positioned by the form into taking up reading and looking vantages rooted in the Symbolic order (the site of the wounding father). An inherent ambivalence makes this position tolerable to us, since our reading in the Symbolic enacts the very remedy for the harm incurred in the Imaginary that Laurie strives to overcome.

Conclusion: Mirrors Reveal Autobiographical Authority as Mask or *Prosopon*

To conclude, we might consider how all of this fatherly symbolism renders the notion of the Imaginary more obscure. Whether indicative of Marji's individuality in the face of the collective, or David B.'s conflations of trauma and memory, or the inner truth of Kochalka's elf face, the Imaginary seems to envision a world of bodies of the self not yet made flesh. This is the world that the comics, like the history of caricature, avidly puts on display. But the fact of its long-standing power in Western consciousness and art does not make it any easier to comprehend.

In describing the Imaginary as a visual playground of bodies without subjects, without point-of-view, Fredric Jameson comes close to limning the unconscious of the graphic novel form as it is usually rendered:

A description of the Imaginary will therefore on the one hand require us to come to terms with a uniquely determinate configuration of space—one not yet organized around the individuation of my own personal body, or differentiated hierarchically according to the perspectives of my own central point of view—yet which nonetheless swarms with bodies and forms intuited in a different way, whose fundamental property is, it would seem, to be visible without their visibility being the result of the act of any particular observer, to be, as it were, already-seen, to carry their specularity upon themselves like a color they wear or the texture of their surface. (355)

Graphic novels conjure the Imaginary as surely as the latter term connotes "the experience of the image—and of the imago—and we are meant to retain [the term's] spatial and visual connotations" (351). In Kochalka's scene of identity crisis, the mirror leads to a repression of symbol formation at the instant of acknowledging the Symbolic. It is the emergence of alienation in the Symbolic, jokingly hinted at, but immediately repressed. Sandell, by contrast, does not see herself as possessing a body that is, as Jameson puts it, "visible without [its] visibility being the result of the act of any particular observer." The problem with Sandell's imagined body is that it is surmounted by the surplus of having been "already-seen." Perhaps Sandell's insistent restrictions and interpretive negations are a means of compensating for her father's obscene hermeneutic of amplification.

It is only in the mirror, after all, that Sandell shows her I-con achieving a state of equilibrium after being pitched into the paranoid *mise en abyme* of unchecked identifications in the Imaginary. The scene in question takes place in a movie theatre as Laurie sits next to Ben. She grows ever more disconcerted by the film about a couple breaking up, as she can't help feeling that it presages doom for her relationship with Ben. Predictably, solace for these perturbations in the *mise en abyme* is found in a mirror. When Laurie stifles a panic attack by escaping to the movie theatre bathroom, we see her I-con, her mask or *prosopon*, standing before a bathroom mirror telling herself to "calm down" (196). Below it the caption reads, "I took three deep breaths and looked at my reflection" (196).

Although an apt illustration of the devices outlined in this chapter, this moment nevertheless moves beyond the form's reflective mechanisms merely to highlight the ways that reading and looking may perform union. Prominently in this final example from Sandell, our reading amounts to a healing that brings alterity to a state of relation by balancing the Imaginary with the captioning power of the Symbolic. And yet—however satisfying these associations may be affectively—Kochalka's elfish *prosopon* is never far behind, snickering all the while. Ultimately, the joke is always on us when we ascribe feeling to images so deliberately illustrated to disrupt conventions of visual verisimilitude.

And so it is finally amidst all of these games of *prosoponic* peekaboo that the predominance of the mirror in graphic memoir mourns the death of the author as well as the death of reference. As with the "real" face of Kochalka's hero, the genre expurgates its dead (reference, the Real, mimetic verisimilitude) from symbolic circulation in a manner reminiscent of Roland Barthes's comments about seeing himself in a photograph: "[W]hen I discover myself in the product of this operation, what I see is that I have become Total-Image, which is to say, Death in person" (14). Even so, autography tantalizes by so boldly manifesting that perplexing relation of personhood and presence. If, according to Paul de Man, *prosopopoeia* (the giving of a face to something) is the central "trope of autobiography, by which one's name. . . . is made as intelligible and memorable as a face" (76), that trope is vigorously literalized in graphic novel autobiography. But in the world of the comics there is no such thing as an ordinary face. Rather, the mask of graphic novel autobiography conforms to the ambiguities of the masquerade, its secular revelry and sacerdotal ritual. It reveals the face of the author by hiding that referent either to murderously satirize reference altogether or to mourn its loss. No matter the intention, the effect is to presume the true face of authorship *in absentia*—a textual exile by psychic necessity for author-artists and reader-viewers alike.

2

The Child in and as the Comics

... children are not grown-ups. They are not interested in these rarefied matters.
They do not know what the word "picaresque" means; they do understand
Hans and Fritz when they are sticking hatpins in the Captain's ample backside.
—Coulton Waugh, *The Comics* (45)

What does the face of American comics look like? If one were to picture a child, the reasons for doing so are historically sweeping. From Richard F. Outcault's *Yellow Kid* to Charles Schulz's *Peanuts*, the child has been the default actor of American comics since the commercial inception of the form. Regardless of the graphic novel's pretensions, the child or youth remains an emblem of the comics and an archetype of its mediation.[1] Indeed, for all their work to elevate the medium, graphic novels seem loath to quit their children. In the vein of Wordsworth, the child I-cons of autography romanticize youth's vistas and vicissitudes to affirm the enduring appeal of the "romantic, Western vision of the sentimental child" (Fass 255).

But the child of the comics is no mere instrument of sentiment. Like the mirror, the child is not just a recurring subject of the comics but a formal correlative as well, fostering philosophical reflection on the complicated nature of temporality. Works like *Persepolis* transfigure the past into a conceit of the narrated present.[2] As Hillary Chute puts it, "the comics form not only presents a child protagonist and an adult narrator but also gives voice simultaneously to both perspectives, even within the space of a single panel" (*Graphic Women* 5). The resulting fragmentation of the panel yields distinct ontological domains. In that of the caption, words mediate the present as an effect of

57

authorial knowledge—explored in the previous chapter as an effect of the Symbolic. In the domain of the image, the past is a stylized opacity. Even so, these zones are not separate and their porous division compounds the juxtaposition of time, not to mention humor and pathos.

Because they signify between text and image comics seem to possess an intermediary eloquence. Jared Gardner lauds their ability to express a host of "gray areas" ("Archives" 790), but none more absorbingly than between past and present. Most critics of *Persepolis*, for example, notice its splicing of the drawn past-time child with the present-tense captions of the adult and tie that splitting to a range of cultural politics surrounding the story; however, few go on to theorize what such a structuring suggests about comics *tout court*.[3] This chapter aims to correct that critical scarcity by investigating the comic form's association with the child.

All protestations aside, comics and graphic novels have been historically linked to the child and still connote children and children's reading. This is not to say that the medium is essentially juvenile, only that it signifies such a quality (call it juvenility) regardless of content due to formalistic, historical, and even phenomenological liaisons with imaginary children. Nor is it my intention to rehearse that history here.[4] Rather, I want to historicize both the championing and the denial of the child's perspective in the comics form, locating that ambivalence in the picaresque workings of Outcault's *Yellow Kid*, which today's iconic child extends. And as my analysis of Joe Sacco's *Palestine* (1993) will demonstrate, the child in the comics uncovers juvenility in even the most serious of graphic novels. The primary forms it takes are examined in later sections, which analyze the prophetic child in Kyle Baker's *Nat Turner* (2008), the queer child in Ariel Schrag's *Awkward* (1995), and the melancholic child in Chris Ware's *Jimmy Corrigan, the Smartest Kid on Earth* (2000). My aim throughout will be to track the ways childhood engages the comics—that is to say, appearing before us as an effect of our successful training in dialogical reading and seeing, curricula inherent to every comic.

Not Just for Kids Anymore—
Insistences Upon the Maturation of a Form

What has childhood come to mean in American comics? If every emblematic child is also a theoretical imagining of origins, what sorts of origins do comics kids propose? At the dawn of the newspaper age, the unprecedented popularity of comics about kids (e.g., *Little Nemo, Hogan's Alley, Katzenjammer Kids, Yellow Kid*) incited some officious civic leaders to intervene on behalf of child readers who, in their view, were beguiled and morally compromised by the new medium. One in particular framed the issue in terms of the allure of the comics page: "The avidity with which many children seize this pernicious sheet, with its grotesque figures and vivid and crude coloring, amounts to a passion, which wise parents should regard with alarm and take steps to prevent" (qtd. in Walker 23). Arguments about the prurience of comics reached a scandalous peak some five decades later in what has become the infamous thesis of psychologist Fredric Wertham, whose *The Seduction of the Innocent* (1953) argued that comics use images to make reading a matter of picture decoding, so that even children "with good reading ability, are seduced by comic books into 'picture reading'" (139).

It goes without saying that these arguments clamor to protect virtual rather than actual children. To be sure, moral panics take root in the cracks of volatile social ideals, and at the dawn of the twentieth century the ideal of the child was a busy epicenter of cultural changes regarding labor laws and compulsory education, to name only a few issues. The case against American comics gained momentum from a general suspicion of visual media, shaped by religious prohibitions against the idolatries of the image. These interdictions, along with the ongoing homogenization of bourgeois values in the early decades of the twentieth century, find odd resonance in the historical tumult over the alleged irreverence of the comics and their eventual censorship in the Comics Code.[5] Instead of pursuing a linear history of the convergence of children's pictorial literacy and the obscenity of the image, however, we would do well to consider the paradox that that convergence relies upon: comics promote adolescence and its rejection; they encompass both the view of (or as) the child and the child's view under verbal erasure. It is this paradox that lies at the heart of the comics' formal preoccupations with the child.

Even when contemporary critics refer to comics having grown up, as does David Hajdu in a 2003 piece for the *New York Review of Books*, the proclamation highlights by implication just how immature the form is still thought to be: "Hyper-energetic, crude, sexually regressive, and politically simplistic, comics—like rock (and, in recent years, hip-hop)—give fluent voice to their audience's basest and most cynical impulses. These are their virtues, arguably, as outlets for emotional release and as social counteragents." Never mind that two of the graphic novels this critic goes on to appraise—Joe Sacco's *Safe Area Gorazade* (2000) and *Palestine* (1993; 2001)—are anything but "politically simplistic" (Sacco represents an all-important deviation from the rule for Hajdu, a point to which we shall soon return)—the value of the comics lies in their ability to limn rebellion for Hajdu. Thus, comics are defendable insofar as they counterpoise their other, the establishment. The real object

2.1 Ontological dichotomy from *Persepolis* (6). "East/West Dichotomy" from *Persepolis: The Story of a Childhood* by Marjane Satrapi. Translation copyright © 2003 by L'Association, Paris, France. Used by permission of Pantheon Books, an imprint of the Knopf Doubleday Publishing Group, a division of Random House LLS. All rights reserved.

of criticism is less the purportedly countercultural art form than the status quo, which hovers in the background of these fantasies of resistance as an invariant standard. In Hajdu's thinking, rock, rap, and comics emerge through simple negation: they are what they must not be, neither serious nor sage.

Ironically, one of comics' most notable affordances is their ability to reconstitute binaries (like the one driving Hajdu's slippery argument) as visual metaphors. A prominent example may be seen in Marjane Satrapi's autobiographical avatar Marji, whom Satrapi depicts as a dichotomy of Western and Middle Eastern cultural values (Fig. 2.1). Like Hajdu's binarizing of comics as a non-serious opposition to dominant culture, Satrapi uses recognizable cultural symbols in stark contrast to convey a less stable cultural fusion.

With an economy of expression the panel not only displays but subtly disrupts the binary, indicting even while relying upon the logic that organizes Middle East and West in strict opposition. One is initially led to presume that the Western left half of the panel, with its mechanical gears and tools, signifies the "very modern" aspects of the family mentioned in the caption. The mechanical side neatly balances the leafy crescents of the unmistakably Arab side of the panel. Yet to which sentiments in the caption do these Arab designs correspond? The veil Marji wears only on one side of her body certainly pertains to the statement, "Deep down I was very religious," but the arabesques do not. In fact, either the gears or the arabesques could illustrate that the family is "very modern and avant-garde." The visual binary of the image does not give viewers the clear-cut categories promised in the caption. And, crucial to our purposes, this lapse seems dramatic, perhaps even instructive.[6]

Carrying over the lessons of the opening two panels discussed in the first chapter (while looking forward to the capacity of comics to morph into picture puzzles—the subject of the following chapter), this single panel offers training in synesthetic reading. It fuses visual and verbal signs into what at first appears to be an unambiguous representation of opposition. On the one hand, complexities of origin and identity are visualized through juxtaposition and mirroring. On the other, to apply this principle of opposition is to witness other aspects of the panel conspiring to undo its paradigmatic value. Some of these lessons overlap with those encountered in the previous chapter on mirror moments, of which this panel is yet another example. But whereas the aim of the first chapter is to posit the mirror as a metaphor for the unconscious operations of comic structure, the point here is to notice what happens when the mirror breaks. What happens when the reflections proposed fracture our trust in the text's organization of meaning? If the focalizer of interest in the first chapter is the I-con, here it is the archetypical iteration of the I-con in the child—the comics' standard for both conjuring and dissolving a central opposition of past and present.

Our inability to unequivocally coordinate image and caption is crucial to *Persepolis*'s lessons about cultural identity and the hybridity of its child protagonist. Genetic and cultural inheritances do not cohere in actuality with the rhetorical devices so often used to symbolize them. Some identities, like Marji's, are better communicated by the failure of clean divisions and one-to-one correspondences. What does not fail, however, in Satrapi's visual exemplum against monocultural essentialism is the primacy of the child. Indeed, Satrapi's memoir advances a logic of identity—what Baudrillard in another context describes as "ideal coextensivity"—which locates the iconic child as the substratum upon which sexual, classed, and social influences accrue.[7]

This capacity to speak ideology as a type of picture language is not unique to *Persepolis* nor is it an observation about comics exclusive to academic discussions. In a 2004 *New York Times* article aptly titled "Not Funnies," Charles McGrath acknowledges childish qualities in the medium, but claims them to be the means to a salutary destabilization of elitist categories of high art and serious literature. After an eloquent series of close readings, McGrath concludes by promulgating the childishness of comics as a misunderstood asset:

... no matter how far the graphic novel verges toward realism, its basic idiom
is always a little, well, cartoonish. Sacco's example notwithstanding, this is a
medium probably not well suited to lyricism or strong emotion, and (again, Sacco
excepted) the very best graphic novels don't take themselves entirely seriously.
They appeal to that childish part of ourselves that delights in caricature . . .

Leaving aside the fact that it is only in stigmatized relation to unexamined
notions of adulthood that "that childish part of ourselves" is ever knowable,
McGrath is boldly onto something here. Echoing the logic of Hajdu's essay,
McGrath makes seriousness and its child-laden inverse the benchmarks for
assessing the cultural value of comics. Despite perpetuating romantic notions
of the child that stirs within, McGrath guides us to an intriguing question:
Why is it that the most commercially and critically successful graphic novels in the US—autographies like Spiegelman's *Maus*, Satrapi's *Persepolis*, and
(yes, even) Sacco's *Palestine*—foreground rather than sublimate the medium's
childishness?

I want to join McGrath in wondering if the power of the medium lies in
its eloquence for signifying the synapse or the space between, which the child
incarnates.[8] To be sure, the child rises to the level of an imperative in the comics, whether we want it to or not. It should be noted that many comics sidestep
the issue. They counteract the form's tendencies toward childish distortion
with adult storylines and voices to assert perhaps the more culturally mature
aesthetic of caricature or satire. If there is a child in us who finds caricature
appealing—to return to McGrath's formulation—the history of caricature
reared it to maturity long ago.[9] Anyone glancing at the difference between
a political cartoon and a comic strip from the same major newspaper, for
example, would likely recognize the distinction to which I allude.

What, then, is the present appeal of comics for adults? The recent surge
of comics memoirs, along with such fictions as Chris Ware's *Jimmy Corrigan*,
cognize the world from a perspective readers may believe themselves once to
have occupied. These are not texts for real children, but rather textual devices
for the rehabilitation of imaginary ones. These are texts for children that never
were. As Jacqueline Rose presciently argues, children's literature and literature
of children presume as their primary but unstated subject the "impossible
relation between adult and child" (1). That relation is impossible for making it
seem as if adults come prior to children, producing them, but never necessarily meeting them in the space of the fictions at hand. In this way, the mask of
the child signifies both the condition and cognition of story. Never simply a
symbol of individual identity in the making, the comics child imagines (and
images) the social order at a point of incipience and in so doing reactivates
the picaresque tradition out of which it grows.

A Picaresque Genealogy from Yellow Kid to Marji

Autobiographical graphic novels are not the first to spotlight dichotomies of experience and innocence, voice and view. From *Humphrey Clinker* to *Huckleberry Finn*, the journeying youth, or picaro, has long charmed audiences with a mischievous disregard for propriety. What permits Huck or Clinker access through social space derives in part from the license granted to humor. Their class position also has something to do with it, as one critic observes: "[T]he *picaro* observes society from below, from his position as *lumpen*"—and it is this initial perspective, according to critical consensus, that "gives us the key to [the picaro's] demythifying realism" (Cruz 114). At the apex of the picaro's upward and myth-razing view is the elevated reader, newly appointed emissary of the community the picaro has yet to join. Through ordinary acts of sympathy and feeling, readers are empowered to absolve picaros of their trespassing.

In many ways, the picaresque enjoyed a renaissance in early twentieth-century comics. Undaunted by boundaries, Little Nemo and Yellow Kid were also pioneers of history. They crossed over into urban spaces newly configured by capital: materially in the newspaper and diegetically in raucous tableaus of the city and its denizens. Indeed, the Yellow Kid illustrates Walter Benjamin's thesis that the sign-carrying sandwich man (like the prostitute and the flâneur) organizes public space as well as life itself around spectacles of consumption.[10] Moreover, the Kid foregrounds the role youth plays in maintaining new forms of sociality.[11]

The graphic novel child foments crises of community and spectacle that the Yellow Kid and Little Nemo helped to realize. A glance at *Persepolis*, Clowes's *Ice Haven*, or Thomas Jenner and Angeline Perkins's *Kellie's Diary* is sufficient to aver Brian Walker's claim that the comics "never outgrew the bad reputation of their obstreperous youth" (24). But before the Marjis and Jimmy Corrigans of the graphic novel, the Yellow Kid put youth at the center of social, historical, and psychic volatility. "A Turkey Raffle in Which the Yellow Kid Exhibits His Skills with the Dice" (Fig. 2.2), a cartoon by Richard F. Outcault from the *New York World* (1896), shows the jubilant Kid with a dead turkey over his shoulder. In opposition to the Kid's bounty, the unlucky throng must redirect hunger using shabbily inedible substitutes: a map of Turkey or a rickety booth touted as a Turkish museum. Even while emulating the Kid's exclusive grasp of the signified, reader-viewers are forced to mirror the unfulfilling spectatorship of those who lose to the Kid. And the comic seems aware of this jibe, compensating for its equation of fanciful looking and factual loss by elevating and empowering readers. Our viewing of the scene is tantamount to consuming the social, surveying the social order as an object of panoramic totality.[12]

2.2 "A Turkey Raffle in Which the Yellow Kid Exhibits His Skills with the Dice."

Thus, the comic affords panoptic control over the sprawling threat of the social. It does so even while impugning voyeurism as deprivation. Especially after 1896, the average page of the *Yellow Kid* contained areas of focus that viewers must seize, in effect, to conquer the narrative puzzle of the page and solve the rough joke that the Yellow Kid unfailingly tells.[13] Reading comics, therefore, has instructional implications for those attempting to thrive amidst sweeping social change. What could be better practice for negotiating the new demands of urban existence than unifying visual particularities into an amusing totality? As subjects of growing state power, changing cultural pressures, and rapidly increasing market demands, early twentieth-century readers could hardly fail to enjoy comic heroes, who like their picaro forebears, stand aloof from subjection, remaining open and fantastically inchoate.

Not yet adult, not quite child, the picaro commits violations to an established order that is not yet established to him. His infractions beg for a punitive consequence that never comes. Fair penalty would require moral awareness, which would in turn dissolve the picaro's defining narcissism. According to one critic: "[T]he most endemic ailments of the self that the picaro suffers . . . are the maladies associated with narcissism, the unhappy consequences of such self-concentration, even self-adoration, to the degree that the surrounding world is lost or missed or rebuffed altogether" (Sherrill 96). Like the juvenile delinquent postulated in legal discourse, the picaro's intellectual and emotional distance from the world is exculpatory.

To be sure, much of the humor in Outcault's strip results from seeing the Kid out of place at the center of some political imbroglio.[14] The Kid exports politics from one imaginary scene (usually an unmarked bourgeois landscape) to that of the Lower East Side tenement district, where signs and slogans vie for attention against undergarments hung out to dry. Outcault's characteristic "cacophony of signage" invents a new kind of newspaper reader.[15] The ideal reader of the strip is coached into being just as indifferent to the symbolic order as the Kid, becoming primarily a viewer of the imaginary—a member of a satirical mass public who is neither the Lower East Sider nor the gentleman of politics.[16] The ideal viewer thus inhabits an especially hybrid space that holds the real both in view and at bay.

Whether the Kid is drunk at an Oktoberfest, where everyone pretends to be German, or marches through the slums with ungrammatical banners held high, he remains an emblem. Reading him (literally), viewers are caught in everyday acts of urban spectacle. Because the Kid is visually marked as a child and absurdly bedecked in his articulate nightshirt, he seems just as much of a dreamer as Little Nemo. The ever-changing writing on his shirt pushes him several degrees further into the realm of the object, nearly on a par with the ideogram. Ironically, though—and one wonders if this point needs justification for enthusiastic readers of historical comics—these added touches of abstraction do not necessarily put the figure of the Kid at a further remove. Rather, they secure his relation to the real (as is the case for all comics kids) through fantasy. The real city lurks behind the fantasy, for as Judith Butler cogently explains: "[T]he boundaries of the real against which [fantasy] is determined are precisely what become problematized in fantasy" (110).

Summarized in this way, it is interesting to note the similarities between current child heroes of the graphic novel and the child's embodiment of social rebellion in the early strips. Then and today, children merge the political and the social. They trigger temporal confusions indicative of and resistant to reigning ideologies. As Scott Bukatman argues in reference to the way

2.3 Marji asking, "Where are you?" from *Persepolis*. "Where Are You?" from *Persepolis: The Story of a Childhood* by Marjane Satrapi. Translation copyright © 2003 by L'Association, Paris, France. Used by permission of Pantheon Books, an imprint of the Knopf Doubleday Publishing Group, a division of Random House LLS. All rights reserved.

that *Little Nemo* "speaks eloquently to the condition of kinesthetic knowledge" (96–98), comics translate particular types of knowledge into ontological spaces that readers inhabit.[17]

Take, for example, a scene from *Persepolis* (Fig. 2.3) in which young Marji converses with God in her bedroom. Having decided to attend a demonstration, she tries on hats and poses in her mirror first as Che Guevara, then as Fidel Castro. Marji looks for God who has disappeared, leaving unanswered her question: "Don't you think I look like Che Guevara?" Marji's allegorical search for God recurs throughout *Persepolis*, but it begins here as she first addresses herself and then the reader on the other side of the panel. The sequence correlates panel and mirror as Marji turns away from her own reflection to face us and ask: "Where are you?"

Insofar as the mirror is the metonym of the comics panel, this one makes reader-viewers proxy to divinity. Our position on the other side of the grand frame-up of the comics panel mirrors the existential predicament of the seeker of divinity. And, as with her picaresque ancestors, the provocations Marji sets in motion are conceptual as well as comedic. Whether the girl in the hat looks like Che or Fidel is not only farcically cute but ironic, given that the entirety of the world that creates this proposition is an exaggerat-edly drawn one. The adult cartoonist stages a world that her avatar cannot yet comprehend in order to illuminate the lesson that Marji is in the pro-cess of learning: identity is not reducible to appearance. At the same time, the scene embeds a poignant lesson for the reader, suggesting that identity for the reader *is* reducible to cognitive practices preordained by the artist. We are, in other words, only what the comic prepares us to be. For the most part, this means that we are beholders, sorters, readers, connectors, question-ers—many things, but seldom speakers. Rarely do we speak aloud to comic characters even when they speak to us. The scene trains us to become aware of the agnostic implications of our inadvertent refusals of address. As with the Kid's turkey shoot, we are potentially uncomfortable with our spectatorship, pulled out of naturalized practices of viewing and dragged into monological spaces of immanence reserved for Gods and authors.

Of Picaros, Gods, and Conservativism

Even as the iconic child allegorizes the loss of divinity, it is misleading to sweep the I-con of comic art under the rug of religious orthodoxy's suspicion of the image. In its ecclesiastical role, the icon is not "merely a symbol of the archetype, but the represented becomes present through the icon" (Galavaris 3). It is this emphasis of the icon as vehicle more than symbol that has caused some comics scholars to note an inherent oscillation in panels requiring clo-sure between traditional notions of the idol and the icon.[18] The idol applies when the dialogical encounter between the viewer and the comic enshrines the image, emphasizes the distance between viewer and image, or plays up the the image as a displacement of the Real. A Luciferian copy, the idol pro-fanes the sacred—in this case, the Real. By contrast, the icon applies when, as Patrick Doolan explains, the image is secondary to the sacred encounter for which "it acts as a catalyst" (99). It is not the image but the encounter with it that consecrates. The theological is thus another way of getting at the tautol-ogy the iconic child presents. The child is both an ironic and sacred naïf who harbors the wish for cosmic closure.

The history of the picaro clarifies the important cultural work that nostalgia accomplishes in our age of lost gods and children. Children are handy projec-tions for desires of origin not easily articulated by adults. Like the Yellow Kid who, despite buffooneries of dialect and situation, stands exclusively at the center yet far from the madding crowd to which he belongs, so stands Marji. We identify with that part of them that stands alone, exalting the individual as well as the individual's consequential loss of community and divinity. It is an encounter with categorical crisis that the child as icon evinces, since the child embodies a central phenomenological paradox of self-identification in naming both the person we continue to be as well as the trace of our having been. Hence, the ontic waltzes with god, the crowd, the real, and with modernity in comics all radiate from a central irreconcilability of two temporalities—past-time and passing time. An icon in the classic sense, the child transports us to an encounter with this irreconcilability.

The contemporary child of the graphic novel carries on the picaro's efforts by translating crises of community into crises of spectatorship. Both Marji and Yellow Kid forcefully presume their own singularity amidst the masses they resemble but whose fate (as object) they transcend. Through the formal design of the comic text, they reflect the dialectical negotiations of a reader who both identifies with and lords over the picaro, experiencing both solidarity with the rebellious individual and visual dominion over all that is seen. The comics child moves beyond the detail (the single event, scene, or panel) to apprehend totalities (episodes, narrative closure, history).

Ultimately, the history of the picaro sheds light on one of the most captivating paradoxes surrounding the comics child, from the Yellow Kid to Marji: the reader may become the not-yet subject that the picaro models as well as the very logic of subjection that the picaro is fated to obey. And the zone of this logic corresponds to a futurity of godlike immanence on the other side of diegesis. That there is always an "other side" to literature's terrible and thrilling verisimilitude coincides with the certainty of there being a child "self" on the other side of every adulthood. Both certitudes have theological implications, suggesting an optimistic universe thick with unseen yet benevolent presences. But this is not the only way to read these scenes that predicate the divine reader of the Kid's slang-ridden shirt or Marji's god-search. Particularly in the latter, we are forced to pantomime an absent god in the same position as the mirror and the panel's fourth wall, which is to predicate divinity as a supreme device for the dislocation of citation, a force that makes referent and reflection the same.

To what extent does this force and the textual conditions giving rise to it ramify the genre or the form at large? This is the question taken up by the following sections, for we have yet to prove in full the thesis that opens this chapter: that the child inheres as both the default subject and structure of identification in US comics. The history of the picaro has helped us to flesh out that association, but before examining key permutations—the prophetic child in Kyle Baker, the queer child in Ariel Schrag, and the melancholic child in Chris Ware—we must first ask whether any graphic novel or comic would have the same effect in the absence of the child? If there is truly something in the form and not simply in the content (if we momentarily allow this admittedly false binary), then would not even the least childish sample yield similar results?

The Child Even in Joe Sacco's Exceptionally Non-Childish *Palestine*

To understand how the iconic child construes even the ostensibly non-childish graphic novel, let us turn to a text that, next to *Maus*, signifies as the great exception to the inferiorities that plague its generic peers—Joe Sacco's *Palestine* (originally published in 1993, reprinted as a graphic novel in 2001).

The second chapter of *Palestine* shows our journalistic hero being carried into the hospital wards of Nablus to "take pictures" of the "Public and Private Wounds"—as the chapter title informs us—of various Palestinians. Sacco's I-con is toted doll-like, fish lipped, and Annie-eyed (due to pupil-free glasses). His camera bag dangles behind him as he is himself dragged like a purse—the feminized, objectified capstone to a general infantalization. But he willingly endures it all to apprehend the "something [that] *always* happens" (28). Is it merely for denotative value that the caption accompanying the image of Sacco being carried attributes this rough tour to "the kid who's caught five rounds"? Or are we to infer a witty doubling of the reference, since the only figure in this panel possessing the child's vulnerability is Sacco? Nor is this the only insinuation of hero and child. Sacco is plied relentlessly to take milk by a man he refers to as the milkman and begins the text-heavy narrative of the chapter with the claim that "it's a good idea to get the kids on your side . . . I've smiled and beamed my way into their little hearts. Kids can be exhausting" (41). And smiling and beaming is precisely what Sacco's avatar does for reader-viewers, as the mask of his I-con manages our responses to the authorial voice of narration. Perhaps we too are exhausting, standing as every comics reader must in the limit space of reception ever awaiting address.

If there is nothing overtly childish about Sacco's comics-journalism, at the very least we might notice how the enervating child plays the text's primary addressee. Juvenility illustrates the face of reception in *Palestine* when Sacco places viewers awkwardly close to a semicircle of some dozen or so children (Fig. 2.4), who personify the communication challenges of his project. All heads turn towards us, smiling, as a few ask questions—two of which are laughably identical: "What is your name?" "What is your name?" (41). Stammering, crowding, solicitous, do the children not address us at this moment and are we not meant to feel the burden of these questions? Standing in the

2.4 Children interviewing the interviewer in *Palestine.*
© Joe Sacco, images courtesy Fantagraphics Books.

place of Sacco's I-con, we experience just how exhausting childish inter-
locutors can be. Rather than anything essential to them, it is the sharpness
with which their beaming ring of toothy glee contrasts against the wall of
stone-faced adults, shocking us back to the hardships of life in Palestine.
Finely crosshatched for detail and expertly composed, the scene visualizes a
dynamic familiar to the comics, in which child and adult come face to face to
recognize if not to bridge the chasms between them.

In its second chapter, *Palestine* invokes that definitive chasm once again,
this time via an allusion to children's cartoons. The chapter opens with Sacco
hailing a taxi to escape scenes of escalating or potential violence and spending
his nights "shaking [his] bootie" at a nightclub in Jerusalem while "watching

Tom and Jerry brain each other on the video screen" (28). A musical word balloon in the background of a dancing Sacco contains the absurd lyrics "Take off your pants-pants" (28). The balloon links Sacco with the video image of Jerry the mouse, who appears in the same rifle-toting pose seen in an adjoining panel, where a frightened soldier stares off-panel to the space where earlier Sacco has made his enviable taxi-escape.

The reference to the *Tom and Jerry* cartoon offers an analog to the violence of the Palestinian-Israeli conflict. Both are episodic, seemingly without end, and for Sacco in any case, visually horrendous and personally innocuous. Interestingly, the impossibility of the violence—given its fantastic context—withers as a defense against the charge that *Tom and Jerry* cartoons increased the violence shown to children on TV just after World War II.[19] As Stephen Kline implies in his commentary, there is something about the cyclicality of cartoon violence, its sheer repeatability, that is exculpatory: "Friction, resilience, the mechanics of the lever and the spring, and the flexibility of the body were the endlessly repeated visual ideas in the *Tom and Jerry* series, so it didn't matter that there was no pain and no lasting hurt" (116). The effect of the contrast between the popular children's cartoon and the surrounding geopolitical clash recalls Spiegelman's animal mask strategy in *Maus*.[20] If the irony works at all, it does so on condition of our willingness to assume the position of the child in relation to a spectacle of high seriousness, which, like caricature, liberates insofar as it remains on some level inappropriate to the context.

So long as we are inappropriate viewers—children who make light of what we see—we enlarge that which is seen, making the spectacle responsive to connotations that exceed and subvert it. This dialectic, so similar to the interplay of words and images in the comics form, is used here to put the serious at a distance and to suggest the intricate interlocking of locations of identity (child and adult; here and there; then and now). Were readers of comics to embrace the childishness of graphic novels, they may see, for example, the rifle held by Jerry in Sacco's illustration to be the primary icon through which the secondary yet more seemingly deadly rifle—held by the soldier—acquires meaning. It is not necessarily the case that the play gun of representation is any less potent than that of the soldier's rifle. Indeed, as several social science experiments in the 1990s indicate, Palestinian children spend a substantial number of hours per day imitating not just the military skirmishes between Palestinian heroes and enemy Israeli combatants but also, less grandiosely, the role they already play as children in the conflict, pretending to throw stones at Israeli tanks.[21] Likewise, when reading from the child's perspective readers risk an identification that is fantastical and pedestrian, childish even.[22]

2.5 Sacco taking pictures of wounded children in *Palestine*.
© Joe Sacco, images courtesy Fantagraphics Books.

A central equivocation of *Palestine*'s second chapter, then, is that we "take" the pictures Sacco shows himself taking. Taking a picture is a metonym for reading as the child. Just as Sacco takes pictures of the wounded in the hospital while asking his subjects for their consent to have their picture taken, so must we consent to see these pictures as consonant with reality. We do so because of and despite the fact that these images are carefully, exactingly, but nevertheless obviously drawn—and thus neither material enough, as they appear to us in printed copies of the book, to physically "take," nor realistic enough for us to mistake for photographs.

If these images are to move us as evidence, they must become fantastically tenable, just as they seem to be within the book. After being asked if he wants to see the children, Sacco is again carried off, this time dragging the very panels of the comic in tow. His fingers seem able to wrap around the first of a series of four images (Fig. 2.5) arranged as panels coming off of the page three-dimensionally. The one on the bottom left even has its four corners folded into what appears to be the triangular pockets of a photo mount for a frame or album. The images become impossibly more than they are, transcending two-dimensionality by virtue of our investments in iconic abstraction, of course, but also because of a reception context reminiscent of children's material reading. As Valerie Krips explains, "[t]he children's book should be understood as both a trace of and metaphor for the past [. . .] it combines materiality with symbolic power [. . . .] the object around which rituals of childhood are enacted and imagined" (33).

We take pictures; Sacco takes pictures. And in this storytelling exchange, the iconic is our primary currency. It alone gives. Visuality assimilates even touch for Sacco, whose ubiquitous and often enlarged hands, according to Rebecca Scherr, underscore the "emotional and corporeal forms of evidence that occurs through a haptic, visceral engagement with the pain of others" (20). Words entail fewer injurious seizures (takers) of emotion or memory. On the one hand, words are deceptive objects deposited into pockets (captions) where they remain lost and invisible, while, on the other, they have potential by mimicking images, erupting from their repositories, like the Yellow Kid's verbalizing nightshirt. In this way, words can be dangerous. Rather than anchoring images, they sprawl visually and need anchoring themselves. But whatever the specific power of words or images, their intermedial relationship contributes to the pedagogy of innocence that infuses Sacco's aesthetics and which *Palestine* everywhere imputes to children, as martyrs of history, as addressees of narrative, and as advocates for the hegemony of images.

A telling interchange Sacco chooses to include at the start of this chapter hints at the subordinate status of words. It comes as evidence of those unchoreographed "intimacies with fellow passengers" (28) that he experiences while escaping scenes of conflict in taxicabs. This time, instead of witnessing Sacco's avatar taking a picture, we see him taking an address of a desperate young man who pleads with him for help to "get out of here!" The harried young man "scribbled his address," Sacco reports, adding somewhat coldly: "I put it in my pocket and forgot about him forever" (28). This message in a bottle cannot drift across its ocean of difference to reach us, Sacco contrastively suggests, because, unlike the pictures "taken" of the wounded in the hospital, it is rooted in a ground of writing. Words are not just more ephemeral than the ever-present ground of the graphic field but obliterated by it as well.

The general image of the man wanting to leave and giving Sacco his address, however, has not been forgotten. If we believe the caption, that Sacco "forgot about him forever," we miss the truth that our own eyes take in: that Sacco has not forgotten the man at all and has in fact enshrined this moment as a visual exchange whose durability in memory withstands verbal erasure. The whole truth of this scene can only be apprehended as a conflict between memory's visual tools—pictures given and taken—and verbal utterances falsified by pictorial counter claims.

I have restricted myself to one representative chapter of *Palestine* to make my point, but there are other linkages to children—chapter titles and occasional captions referring to adults as kids or boys, which become informal terms of collective community; scenes where Sacco portrays himself drawing the attention of children, or those fewer instances where his captions tell us about his magnetism for children explicitly: "[S]ometimes, on the way to one place or other, we'd attract a crowd of kids . . ." (185). There is also the fact that there are more scenes of children guiding Sacco than adults, as when, near the end, "kids say they know" where to find the "grave of Hatem Sissi, the first person killed in the intifada" (223). And, finally, there is the boy who ends the book in the rain, detained by Israeli soldiers from whose perspective an imaginary future (as well as a hopeful conclusion to the graphic novel) is made possible. On a conceptual level, the entirety of Sacco's project is predicated on the assumption that he will go into the region with a blissfully ignorant curiosity. This pedagogy of innocence, as I have characterized it, is the mindset not only of the tourist but also of the child. That connection is explicit within the tradition of the Bildungsroman, in which inexperience becomes the necessary precondition for a definitively modern narrative of growth through the acquisition of experience and knowledge.

But this is not the ordinary kind of positivism that touts the beneficence of knowledge while concealing a regressive nostalgia for other absolute values of the Enlightenment such as a sliding scale of human value. Nor does this positivity support the Enlightenment's evidentiary correspondence between optic proof and knowledge, a notion kept alive in everyday newspaper photojournalism. Indeed, Sacco's text maintains a childish insistence on the validity of the visual or of "taking pictures," without actually endorsing that validity in practice. Rather, lived reality bristles with fictionality in Sacco's universe. The subjectivity of his vision saturates every panel, braiding the perspective of the artist into every stylized reflection of what he has purportedly seen.

As the foregoing analysis has intended to demonstrate, even in Sacco's *Palestine*, the child emerges as both the depicted subject and the general addressee of history. In some ways, the child names the space of enunciation or the code of the comics more generally. By the latter, I mean to build on Roland Barthes's observation about photography which seems to have no code "between the object and its image" since the photographic image, while not being reality, achieves a "perfect *analogon*" of reality or what Barthes calls "analogical perfection" (*Image Music Text* 17, emphasis in original). Drawings, particularly those in comics, are steeped in code. Hence, comics comprise a language of analogical imperfection, laden with systems for approximating reality through hyperbolic, grotesque, and subversive forms of analogy. Whereas Barthes proclaims elsewhere that "there is no drawing without style" and "like all codes, the drawing demands an apprenticeship," I would like to treat this statement the way Barthes approaches the photograph. I want to suggest that the comics propose a drawing code that requires no apprenticeship. This is not to suddenly reject the premise for this book as a whole, but to introduce two levels of apprenticeship: the one, which entails the various pedagogies particular to specific comics texts, artists, styles, and subjects, and the other which pertains to ubiquitous features of the form. As Scott McCloud makes clear throughout *Understanding Comics* (and announces in his subtitle), the form articulates invisibly, in a manner so routinized or sublimated as to be learned without the viewer being conscious of apprenticeship.

It is on this level that the child signifies in the comics—as the unquestioned, inevitable, sometimes unwanted face of the genre. In addition, therefore, to limning rebellion like the Yellow Kid or Marji, or embodying a subjective vulnerability that initiates narrative desire as with many confessional or trauma narratives, or founding communities from the position of political or historical incipience, the comics child also denies any presumption of innocence. Indeed, in some cases the child is a space-clearing agent, not unlike Walter Benjamin's notion of the primitive but positive barbarian, who destroys not out of malice but to hungrily make way for the new.[23]

Three types of space-clearing agencies perpetuated by comics kids remain to be explored. The first is the child that calls forth community and traumatic history so as to demystify trauma. This child bears resemblance to Satrapi's Marji and Sacco's Palestinians, but its most complex fruition may be found in Kyle Baker's *Nat Turner*. The second is one of the most unique cases of the comics child: an acclaimed graphic novel about childhood actually drawn and told by a *de jure* child, *Awkward*, by fifteen-year-old Ariel Schrag. Because of its uniquely authentic claim to adolescence as a space of authorship rather than remembrance, *Awkward* exposes the disturbingly typical desire for youth, or what I shall call "pedographic narrative desire," which defines much autobiographical graphic memoir. And, finally, the child functions in Chris Ware's *Jimmy Corrigan* as a provocation to epistemology. Along with Ware's lavish choreography of panel arrangements, the figure of the tragic child intersperses scenes of adulthood that deceptively lull reader-viewers into simplistic interpretations of causality elsewhere repudiated by the text. In all three the iconic child of the comics forges new textual spaces of possibility— of history, identity, and knowledge—not just to read or to view but to inhabit.

The Prophetic Child as History in Kyle Baker's *Nat Turner*

Kyle Baker's graphic novel *Nat Turner* takes the comics' layering of temporalities to a whole new level, seeming to circulate in our time and in that of American plantation slavery. Told in a visually dominant style, *Nat Turner* pays homage to the wordless graphic novel tradition of Frans Masereel and Lynd Ward, recoding wordlessness as subversion.[24] That the story is told almost entirely through pictures means that it would have been intelligible even to illiterate slaves. In this way, *Nat Turner* both memorializes and performs insurrection. To contextualize the 1831 Virginian slave rebellion, the narrative reimagines the slave insurgent as a prophetic boy, supernaturally in touch with the harrowing slave ship experiences of ancestors that he could not have witnessed himself. The pictorial simulates prophecy and scripts the child as history's author. Unlike *Persepolis* or *Palestine*, which envision the child as a primary actor or addressee of history, Baker's child incarnates revolution and retributive racial violence against white oppressors. In accordance, the image is formally extolled throughout the text as the just usurper of the authority of speech and writing.

In the preface, Baker wrests Turner from the oblivion of history: "Who was this man who was important enough to be mentioned in *all* the history books, yet is never spoken about at length?" Turner's exile from official records of the national past transfers to the graphic novel's essentially wordless structure. *Nat Turner* is so logophobic that characters even speak in pictures whenever speech balloons appear, scant as they are. The same capability of literacy to change history, which Baker ascribes to Turner in the preface, returns at the very end of the book. There, a slave child purloins a copy of Thomas Gray's *Confessions of Nat Turner* (1831) after Turner's execution, stealing away into the shadowy night with the book clutched in her arms. Baker's valorization of the child reflects the consensus of race and diaspora critics, who claim, as does Landsberg here, that "[j]ust as the child is the site of trauma [. . .] the child ultimately must be the agent of recovery, creatively producing his or her own genealogy or memory narrative" (88). If any child signifies new beginnings, one armed with contraband (subaltern literacy or memory) assures revolution, the most forcibly *new* beginning imaginable. Is it surprising then that Baker's "i-con" for reading as rebellion is not Nat Turner the adult dissident but Nat Turner the prophetic child?[25]

Baker suggests that young Nat possesses literacy automatically, mythically, "with the most perfect ease, so much so, that [he has] no recollection whatever of learning the alphabet" (86).[26] Turner's childhood reading is a visionary activity. With eyes agape and Bible in hand, young Nat is shown imbibing the history of Egyptian slavery as the represented forms he reads about (shackled hands, slaves bearing immense blocks, pyramids in the distance, Moses parting the Red Sea) materialize in the very space he occupies. Interestingly, Baker imputes to him the same radical fusion of mentality and tactility that Walter Benjamin admired in all children, according to Susan Buck-Morss: "What Benjamin found in the child's consciousness . . . was precisely the unsevered connection between perception and action which distinguished revolutionary consciousness in adults" ("Dream Worlds" 320). That ideal reading is always picture reading (perception plus action) is one of the primary lessons of the text. Thinking like a revolutionary is thus similar to reading iconically in the orthodox sense of iconic, as a material encounter with spiritual or mythical significance. And to read this book, Baker intimates, is to experience liberation from history's injustice, which is precisely the image the book opens and leaves us with: a slave in the dark having gotten hold of the very book we read, a representation in the words of Qiana Whitted of "the dangerous freedom of the disembodied black subject who *reads* and *sees*" (85, italics in original).

As a project of historical revision, *Nat Turner* causally links the rebellion to the Middle Passage. Recounting the slave capture of an African woman, presumed to be Nat Turner's ancestor, the graphic novel dramatizes a scene she witnesses en route across the Atlantic: an African father would rather surrender his baby to the sharks than to slavery. At the beginning of the ten-page sequence, Baker arranges the panels so that we see the increasing awareness of Turner's foremother. She seems to know what the African father is set to do. And yet to view her concern merely as horror is to confuse Baker's representation of Afrocentric remembrance with the kind of memory-work Toni Morrison undertakes in *Beloved*. Indeed, Baker's approach to the historic slave ship perfectly illustrates Molefi Kete Asante's insistence that true Afrocentricity evinces a consciousness not simply of oppression but of victory: "The victorious attitude shows the Africans on the slave ship winning. . . . no one can be your master until you play the part of the slave" (65). From an Afrocentric perspective, the fatherly hand that cradles the infant's head in one panel is just as loving as the one that drops the infant into shark-infested waters a few panels later. By contrast, the white hand that catches the infant at the last minute is a contrapuntal force to the African ethos of death before slavery (53). When, in the very next panel, the African father bites that white sailor's hand to make it drop the child, viewers are forced to reverse the standard valences of rescue and violence. Panels of hands clutching the infant juxtapose those of the awaiting shark and the African parent biting the white arm. We do not see the shark bite the child, nor must we. The first bite of the father shrouds and renders ghostly the second one that goes unrepresented. We see the violence of the African male defender so that we do not have to see the violence of white oppression that it forestalls. The grim sequentiality of the Nat Turner rebellion imbues this opening scene, setting in motion a logic of substitutions whereby history is redefined as an economy of image exchanges.

Indeed, the slave infant serves as the raw material of revolutionary history, the *casus belli* and traumatic origin of Turner's rebellion. It *forever* falls toward its toothy disaster like characters in novels, dreams, or myths frenetically ossified at an eternal brink of disaster. It is never fully sighted (cited) as corpse. Its persistent status as the moribund fetish of Middle Passage remembrance culminates in its transfer from diegetic image (of action happening in the real-time narrative) to aural icon—a pictogrammic sign of speech content. For, by the last page of this opening section, the scene of the baby that drifts into the mouth of the shark reappears as a speech balloon spoken by the young Nat Turner (Fig. 2.6).

The utterance is prophetic in more ways than one. The image-story in the speech balloon mirrors a panel witnessed earlier. In consequence, the past is made to come again, to return, as it were, in a space reserved for the present. History is a radical typology in this sequence. It recurs as oracular vision and Baker seems intent on affirming those claims attributed to Turner in the *Confessions* that: ". . . the Lord had shown me things that had happened before my

2.6 Young Nat narrating from *Nat Turner* (57).

birth" (qtd. in Baker 57).²⁷ Curiously, this panel also metaphorizes the reception context of the graphic novel; as visual hearers of the story Baker retells, we are like the listeners of Nat's pictorial shark story. As Qiana Whitted has argued, through these scenes of Turner's pictorial storytelling, Baker "furnishes a more direct, systemic justification for the traumatic pain and rage that inspired the revolt" (87).

As with Turner, Baker utilizes a language of picture-history and prophecy in order to constitute a particular type of community. Not insignificantly, Baker portrays the young Turner's audience—our readerly counterparts—open-mouthed in awe of the tale and, disturbingly, in imitation of the shark. The composition of their assembly emphasizes the value of facial expressions in mediating an affective (and thereby redemptive) relationship to the present story as well as to the traumatic past it represents. The distinction between these two temporalities, and between Turner and Baker, productively unravels in the slack of creative nonfiction's permissive contract with readers. According to this scene of the young Nat narrating, everything we have seen in the graphic novel so far becomes eerily congruent with two other narratives—the visions that motivate young Nat to rebel and the retelling of them to an audience of incipient revolutionaries, whose position mimics our own.

Ultimately, Baker's choice of a pictorially dominant comic suggests that this history is best experienced not in lexical or verbal terms but as a soteriology of icons and idols—a vision, in other words, immediate and materially present. But Baker's child is not a progressive genealogist in the sense that Alison Landsberg describes, using Lauren Berlant's notion of the infantile citizen whose "insistent stupidity" subverts the national order, rather than "constructing a livable present tense" (90). Baker's child genealogist interpolates the livable present with the funerary past. Even more radical than prosthetic memory, where narratives enable knowledge of past times never experienced, Baker utilizes the comic text to replay the past as a traumatic immediacy, which recalls Walter Benjamin's famous dictum: "To articulate the past historically does not mean to recognize it 'the way it really was' (Ranke). It means to seize hold of a memory as it flashes up at a moment of danger" ("Theses" 247).

Nat Turner's preoccupation with infanticide helps us to understand the dangerous materials Baker wrestles with. Even though Baker professes a heroic view of Turner's rebellion in the preface, the exact meaning of that event in the story remains ambivalent, organized as it is around scenes of child murder. A primary example is that of the infant and the shark, but two others bear mention. One is easily the most memorable image of the graphic novel: Will, the muscle to Turner's leadership, axing the head off of a young white boy. The other uses "speech" balloons to show Turner deciding whether or not to return to a mansion to dispatch a sleeping infant, the lone survivor of a recent raid. The images that occupy the formal place of speech depict scenes familiar to readers of slave narratives in which children are wrenched from anguished mothers at the auction block. They illustrate warrants for the decision Turner finally makes, ordering Will and another man to finish off the sleeping white child. The picture of Turner's agonized face probing collective memory for guidance offers an interesting commentary on ethics, since the two insets containing the ethical warrants exist in the same panel as the agonized face that must make the decision. Here again, a politically conscious form of living through and beside history mirrors the position of the reader of comics, who likewise scans an image for affect and meaning in the presence of proximate images vying for attention.

The pictorial simultaneity of the comics and Baker's choice of nearly exclusive pictorial units of narrative information replay diasporic trauma.[28] Throughout *Nat Turner*, Baker establishes a clear chain of historical causation, turning "the horrific historical memory" (Brooks 5) of the Middle Passage into a kind of tableau, a magical telos through which the historical memory of the Nat Turner Rebellion may be understood.[29] The narrative thus defies that condition of historical trauma which Baker and the rest of us may be working against; namely, the disconnection of traumatic events as they exist in an unnarrated state, where the relation of one event to another is unfathomable.[30]

The Queer Child and Pedographic Narrative Desire in Ariel Schrag's *Awkward*

Ariel Schrag's year-by-year set of high school diaries departs from the throng of graphic novels that merely curate childhood. Although *Awkward* (1995) chronicles the author's freshman year at a Berkeley California high school, it does not do so from the adult's backward glance. Instead, it is drawn and written by a fifteen-year-old Schrag during the summer after the experiences recounted. Almost no other published autography about youth or childhood is written by an author at a comparable age. Contemporary webcomics, of course, are the exception to this rule, but even those that rise to the same level of completeness and legibility are seldom by comics memoirists as young as Shrag was when composing *Awkward*. The usual fare tends to be written by artists closer to age twenty than ten, as with Adriana's *Teen Angst* (2008), which is the first recommendation given on the site Web Comics Nation after clicking on "Autobiographical/Slice of Life."

Plagued by SAT preparation and given to ambivalent fits of self-loathing and offbeat wit, Adriana draws a supposedly self-reflexive image of herself, naked from the waist-up but with her back turned to viewers. The accompanying caption within the cartoon sadly declares: "I woke up with the crushing certainty that I was hideous, unlovable." But another caption from the presumed self-portraitist accompanies the cartoon, this one in a tinier font and appearing just below the panel. It reads: "This is funny because I am almost never without a bra." The "I" of this second comment assuages through humor the melancholy uttered by the other authorial voice of the cartoon. It seems to account for the potential titillation uttered visually by the supposedly same authorial entity that draws the cartoon. In addition, it testifies to the wild disregard autobiographical webcomics have for the juridical guarantees that found autobiography's pact (a la Lejeune). We cannot verify Adriana's true or singular identity. Oblique as it may be, *Teen Angst* offers a more mature I-con than Ariel of *Awkward*. Yet the webcomic's panels are often one-offs, presented with less regularity than Schrag's page-based panel gridding. Nor does *Teen Angst* bear much fidelity to an aesthetic of self-coherence and internal unity, since the overall arrangement of the panels change from one post to the next. Although Schrag's first autographical volume may be seen as her least successful, it nevertheless maintains a greater unity of form than many webcomic diaries. But then, perhaps, the real difference is that Schrag's vital statistics, always already a legal discourse, are vital indexes for the I-con that takes shape in *Awkward*'s pages. The fact of Shrag being a minor and an author operates as a loaded form of comics juvenility, soliciting what I shall call a *pedographic* context of reception.

Aside from her precocious talents as a cartoonist, Schrag's salacious experimentation with drugs and sex may help to explain the rarity of her example. Life stories that confess as much mischief as Schrag's could activate the same moral panic that springs into litigious action whenever minors and the illicit are aligned, putting both parents and parent publishing companies in jeopardy. It is difficult to imagine, after all, an audience for Schrag's work exclusively made up of fourteen- and fifteen-year-olds. So, as adult readers scan Ariel's first loves and awkward groping under covers, a dangerous aura of pubescence charges the cartoon. Unlike most other graphic novels about childhood, *Awkward* literally authorizes sexualized youth. But as we look upon Schrag's eroticized pictures (notably, we might add, at a time when it is illegal in most American states to traffic in "dirty" pictures from a fourteen-year-old), we soon realize that she may be far more interested in grossing us out than turning us on. For, as it turns out, Shrag has a penchant for the freak show aesthetics of trashy bathrooms at L7 and Marilyn Manson concerts.

2.7 Women's bathroom from *Awkward* (9).

Even so, the non-normative erotics of the text and the author's unique status as child help to queer the typically empowered position of the reader.[31] To be sure, the adult reader is liable to sometimes feel uncomfortably addressed as an age-inappropriate interloper. But could not the same be said of all of those other memoirs that disguise their adult authors in the drag of childhood? As Katherine Stockton says of the queer child who generatively subverts childhood studies: "A gay child illuminates the darkness of the child" (3). According to Stockton, that darkness is thickened by impositions placed upon all children to live out other people's notions of childhood, children who "grow sideways as well as up [. . .] in part because they cannot, according to our concepts, advance to adulthood until we say it's time" (6). No other text exemplifies the sideways movement of the child—queer or otherwise—than Ariel Schrag's *Awkward*.

One telling panel in *Awkward* (Fig. 2.7) hazards obscene entrance into the women's bathroom at one of the many concerts Schrag attends. What makes the scene visually disorienting is Schrag's systematic indifference to shading. Just about every object in the panel lacks contrast, and individual elements are difficult to construe. From still-lit cigarettes pluming smoke on the floor to the entwined bodies muttering in squeezed fonts, Schrag's marks drift off the page. Her lines are subsumed by white undifferentiated space. Rather than marking surfaces with shadow, Schrag conveys depth through the relative size and placement of images, creating a sort of delayed recognition.

The *prima facie* illegibility of *Awkward* may lead some readers to see it as the starting place for a developing artist, whose skill with chiaroscuro and pointillist shading grace the pages of *Definition* (1996), Schrag's second book, only because those skills were learned then. However, a less simplistic telos of development posits *Awkward* not as the juvenilia of the budding artist but as a sustained effort of pictorial grotesque. Moreover, while Shrag employs flatness and linearity to riff on the Sunday funnies, her diaries are most influenced by their Bay Area origins. Aside from 1990s grunge music, *Awkward* makes stylistic allusions to the hectic protocols of "zine" culture, particularly through its Magic-Marker monochromania and copy machine effects of graininess.

After focusing beyond unshaded forms in Schrag's bathroom, viewers may discern the platform at mid-distance that anchors the scene. There, on what must be the sink, a lesbian couple lies entangled. The woman on top, who sports a Mohawk and combat boots, blithely proclaims the "girls bathroom just the funnest place to be." A second couple beside them similarly shows one woman handling the breast of another. Unseen behind a stall, another woman delivers a speech that is more arresting than either of these sketches: "So like guys, I was putting my hand down to masturbate but I kept pissing on my hand! I mean I wanted to see what's goin' on down there, but just couldn't stop." The miniature pair in the bottom left foreground survey this scene from a space that is in balance with the bottom right caption: "Meg peed. But I wasn't exactly in the mood . . ." Both the caption and the foreground children set the bathroom at an even greater remove. Interestingly, the caption projects an un-viewable act by one of those foreground children, whose innocence at this moment is heightened by her foreshortening. We do not see Meg traverse the drawn distinction between foreground and the rest of the panel. The comic refuses the inner space of bodily excess. Indeed, the strange commingling of urination and masturbation is perhaps made all the more graphic for being un-pictured, indicated only in the words of a bizarre speech presented for its shock value—perhaps apropos of the setting—as a type of graffiti.

A related situation, in which something is conveyed only in words, may be found in the notes that pass between Ariel and Meg on the facing page. As a series, these handwritten testimonials of same-sex desire structurally mirror the bathroom scene. In one note, Meg explains why she considers herself a freak, because "I like girls as suck friends," to which Ariel replies with a thoughtful yet tentative admission of queer solidarity: "Well sometimes I *do* like girls. It's hard to say, I don't know, but I definitely don't think there's anything wrong with it" (8). These borderless, free-standing notes on the verso page confront their counterparts in the bathroom, as if to suggest there may be something "wrong with it" after all—not necessarily with liking girls but with some of the disorderly women who do.

2.8 Emotional lady grabbing Meg from *Awkward* (10).

Confirmation comes on the following page. A woman similar to those from the bathroom—crude, inebriated, older—puts Meg in a lecherous chokehold (Fig. 2.8). While doing so she exclaims: "You are one fresh bitch!" (10). Another moment as aware of the intergenerational tension between the world of the author and that of the adult reader occurs in *Definition* when an arts mogul aggressively asserts his passion for Ariel's work at a comics convention. The reader necessarily shares affinities with these aggressors that intervene upon an otherwise hermetic world of youth. The adult interposes as a kind of violent absurdity in Schrag's universe. As a result, we are better able to see a property so common to autography that it deserves its own name— call it a *pedographic* function, whereby the fantasy of youth as a closed circle is punctured and shown to be an objectification of the adult spectator. In this way, *Awkward* could incite the same negative reactions to teen eroticism that, according to W. C. Harris, equate "sex with corruption and knowledge with the death of innocence" (159).

Like the scene in the bathroom, this one of Meg being accosted is pedographic. It puts the iconic child in violative proximity to adult eroticism and by implication the presumptive reader-viewer. As with most comics, our spectatorship allows for unrestrained visual access. We glimpse sequences that characters within the panels are blind to, such as the figure from the panel just prior to the one of Meg's molestation. That figure's hand transgresses a formal border in thematic parallel to the transgressive adult hand that clutches Meg. These gestures reinforce readers' scopic authority, linking our penetrative eyes to their boundary-crossing hands and precluding identification with reviled adults within the panels as a result. Thus, *Awkward* solicits and apologizes for a pedophilic form of scopophilia. The narrative and its implied lessons in reading and seeing circulate within a queer economy of desire not just in the sense of the homosexual identity that Meg espouses or the one that Ariel will proudly adopt in later books. Rather, the text solicits an unconventional erotics of adolescence as a bacchanalian openness, presenting the supreme fantasy of there being no fantasy to preteen sexuality at all.

But there are two primary fantasies that organize this autography, and the scene with Meg depends upon both of them. The first fantasy is one that comics and cartoons relentlessly indulge in of a world thoroughly expunged of its bothersome adults. Toward that fantasy, this panel and the one of the women's bathroom reveal in a flash how Schrag's premise hinges on intergenerational spectacle, which leads us to the second fantasy. Although Schrag includes no intelligibly nude drawings of herself or others in *Awkward* (the first such drawing comes in *Definition*), there is yet the suggestion that the book's displays of early teen eroticism exist for the prurient interests of adults.[32] Indeed, insinuations of pedophilia are especially problematic in the context of queer literature, as Harris makes clear: "The readiness with which even gay-sympathetic straights [. . . fall] back on the pedophile narrative marks how viscerally heterosexuals, regardless of their feelings about homosexuality, cringe before the bogeyman of intergenerational sex and teen eroticism" (159). Harris does not expound upon texts like Schrag's that seem hell-bent upon raising such bogeyman for ironic ends.

For if these panels stir anti-pedophilic outrage, they do so without much help from Ariel, who smugly describes Meg being grabbed with characteristic understatement: "During [the song] 'Can I Run' the lady next to us got a little emotional" (10). Ariel's euphemism is not without its larger purpose. It exposes the dialogical nature of the pedographic and its commingling of emotionality or sympathy and sexual violation. Furthermore, the Dionysian structure of the narrative, with its raucously episodic emplottment, counteracts the initial impression of a moral turnabout in the page-to-page juxtaposition of the classroom notes that admit to a queer orientation and the subsequent travesties of lesbianism. Merely a hiatus, the pedographic represents neither an indictment nor a wholesale denial of lesbianism as evidenced by the autobiographer's continued obsessions with actress Juliette Lewis or her less fantastic but no less unrequited adoration of older girl, Margaret. Ariel has such a visceral reaction to Margaret that, when holding hands, the two dig their "nails so hard into each other her finger started bleeding." And, while hugging her, Ariel reports: "I looked up to her so much I could have cried. I wanted to kiss her, I loved her so much" (24).

The fact that Ariel embraces a fluid, unlabeled sexual identity (the phase of determinative labeling begins with the opening panels of *Definition*) and still pursues sexual intimacies with boyfriends demonstrates the extent to which *Awkward* operates within a queer temporality. Like the iconic child, *Awkward* presents the fantasy of being almost pre-cultural, of existing prior to consciousness. Ariel's refusal to name her orientation coincides with the narrative's boisterous, un-centered plot. Each associates to an ontology of delay that Katheryn Stockton defines as queer temporality. According to Stockton, sexuality forms as a belated recognition in the case of queer childhood, so that representations of queer development come to possess a horizontal or "sideways" movement, a temporality that "spreads sideways—or sideways and backwards—more than a simple thrust toward height and forward time" (4).

In the queer temporality of *Awkward* existence unfolds as a type of seriality. Ariel's life, like the comics form, spatializes time as so many concerts, conversations on the phone, and revolving cliques in sequence. Repetition not only refashions development as sideways movement, it also amends the human posited by the text. As Judith Halberstam puts it: "[Q]ueer temporality disrupts the normative narratives of time that form the base of nearly every definition of the human in almost all of our modes of understanding" (152). In addition to those gays and lesbians eager to raise families in a post-Obama regime of political sympathy, if not support, there is a more anti-conformist impulse within gay culture to oppose heteronormativity by living in the "stretched-out adolescences of queer culture" (Halberstam 153). *Awkward*'s pedagraphic design shows us what that protraction looks like. It privileges a "persistent present" resistant to models of time that would constrain the present according to a reproductive logic. Thus, *Awkward* upholds Halberstam's claim about queer temporality, in which "the past represents the logic for the present, and the future represents the fruition of this logic" (Halberstam 11). Undoubtedly without intending to, Schrag plots her life as a series of crushes, cliques, and concerts in perfect illustration of the "persistent present" of queer temporality.[33]

And, as with the Yellow Kid, Schrag's I-con maintains individuality in the promiscuous midst of grotesque forms. When, in the bathroom scene, Ariel faces the viewer with enlarged eyes, her shocked look is a plea for recognition in a world gone awry, much like the looks the "straight-man" gives to the audience in comedy. Ariel's search for the viewer's gaze suggests that what she witnesses is so alienating that her only means of rescue from it lies beyond its diegetic bounds. Looking thus becomes the means to an imaginary transcendence. The scopic community that results between viewer and I-con echoes *Awkward*'s structure. In keeping with the straight-man of comedy and the comics child in general, Ariel's look opens onto special exits through the fourth wall of mediation. In so doing, Schrag's iconic child exhibits a range of family resemblances with others encountered in this chapter; it marks the site of social rebellion as well as impossible origin and enacts a fantasy of pre-cultural ways of being and knowing. More typical of the comics child, Ariel's looking and seeing help to found community through a revision of temporality and the compulsory logics of sequence and causality that structure the comics form.

Towards Conclusion: Chris Ware's
Jimmy Corrigan, the Saddest Kid on Earth

That the child limns rebellion has been of mantric concern throughout this chapter, yet few texts are as demonstrative of the formal implications of that rebellion as Chris Ware's *Jimmy Corrigan: Smartest Kid on Earth* (2000). The first break from convention comes at a paratextual, pre-narrative stage of the book in the extensive prefatory information on the inside cover. There, an exam appears that readers are to cut out and send to the author with a $20 check. Presumably, we would pay for the results to such questions as "Your relationship with your father was a) strained or b) distant."

As with Schrag's bathroom scene or the Palestinian children who question Sacco, Ware's preludial materials prime readers for the demands that lie ahead. Their placement poses a challenge of connection: How do the gag questions and tests precipitate the story? A possible answer comes in the first four narrative pages that follow the tests, dramatizing the washed-up superhero actor who sleeps with Jimmy's mother. This second opening establishes the anxious premise of the graphic novel, so that when Jimmy's estranged father sends for him, we may further appreciate how that offer spins Jimmy and the text into reveries of Oedipal anxiety and a somewhat futile quest for reunion that is darkly funny and impressively baroque. To begin (again) with the TV actor and the mother is to affirm classical psychology's etiology of childhood, which presumes the causal origin and telos of the ego to be located in childhood. Similar to Baker's enlistment of the child in *Nat Turner* as the sentimental (and simplifying) *casus belli* of historical (and complexly unnarratable) trauma, the trials of young Jimmy are shown to be part of a broader historical formation of father-son dysfunction. Indeed, one of the parallel story threads that readers must braid together involves an eerily similar little boy around the time of the Chicago World's Fair of 1893.

The child is an obvious prime mover of Ware's plot and theme, but it also functions as trope, both icon and i-con.[34] As trope or figure, the child is significant to *Jimmy Corrigan* in three principal ways. First, as a visual symbol the child is made legible through commercial iconography, which transforms the sentimentality that would yoke children to pre-socialized experience into a naïve desire for participation in commodity culture. Second, because scenes of Jimmy as an innocent child contrastively establish the hopelessness of adulthood, childhood once again is shown to facilitate an abstract yet intensely formative meditation on the nature of time, as we have observed in Baker and Schrag. Buying into the circuitous temporal logic of Ware's multigenerational tragicomedy means that the causal relations tying past to present are never as arbitrary as they appear. Especially in the case of dysfunction, the present is represented as an ongoing condition, the symptom of an eternalized malaise. Third, the trope of the child bundles the crisis of development in with crises of sequence and "closure"—in both McCloud's usage and that of pop psychology.

Nevertheless, *Jimmy Corrigan* is not strictly about childhood. An anachronistic idiom of boyhood adventure—complete with superheroes, robots, and cowboys—intensifies the ennui of adulthood in Ware's universe. At its simplest, childhood in Ware activates the less salacious side of the same dynamic of pedographic narrative desire that impels Schrag's *Awkward*; it plays upon childhood vulnerability through an iconography of abuse conspicuous in autography, from Phoebe Gloeckner's *A Child's Life* (2000) to Debbie Drechsler's *Daddy's Girl* (2008) and David Small's *Stitches* (2009). Not based overtly on abuse, Jimmy's pain and the geometry of the panels that convey it suggest an ontological death of a thousand cuts. Close-ups on an alarm clock, the milk and cereal box, a red bird atop a stark tree branch, and other panelized slivers of kitchen drear organize the opening four pages in the same way that the adult Jimmy's perfunctory "Ha ha" sadly punctuates his dour and lonely life in later scenes.

If we did not come to the text with knowledge of the child as a tropological device, the prefatory tests in *Jimmy Corrigan* bring us quickly up to speed. In particular, they call attention to the way the child initiates and interrogates narrative causality. On the opening inside cover, in an entry numbered "3. Role," readers are invited to enter the text thinking of a time when, "waking up one hopeful, sunny morning, we feel the innocent child within us reanimate, a feeling only to be shortly dispelled by the masked lie of adulthood staring back at us in the bathroom mirror."[35] The point about the mirror is significant. Young Jimmy first appears in front of a mirror where he fashions a red mask for himself in anticipation of the superhero actor he is to meet at the car show. It is this failed surrogate for the absent father who eventually gives the boy the moniker of "a real smart kid" as well as his own orange mask at the end of the sequence.

As with the mirror moments in Chapter One, this one loads up the drawing with subjective, iconic significance.[36] The mask ornamentalizes the real as the imago in the mirror meets its ego in the panel. Once again, affect and substitution flood the image with meaning. Ware's expert manipulation of the unlikely truths that the comic image may be called upon to express closes the scene as young Jimmy wears a mask to dutifully report the actor's farewell— "Mom! He said to tell you he had a real good time!" Like the child in *Persepolis* who queries readers who stand in for a lost god, this scenario imparts an uncomfortable reading lesson.[37] To be sure, the hopefulness of young Jimmy seems to have uncharacteristically carried over onto the "masked lie" of the adult, leaving the latter comically identical to the former. That the young Jimmy looks like the older one, dresses just like him, and even finds himself in the same emasculating scenes of miscommunication with his mom all point to Ware's repudiation of the child's standard priority. Ware's child is not simply the site for an impossible origin, as is the case in Baker, nor does the child protract and thereby defy the temporal norms of adulthood, as is the case in Schrag. On the contrary, Ware's child exists in a state of fantastical continuity with its partner figure, the childish adult.

Continuity facilitates the commercial logic that pinpoints the child as a locus of consumption. Consider, for example, the panels that recur every few pages or so to redundantly announce the title of the graphic novel. These typically feature a grandiose font beside an image of young Jimmy rocketing through space or posing strong and proud. By interlarding these "superlative" panels of the young Jimmy into the narrative of the elder, the text psychologizes the latter through the child. The child is thus the unconscious source of bombastic renaming rituals that poke through the Symbolic. Different from McCloud's standard types of closure, these embedded title panels contain uncloseable repetitions of the child and thereby give rise to a critique of knowledge, which casts doubt on the comics' insistence on one-to-one causalities of incident and event.

To explain, let us consider the opening instructions to the graphic novel, which highlight a typical two-panel illustration of comics closure. In one panel, we see an anthropomorphic mouse holding a sledgehammer aloft, while a cat lies prone at its feet. In the second panel, the mouse's dropped hammer contacts the head of a now decapitated cat. But that is far from being the end of the matter. The opening test elaborates on these two panels as if the entirety of the comics form hangs together in them. One lesson we are to learn from it all is that the sequence of the two panels forms the basis of narrative causality. We are encouraged to commit the reasoning fallacy of *ad hoc ergo propter hoc* in order to read sequences correctly. If B comes after A, in the comics, then A has caused B, and A is almost always the temporal antecedent of B. This rebellious blurring of correlation and causation parallels

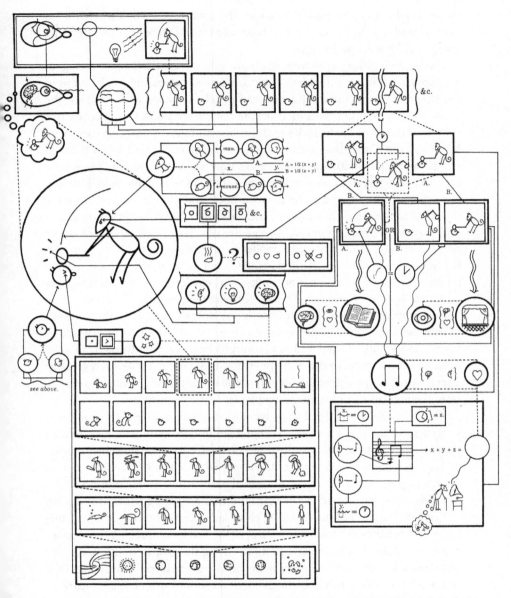

2.9 Elaboration of mouse and cat-head from inside cover of *Jimmy Corrigan*. "Inside Cover" from *Jimmy Corrigan: The Smartest Kid on Earth* by Chris Ware. Copyright © 2016 Chris Ware

the reversal within the panels in which the mouse violently dispatches his natural predator the cat. Out of that reversal a crucial piece of Ware's puzzling critique of knowledge emerges.

Deliberately risking epistemological overkill, Ware includes an extravagant concept map (Fig. 2.9) elucidating the convoluted causes and implications of the single action in the mouse-cat head panels. In scope and intricacy, the chart is overwhelming. Vectors from the main panels link to adjacent strips that summarize the life histories of the mouse and the cat, tracking each from birth to death. Other lines emanating from the main panels explain through images and quasi-mathematical symbols how the heart, eye, and brain read the three squiggly lines surrounding the cat's head where the sledgehammer impacts it. Through an icon of an open book and that of a curtained stage in a theatre the chart illustrates comics reading as a synesthetic experience of literature, drama, and music. A sequence of mini-circled images of an ear hearing musical notes comically implies that the mouse got his sinister plan for hammering his feline nemesis while listening to music. And if all this medium muscle flexing were not enough, tiny clocks between images portray gutters as hinges of durational time. In the reverse bathos of the exam that moves from the stock routine of the funny animal pratfall to these scenes of sublime instruction, observers become pupils of the sheer magnitude of Ware's project, its sensual and temporal precision coming through in spite of its childish actors. To drive the point morbidly home, Ware even gives us a seven-panel sequence at the bottom of the exam that traces all of existence from the big bang to our impending planetary decomposition.

The relationship of this expansive and intricate configuration of panel sequences to the tiny panel pair is central to understanding how Ware uses instructional pictorial genres allied to comics (blueprints, flowcharts, how-to diagrams, commercial signs, musical scores) to reflect the complex nature of meaning in *Jimmy Corrigan*. As with the miniature visual allusion of the cat-and-mouse cartoon in the background of the opening panel in *Palestine*, an unlikely inheritor of the childlike, child-laden aesthetic of the comics, this scene also initiates the narrative project of the text by embracing the iconography of childish entertainment. Reminiscent of the picaro tradition, the cat-and-mouse test in Ware compares to the mini-titles that recur throughout the text. Both translate crises of community into crises of spectacle or closure.

In Ware's world, those crises are not just temporal, epistemological, or psychological, but ontological. Lonely and resentfully haunted by its supposed converse—the innocence of childhood—Ware's adult world has either banished or psychically cannibalized its children, a fate shared, not coincidentally, by superheroes in the text. This imagined adult world occupies a temporality that is pessimistically queer in the sense that it reproduces no children save for the obscene adolescence that Jimmy incarnates. By focusing on the tedium of adulthood, its castrated dreams and decapitated cat heads, Ware's aesthetic of the child works retrospectively in futile search for the psychic or cosmic culprit whose ball-peen hammer has crushed the joy from this world at some irrecoverable moment of origin.

What could be simpler than this primal scene of children's spectatorship of cat-and-mouse violence? As with an Itchy and Scratchy cartoon, embedded like *Hamlet*'s "Mousetrap" in *The Simpsons*, the cat-and-mouse morality play tugs at the structures that house it. In Ware, the rhizomatic and didactic energies of the pictorial footnotes to the pratfall suggest both an unbounded optimism in the explanatory power of pictures as well as the postmortem horrors of their mechanization. To grasp the optimism, we might borrow from Kathleen McDonnell's insight that the Itchy and Scratchy cartoon "is also a celebration of animation itself and its freedom to depict the forbidden and impossible, 'without consequences,' subject only to the limits of imagination" (123). But while Ware obviously lauds the comics, an effect of his ecstasy of tangential information is that it squelches not only the primacy of the first two panels, but also their legibility. The mass of information that erupts from the bigger pictures threatens to smother all that the smaller ones hope to explain.

Luckily, images like cartoon bodies do not expire. As Phillip Cole observes in the violence of Itchy and Scratchy, Scratchy's eyes always survive the variously gratuitous exterminations of his body: "[W]atching the whole process. . . . [so that] throughout whatever is happening after his death, Scratchy is a witness, conscious and aware of it" (110). Similarly, Ware's pictorial garden of ever-forking paths visualizes not only the death of simplicity but the end of narrative as well. As we move from origin to contingency, we inevitably lose sight of those distinctions that found narrative acts and set them apart from two-dimensional art.

Childhood names the formal desire for that ideal of origin, whether of formative distinctions or psychic substrata faintly reflected in the mirror. Never merely reducible to innocence, lost or passing, or even one's coherence across the entropic ravages of linear time, childhood operates as a structuring fantasy of comics' subject matter, sequence, and temporality. The past self the child encodes operates as a receptacle of loss, of lost community, or (with Baker and Shrag in mind) communities structured as loss. Beyond these designations, the child also configures lost ways of knowing, as demonstrated by Ware's dissection of epistemological simplicity. Preludial and thus cut off from the narrative proper, Ware's cat-and-mouse test validates non-narrative ways of knowing associated with children's reading, such as the rebus, cut-out activity, or picture puzzle. These material interventions suspend comic narrative even as they reveal its inevitably cryptographic properties—a formal conundrum the next chapter turns now to investigate.

3

Picture Games in Story Frames
and the Play Spaces of Autography

Every artwork is a picture puzzle, a puzzle to be solved, but this puzzle is constituted in such a fashion that it remains a vexation, the preestablished routing of
its observer. The newspaper picture puzzle recapitulates playfully what artworks
carry out in earnest. Specifically, artworks are like picture puzzles in that what
they hide—like Poe's letter—is visible and is, by being visible, hidden.
—Theodor Adorno, *Aesthetic Theory* (167–68)

As seen in the previous chapter, the cat-and-mouse test that begins
Chris Ware's *Jimmy Corrigan* prepares readers for later feats of
visual reading. To be sure, that test is so overwhelming to decode
as to feel more like a baffling dare than a graphic novel. While negotiating its
pictorial elaborations and asides, the test subjects us to its primary lesson: to
approach narrative as a vexing challenge for readers to overcome. To understand reading in this way is to echo Adorno's conception of art forms that
incite "vexation" in readers according to a "preestablished routing."

Adorno's words aptly encompass the theoretical preoccupations of *Reading Lessons in Seeing* thus far. The reflexivity of things being simultaneously
visible and hidden from the last phrase of Adorno's epigraph parallels the
dynamics of the mirror discussed in Chapter One. That is, autobiographical
pictorial authority establishes itself according to an essential mirroring—a
dialectic or a binary—in which the anti-realisms of comic art become a formal
alibi, allowing readers to invest in the psychological realities or reality-effects

of the identities I-cons are meant to convey. That Adorno equates all art to the picture puzzle, a genre associated with children, affirms the priorities of Chapter Two and underscores autography's connections with juvenility. And yet there is a formal juvenility to comics that goes beyond the most typical subjects reflected in autography's mirrors. There is a sense of play in comics, as though the texts, their artists, or authors want to play with readers at least as much as they want to communicate with them. The present chapter takes up this observation to ask: What is produced when autobiographical graphic novels stop showing and telling and start playing?

When a graphic novel renovates its interiors to make room for the ludic (i.e., games and puzzles), returning to the business-as-usual of storytelling is difficult. One example occurs in David B.'s autobiographical graphic novel *Epileptic* (2002, English edition).[1] It appears early on as the plot transitions from the diagnosis of the brother's illness to the family's disillusionment with his medical treatment and subsequent embrace of homeopathic cures, non-Western healing arts, and communal living. Up to this point, and while disorienting at times in style, *Epileptic* has employed a mode of visual storytelling that is more or less conventional. That is to say, the correlation between panels has been fairly evident. And in captions we encounter a familiar autobiographical voice belonging to both narrator and author (though not always together). That voice may also be understood as a device of anchorage due to its primary function of grounding the visual in language and thereby strengthening the ease with which we read. When not damming the fluidities of visual reference, this "voice" of narration speaks directly to the reader from the same space of personal retrospection that autobiographical authority has relied upon since Augustine. But at this particular rupture in *Epileptic*, all of that gives way. Narration itself gives way. Everything is seized by a priority more common to the child's activity book than to autobiography.

As brothers Jean-Christophe and Pierre-François Beauchard (David B.'s given name) are swept up into their parents' search for a life system that would heal the embattled Jean-Christophe of his debilitating epilepsy, the whole family is forced to live a migratory existence. In David B.'s illustrations, epilepsy is much more than the physical manifestations that plague his brother. It afflicts the author-protagonist as well, playing dragon to his inner knight and permeating the text in shadowy configurations, framing panels and engulfing characters with serpentine menace.

But, no matter how grim in aspect, Jean-Christophe's epilepsy nevertheless provides rich prospects for his brother's self-fashioning. Descriptions of various communes, for instance, occasion grandly meticulous displays. In addition to expositional panels that show and tell what the young Pierre-François

3.1 Embedded game in David B.'s *Epileptic* p.48. Excerpt from *Epileptic* by David B. Copyright ©
2005 by L'Association, Paris, France. Used by permission of Pantheon Books, an imprint of the
Knopf Doubleday Publishing Group, a division of Random House LLS. All rights reserved.

experienced, several others diagram the communes' philosophies. What is
more, they do so in a manner that seems intended not only to instruct but to
impress. Pedagogical, lyrically iconic, and frequently humorous, these over-
views of commune philosophy have as much to do with present-tense dem-
onstrations of authority as with the remembered past. They convince even the
casual onlooker to recognize David B.'s (and the comic medium's) prowess for
converting ideas into visual efficacies.

Thus heralded by a ramped-up visual style, an aperture in narration opens
(fig. 3.1). It dilates within a typically surreal panel of inky black and white.
Here, a man's body blends into a woman's; there an orbit of demon heads
swirl. Oceanic waves frame a smiling sun on the right; a crescent moon and
pear counterbalance them on the left. Anchoring what seems to be the prurient obscurantist's alibi for making us look at a picture of oral sex, the salacious
caption bids us to play: "Here's a little game, dear reader. In the drawing below,
can you tell the Yin elements from the Yang ones?" (49).

I stop at this question with every reading and, by taking its "ability test"
seriously, I make it non-rhetorical. Leaving aside for now the arresting power
of its sexual exhibitionism, the halting image conveys more than its content of
words or images. Once prompted, it is as easy as imagining shapes in clouds
to discern symmetries in the panel (although differentiating yin from yang
is another matter). More than a clever authorial intrusion, the visual puzzle
hints at something deeply rooted in the structure of the comics. As we shall
see, a latent potential reveals and unravels itself in this weird and remarkable
invitation to play.

Out of sheer exhilaration or exhaustion the story hereby delivers itself up to priorities beyond mimesis. It stops storytelling, in other words, shifting to an altogether different mode. Of course, this deviation is only a temporary rerouting of narrative demand. We could imagine it having greater disruptive value were it to take up the entire page or if the shapes and symbols decoded for us here were to continue to obtrude upon the backgrounds of subsequent panels. But that is not the case. In panel after panel, *Epileptic* is flooded with images. The yin-yang design is as much the secret key to understanding its torrent of detail as is any one of the communes the cure for the brother's epilepsy.[2] Rather, it would be more accurate to describe this break as having a meta-mimetic relation to the rest of the story. This is so not because it postpones narrative but because it trains us to become better readers of *Epileptic*. At any point hereafter, we are encouraged by this reading lesson to play a game with the pictures. As a result of simply noticing that a shift has occurred, we are thus prodded not only to go on noticing them but also to seek determinative meanings in their cryptic algorithms of symbolic pattern—a mathematics that only adds up to failure, by the way, as most panels in *Epileptic* are idiosyncratic in their symbolism, overwhelming reader-viewers with a minutiae of inky intricacy. They are profuse, to say the least, in terms of detail, ornament, and design.

Despite its brevity, this admittedly small slice of a densely illustrated family history and *künstlerroman* resonates. An artwork in Adorno's sense of the term, the picture puzzle provided at this moment in turn affords a means of engagement, a decoding practice that remains available to us as we navigate *Epileptic*'s notorious intricacy. We are entreated, dared, perhaps even mocked to look at the rest of the autography with as much deliberation as this cheeky panel instructs. But this is no simple matching exercise of symbol to symbolized that we are hereby commissioned to undertake as we read. On the contrary, all the images in this panel and henceforward may assume the function of game tokens, comprising neither mimesis nor semiosis alone but their intersection—a puzzle, to be sure, but a puzzle without a determinative solution.[3]

In what follows, I want to deconstruct the breach and play of this juncture, wondering aloud about the implications of graphic memoir's penchant for ludic interactivity. By "ludic," I am referring to acts of play solicited by the text as well as the textual spaces that these solicitations inscribe. More particularly, I wonder how ludic intermissions interfere with autobiographical identity, affect, and authority.[4] What happens to reading and readers when this shift to play occurs? What is produced? And what are we to make of the scarcely theorized power of comics to morph into puzzle? As the example from *Epileptic* suggests, the strange convergences of puzzle and story in graphic novels have the potential to bring about new ontologies of reading worthy of far greater scrutiny than their ephemeral appearances in individual texts have yet garnered them. This chapter is an attempt at giving these moments their due—at playing along to see where the game in the story leads.

For me, the inquiry itself has its origin in the classroom, particularly with novice readers of comics for whom every panel may become a puzzle to be conquered and solved. More generally, however, my curiosity was stirred by such shifts in autography, shifts from narrative towards play, like those moments whenever the direction of the words in a comic turns on its side or reverses, making us turn our books physically to follow along. How many of us actually turn the book and how many of us pass over this minor solicitation to play? Over the years, students have been eager to discuss these transitions of mode and modality, particularly in autobiographical graphic novels. And my interest in the effect and meaning of such shifts achieved greatest focus over the course of administering the same small-group activity to student readers of Ware's *Jimmy Corrigan*. The task was simply enough. Describe what it might be like to actually cut out any one of Ware's proffered designs such as the carousel or the zeppelin and discuss the function of these embedded cut-outs. The nearly universal response was both a strong desire to cut out the designs and a quasi-mystical fear of actually doing so. This is, after all, a graphic novel and not an activity book.

Let us, therefore, keep in mind this implication of the game's insinuation in a politics of the sacred surrounding the book (having to do with sacrifice, physical mortification, and redemption), a politics heightened by digital culture, which everywhere heralds the death of the book as a physical, codexical object. So, as we examine those moments of medial transformation when comics become puzzles, we shall remain mindful of the ways in which concerns about the inviolability of the physical book are at the same time concerns about mortality, knowledge limits, and the violability and viability of bodies more generally.

Games and Other Visual Puzzles in Graphic Novels

Contemporary graphic novels often contain examples of the ludic. As breaks fundamentally, intervening puzzles and games exaggerate properties literary scholars ascribe to fiction and which Adorno ascribes to Poe's purloined letter. They reason, as does Roy Caldwell, that because fiction "operates in a zone *between* reality and fantasy" the reader becomes a "player reader [who] enters

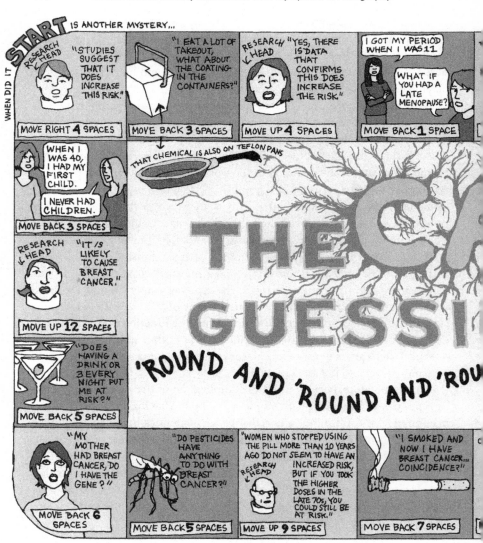

3.2 "Cancer Guessing Game" from Marchetto's *Cancer Vixen* (34–35). Graphic novel excerpt from *Cancer Vixen: A True Story* by Marisa Acocella Marchetto. Copyright © 2006 by Marisa Acocella Marchetto. Used by permission of Alfred A. Knopf, an imprint of the Knopf Doubleday Publishing Group, a division of Random House LLS. All rights reserved.

the game offered by the text" (60). Therefore, it may be the case that the following argument is based more on differences of degree than kind. Such an objection might insist that even though comics routinely switch from narrative priorities to those of the ludic, they do so according to a disruptive property common to all fiction. However, the ludic spaces in graphic memoir under discussion here not only intensify the potential of narration—insofar as the reading of any story (fictional or autobiographical) entails such gaming—they also offer readers the choice to leave the domain of narration altogether, quitting conventional models of reading in order to enter into the textual *ludus* of play, an enclave of activity, gaming, and puzzle-solving hidden in narration's folds.

If we were to limit ourselves, for now, only to those examples which, like *Epileptic*, clearly announce themselves as games, we could point for comparison to Marisa Acocella Marchetto's *Cancer Vixen* (2006) and its page-spread simulation of a board game (34–35). Instead of allowing players to move according to a turn-based system of progress as in *Life* or *Monopoly*, the little boxes arranged in a circle of Marchetto's "Cancer Guessing Game" (fig. 3.2) inevitably lead to recursive loops. These loops finalize the game with a deathly precision not unlike the cancer experience itself. For example, one game box (a term I prefer over "panel" as it captures the emphasis on materiality central to any reversion of story into play) shows a biomedical researcher who says, "Some women who have risk factors never get breast cancer" (35). Along with the quotation, this box contains a caption that directs reader-players to "Move back 4 spaces" (35). Going back four spaces takes us to a box where a different researcher contradicts the first, claiming: "Yes, there is data that confirms this does increase the risk" (34). The caption directs us four spaces ahead, thus interring us in one of the many dead-ends of Marchetto's game.

Through fatalist humor and futile play "The Cancer Guessing Game" orchestrates a thanatological allegory about the dismaying contradictions and corporate corruption surrounding breast cancer treatment. As a model of ludic autobiography, however, it also warns against departing from narrative safe zones, where the illusion of progress is maintained. Every board game literalizes a *telos* of progress, instantiating rules of direction and turn-taking from a beginning towards an objective endpoint.[5] In the "The Cancer Guessing Game," our turn runs aground without the autobiographer and her story. Suddenly left to our own devices, our turns end up being ineffectual, looped into cul-de-sacs of inaction. Cancer and its analogical board game are made to play the other to narrative. Both cancer and "The Cancer Guessing Game" refuse integration and progress, closure and futurity. Moreover, the death that is always figured as a formal *aporia* finds an analog in the circularity of the board game as well as its stand-alone visual quality. Recursivity and stasis are also characteristics of the ellipsis that Ian James detects in contemporary French autobiography. According to James, ellipses denote "an absence or instance of annihilation" by revealing how certain narrative strands "exist in relation to a rupture, or hiatus which exceeds their shared framework of linguistic and narrative representation" (33). Marchetto's game configures that greatest hiatus, death, as non-linearity—death's formal equivalent in the comics, and autography in particular, predicated as they are on sequence and closure.

A different version of the board game appears in Lynda Barry's *Naked Ladies! Naked Ladies! Naked Ladies! Coloring Book* (1984). While assigning specificity to female nakedness, *Naked Ladies!* resists the physiognomic uniformity of female embodiment in mass culture. It does so by providing motivated readers with pinup-style outline drawings to color in and a deck of playing cards to play with, reminiscent of the lecherous "Tijuana Bibles" of the 1960s. Indeed, Barry invites readers to celebrate the variety of her nudes in both a material and a practical way, as we are encouraged to cut out the full deck, with each card bearing a different naked lady. Playing with the cards supplements other textual acts of reading and coloring, imparting a quality of materiality to them as a result. Hillary Chute discusses Barry's "attention to the book as functional object" in *Naked Ladies!*—noting how the "deck of 'cards' of the women" helps to illuminate the book's "sense of play, and of utilitarian purpose" (*Graphic Subjects* 305 n.11).[6] Like action figures from the latest blockbuster, Barry's playing cards make a narrative afterlife possible for her characters and subject. Both the film-themed doll and the Naked Lady playing card convene ludic spaces that protract and suspend narrative finitude. Thinking of it in terms of mortality, for Barry, it would seem, play resurrects what story terminates. Play becomes that space wherein a hitherto monopolized resource of authorial power transfers to an infinite and anonymous collectivity—an audience of reception hereby redefined as recipients of agency via activity.

To the extent that activity distinguishes the ludic from narration, we might also include in our review Barry's famous "activity-book" ending of *One Hundred Demons*. If the ending of any memoir can be said to be a figural rumination on the ending of the autobiographer's life, it is interesting to note that Barry's instructional epilogue defies finality. Designed to be the prologue to a whole new collection of demon-exorcising comics, Barry's ending is rather reproductive, communal, and even boldly messianic. The good news for readers so inclined is that this ending makes possible the production of another text for Barry to be born again in. Resurrection depends upon the completion of a circuit of dialogue established between author-narrator and readers—the positive application of lessons written into Barry's educative life story as part of its curricular capstone.

Other examples that do not announce themselves as games, but which summon play spaces within graphic narrative nevertheless include the choose-your-own-adventure structure of Jason Shiga's *Meanwhile* (2010), the background clutter that may wink and dance for the scrupulous reader in

Julie Doucet's *My New York Diary* (1999), and the "Fearful Symmetry" chapter of Alan Moore's *Watchmen* (1986). In the printed edition of *Meanwhile* color-coded plot choices transform reader-viewers into playful page-turners, rerouting the protocols of reading, as Adorno notes of picture puzzles, according to a "preestablished routing of its observer" (167).[7] A similar rerouting of viewer expectations occurs in Doucet's visual world of animated detritus, which will be discussed further in the next chapter. In all of the examples, in fact, readers are rewarded for their heightened visual attention. In *Watchmen*'s famous chapter, every panel from the first half has a partner-panel in the second half, one often the inverted mirror of the other. Evidence for the pleasure that dedicated readers have taken in playing this advanced form of the visual matching exercise may be found in the countless blogs and Internet fansites that exhaustively record each symmetrical pair of chapter panels.[8]

The symmetry of the beginning and ending of *Fun Home* offers another example. That Alison and Bruce are positioned analogously at both the start and closing of the narrative suggests the need for a recursive review of the middle and a postponement of the conventional notion of closure. That is, in keeping with "the tricky reverse narration" that ensures the failure of there being an end to Alison's story, readers are encouraged to become rereaders. Thus, even a gesture as slight as a duplication of design may prompt decoding practices unmoored from narrative's forward demands. These critical returns and reviews would no doubt underscore the pictorial resonance of those scenes in which Bruce and Alison occupy similar positions, mirroring one another in the style of their expression, shading, size, and placement within the same panel or adjacent ones. More importantly, the very act of going back over the text puts the reader in a state of epistemological solidarity with Bechdel (as author) and Alison (as protagonist). They too suspend the demands of narrative to comment on the perplexities of memory and its limits whenever seeking to reflect the past or the real as it was really lived. By returning critically ourselves after reading *Fun Home*, we affirm its priority of historical criticism and the scrupulous review, particularly in view of the fallibility of our perceptions—our human inability to get reality right the first time through. Even if these affirmations come as the result of Alison's final prompt about the "tricky reverse narration," readers who allow themselves to become reviewers may move from noticing similar pairings of father and daughter, like those scenes of playing airplane at the beginning and end of the narrative, to surveying all the other ways the pictorial both supplements and pushes against verbal scripts of narration. Thus, readers of *Fun Home* may be rerouted in the Adornoean sense to become observers of its underlying picture puzzle, a shift that is available only post-narrative, in the story's afterlife, where two vastly separate narrative spaces may, through their pictorial resemblance, undergo radical forms of closure and connection.

This act of culminating a reading by bringing together two sections of text originally printed apart from one another recalls the tactile amusement available in every last page of *Mad* magazine. There, folding the margins of a picture sutures into being a new, often delightfully obscene image. Many graphic novels similarly incorporate play spaces, puzzles, and other forms deliberately staged as narrative's other in order to lend material dimension to their texts. Such practices create the semblance of middles, pockets, corridors, or interiors, each with its own set of epistemological horizons and ontological possibilities for readers to inhabit. Like the Möbius strip at the center of Alan Moore's *Promethea* (2000), embedded board games or playing cards are invitations to rearrange the page, to physically manipulate the book in one's hands, and to recognize anew the signifying potential of the ground of the text—a normally mute ligature or *tabula rasa* onto which meaning takes shape. As such, these ludic eruptions may depend upon the same practices of tactile and recursive reading that any comic prescribes. But they emphasize these practices to a degree that surpasses routine reading.

Indeed, by definition, the ludic gives rise not just to practices but to *activities* in excess of narration, which compel appreciably more interaction. Some will recognize in these claims an emphasis on action comparable to that espoused by the ludology school of video games scholars.[9] Ludologist Gonzalo Frasca theorizes the difference between games (ludology) and story (narratology) by distinguishing traditional media as being "representational, not simulational" (223) and by more forcefully claiming simulation as "an alternative to representation" (223). Whatever applicability Frasca's distinctions may have to the embedded games in graphic novels is only further complicated by his definition of simulation: "[T]o simulate is to model a (source) system through a different system which maintains (for somebody) some of the behaviors of the original system" (223).

How do we apply these systems to the games in *Cancer Vixen* or *Epileptic*? The plurality of "source" systems in the graphic novels prevents any simple correlation. For example, take *Epileptic*'s yin-yang game, which, it could be argued, models the puzzle-solving so crucial to the plot. Were we to read the game symptomatically we might associate its visual dislocations with the Beauchard family's desperate search to make sense of the empty symbols of both an ineffective biomedical establishment and the esoteric homeopathic discourses they serially endorse. The author-artist's keen and illicit eye for converting a world of ideas into a world of visible objects is mirrored in the game activity. But what remains problematic for the distinction Frasca and other so-called ludologists would like to uphold is that the game, in our case, seems to simulate narrative. The game asks us to un-puzzle drawn elements in order to *read* them better. In this regard, *Epileptic*'s game is an exemplary artifact of *Reading Lessons in Seeing*, tempting readers to play outside of narrative bounds in order to become better readers within them.

Moreover, the uniqueness of such play spaces cannot be defined by interactivity alone, since comics excite interactive reading in general. Scholars of comics typically emphasize qualities of collaboration and closure as the strongest evidence for the essential interactivity of comics reading. As Jared Gardner aptly puts it, "All comics are necessarily collaborative texts between the imagination of the author/artist and the imagination of the reader who must complete the narrative" ("Archives" 800). Likewise, Julia Watson stresses the irregularity of comics reading, which "invites—and requires—readers to read differently, to attend to disjunctions between the cartoon panel and the verbal text, to disrupt the seeming forward motion of the cartoon sequence and adopt a reflexive and recursive reading practice" (28). To an extent, the play space within the comic coincides with the collaborative, interactive, nonnarrational nature of reading comics.

According to Thierry Groensteen, the formal structures of comics "offer the reader a story that is full of holes, which appear as gaps in the meaning" (10). These gaps are an effect of the "iconic solidarity" of the comics, which, according to Groensteen, presumes that "images will be multiple and correlated" (19). All of this pictorial multiplicity makes reading any comic an exercise in puzzle-solving, as Groensteen goes on to admit when describing how gutters and panel borders replicate, in miniature, the gridding properties of the page margin: "Indeed, the empty interstices that separate the panels can actually be perceived as reticular extensions of the margin. From the hollow quadrilateral that it was, these are transformed into a labyrinth" (31). To associate reading a comic with walking a maze is to acknowledge the more challenging participatory demands all comics place on readers. The comics page, as Groensteen characterizes it, "demands to be traversed, crossed, glanced at, and analytically deciphered" (19). Yet, even as the page calls out for a solution, it does so in a language that unavoidably reproduces the puzzle. Any attempt (borrowing from Groensteen) to eliminate the reading puzzle is thwarted by the insistent totality of all the images in the panoptic field; "the focal vision," Groensteen explains, "never ceases to be enriched by peripheral vision" (19).

In spite of his exacting account of the difficulty of determining the proper reading order of comic panels, Groensteen, like many comics scholars, betrays a hint of professional hubris when describing his own effortless ability to determine those unifying threads of narrative continuity: "[T]he story is possibly full of holes, but it projects me into a world that is portrayed as consistent, and it is the continuity attributed to the fictional world that allows me to effortlessly fill in the gaps of the narration" (11). In my view, comics and graphic novels briskly shore up interpretive anxieties (gutters, iconic fragments, pictorial multiplicity, the constant threat of the detail being engulfed by panoptic totality), making *effortless* acts of reading rare occurrences indeed. A different experience reported by readers new to the comics is of perceiving the whole enterprise of deciphering the proper reading order as a puzzle. Rather than allude to the labyrinth, the comics panel is a labyrinth *par excellence* for these readers. We would be justified, therefore, in seeing those junctures where story makes way for the maze or puzzle as emblems of a generic inclination in the comics form.

Self-reflexivity fuels the puzzling comic's transformation into puzzle. Speaking of authorial asides in eighteenth-century novels, Wolfgang Iser describes a reader who "is expected to strive for himself to unravel the mysteries of a sometimes strikingly obscure composition" (*Act of Reading* 102). For Iser, any interruption of an established narrative flow triggers an intensification of the reader's participation: "Thus whenever the flow is interrupted and we are led off in unexpected directions, the opportunity is given to us to bring into play our own faculty for establishing connections—for filling in the gaps left by the text itself" (*Implied Reader* 280).

The scope of interactivity that graphic novels involve greatly exceeds even as it attests to the ubiquity of participation in most other reading situations.[10] Hence, a better distinction than interactivity for distinguishing the ludic or the puzzle space from the comics' inherently labyrinthine structure is the degree to which the reader must foreclose reading altogether in order to fully activate the text. In other words, the defining stress should be placed on the *act* of interactivity, as Kelli Fuery reasons: "[T]o be interactive we must be seen to produce or at the very least participate in something that results in production" (33–34). When wrestling over the semantics of the ludic games graphic texts orchestrate, let us hasten to ask again: What is produced? Does the play space produce anything beyond itself or the structures that make it signify?

Although play need not abandon processes of signifying, it necessitates acts of visual synthesis different from those generally used in comics reading. For one thing, in a textual space of play or puzzle-solving, reference is no longer subordinate to story, plot, or character.[11] At its simplest, the new regime of referenced action conjures a play space that signifies (whether the game is played or not) as liberation from the hegemony of storytelling. As

Marie-Laure Ryan has argued, even a hypertext narrative limits the autonomy of readers by obliging them "to construct a causal sequence of events out of fragments presented in a variable order" (44)—a condition that games or puzzles readily cede, since there is no expectation of a causal or sequential logic in a game except where spelled out in its rules. In short, play authorizes alternative reading pleasures that eschew the teleological positivism of plot and narrative. Freed thus from story strictures, the ludic permits a mode of sustained attention in a space of unusual expansion. It is here where action and reflective cognition meld anew in an altered reader. More to the point, it is here in the play space where readers, like the texts before them, transform.

The Ludic and the Reader in the Margins

An important feature of these narrative moves toward play in autography is that they are *moves* in the first place. In order to warrant the label of "ludic," such a move must also be away from an established narrative norm. Before insisting that this conceptual move from one thing to something else be a precondition for the type of ludic under discussion here, let us first grapple with the effects of treating the ludic precisely as a "move" or a "movement."

There are at least three significant effects of the shift in modality that flanks the embedded play space in autography, which is always also a movement from story to game, from mimesis to *ludus*. First, as breaks from established patterns, such eruptions have as much to do with the reading protocols they violate as with the new rules they bring about. Second, as a result of this break, the reader is invited to become an actor in a play that is, on the one hand, scripted by the text but, on the other, never wholly circumscribed by it. Ludic interventions, therefore, re-enact a fantasy common to textuality—of there being a surplus world outside of the text that is accessible, quite paradoxically, through the very text whose limits are sought to be exceeded. And third, aside from functioning as a break, the embedded play space produces what Genettean narratology construes as a diegetical swerve. That is, it works not merely to violate established patterns (as in *metalepsis*) but, more particularly, to deviate from mimetic priorities. The turn to the ludic seems to entail the reverse of *metalepsis*, which Genette defines in a footnote to *Narrative Discourse* as the moment in "which the narrator pretends to enter (with or without his reader) into the diegetic universe" (101n. 33). In all three of the above effects, an unexpected change in the rules of the game forces narrative to quit diegesis altogether and permits entry (with or without us) into two flickering spaces at once: those designed for our play and those designed to play with us.

By recognizing the move to the ludic as a recession from order, we begin to see in it a kind of revolutionary hiatus. What does it mean for an order (a game, a system of play) to suddenly change its rules mid-play? One possible answer comes from Jean-François Lyotard, during an interview on games and rules. Discussing the precious interrelation of the structural rules that define games and the imagination, Lyotard states:

> There are even some [games] that are not invented yet and that one could invent by instituting new rules. . . . It is in this way that something like the imagination, or the will . . . could develop. And when I say "develop," I do not mean it in the sense of a progress; I mean the fact that one can introduce into the pragmatics, into our relations with others, forms of language that are at the same time unexpected and unheard of, as forms of efficacy. Either because one has made up new moves in an old game or because one has made up a new game. (61)

The recursive relationship between the introduction of "new moves in an old game" and the realization that one may be involved in a game-like social order ("our relations with others") are useful to us for suggesting how David B.'s new move to the "little game, dear reader" implicates the rest of *Epileptic*'s visual narration as a game-work. To be sure, narration has not overtly ceded to game-playing heretofore. That there is a game to play follows a new rule, in other words, which is itself an indication of the establishment of a new order or signifying system.

The game proposes a countervailing efficacy of interactive play that unsettles principles of mimesis in force in most other panels.[12] What is attempted in the "new rule" of the ludic is meant neither to tell nor to show—that other efficacious structure of pictorial mimesis. The ludic panel is finally relational; it hosts interactivity. By staging an explicit turn away from narrative, the ludic, if only for an instant, rescinds that principle of legibility honored by most graphic novels. It ceases to obey the tacit mandate of decipherability governing the portrayal of words and images. And rather than presuppose an easy reception, the game panel calls forth a reader-viewer whose status as player is constituted by the challenges of reception (the picture puzzle only works as a game insofar as playing it involves wins and losses after all).

But how representative is *Epileptic*'s game relative to other graphic novels? *Epileptic* is not *Jimmy Corrigan* (to which we shall return). It does not teem with accessories of playable content, as does Ware's text. And while games are not atypical to most autobiographical graphic novels, as we have seen, scenes of ludic illegibility are certainly more infrequent. It is their exceptionality, in fact, that helps them to carve out diegetic pauses for the non-narrational to inhabit. With that rare efficacy in mind, moreover, we may begin to find interesting analogs for David B.'s picture puzzle in a range of graphic novel tropes. The mirror and *mise en abyme* come forcibly to mind, as do other ludic ciphers found wherever the boundaries of text, author, and receiver productively blur.

By way of example, let us briefly consider the representation of hands in autobiographical projects by Art Spiegelman and Alison Bechdel. Each artist incorporates hands (fig. 3.3) as conspicuous solicitations of the ludic. Both use placeholding hands to map an ideal (illustrated) reader who holds the same thing we do, whose fingers appear where ours must go. In her analysis of Sacco's *Palestine*, Rebecca Scherr rightly links the gesture to the affective priority autobiography gives to contact and connection: "[T]he resonant, emotional quality of many graphic memoirs depends on the reader's apprehension of the hands of the author, that is, the trace of the author's presence" (22). For Hillary Chute, who has gone further than any other critic in her analysis of hands in comics, the hands in *Fun Home* not only emblematize the gap between Alison and her father, but their function also "mandates a baseline manual sensuality" (199) for reading comics tactilely.[13] The consonance of depicted hands holding pictures and our own situation as readers invites us to place ourselves onto, if not *into*, the spectacle in a uniquely physical way. Although momentary or even unconsciously perceived, the game and the new rules it promotes rely upon movements in the physical space of the comic, where real hands and fingers seem to magically touch their figural antecedents. Do these figural hands not resemble our own? Are we not anticipated by them, physically? Such musings inevitably lead to questions more inclined to trigger the gaming mode that interests me here: Can you place your fingers on top of the drawn ones?

Regardless of their fit, hands holding pictures within comics pictographically unite tropes of artists and viewers, text and texture.[14] As a metonym for what Katalin Orbán calls "the reader's 'carnal' hand" (63), autography's handiwork makes trouble for aesthetic philosophy's notion of *seeing-in*, which Michael Newell, riffing on Richard Wollheim, defines as "[p]ictorial seeing [. . . which] involves the veridical experience of seeing the picture surface, and the non-veridical experience of seeing the depicted subject" (30). While we have been less concerned about the "truth" or veridicality of the comics, Newell's distinctions are still valuable when comparing a drawing of hands with its effect: the depiction of an invisible, impossible, and non-veridical subject. Of course, it would be wrong for us to imagine the swelling of the non-veridical to absorb the veridical as a one-step process in the case of autography's ubiquitous hands—hands that "take" pictures (as discussed in Chapter Two)

3.3 Hands in the margins from *Maus I* (100). Graphic novel excerpt from *Maus I: A Survivor's Tale: My Father Bleeds History* by Art Spiegelman. Copyright © 1973, 1980, 1981, 1982, 1983, 1984, 1985, 1986 by Art Spiegelman. Used by permission of Pantheon Books, an imprint of the Knopf Doubleday Publishing Group, a division of Random House LLS. All rights reserved.

in Saaco's *Palestine*, or that grasp simulated photographs in *Maus* and *Fun Home*, or which hold the very book we hold in our hands. All of these guiding hands serve as optic surrogates for tactility.[15] How much more forcefully are we interpellated when even our physicality as book-holders seems to have been accounted for and made tactile by the text? Rather than the classic contract of fictive verisimilitude, this form of *seeing-in* fosters critical reception, as Julia Watson maintains, "call[ing] readers' attentions to our voyeuristic looking at . . . intimately personal acts" (33).

And, as with most published memoir, one of the most intimate acts imagined by the text is that of reading. Never passive, the reader-viewer of much autography has in addition to the participatory requirements of any graphic novel the burdens of *seeing-in* in order to bear witness.[16] To be sure, none of the graphic memoirists mentioned had need of Marvin Leibowitz's claim, based upon clinical observations, that "[t]he sense conveyed by the drawing of hands, then, is of the ability to control the environment, to deal directly with the self-object experience" (96). Indeed, the illustrated hands that hold the text or its adjuncts—pictures—affirm the priority graphic novels ascribe to a faculty Chute refers to as "manual sensuality." Hands indexicalize the presence of the reader in otherwise private spaces of testimony and visual enunciation. They do so even as they dissolve into *mise en abyme*, which, as I have already shown, excites autographic anxieties regarding nature and culture, subject and object. Indeed, hands and the tactile possibilities they engender take on a sacred function in autography associated with the ludic.

Between drawn fingers and real ones, a ritual space of difference arises. The same touch that holds a comic book or graphic novel inevitably conceals images. This is so particularly for commercial book objects, whose publishers mandate dimensions that render the images within them on a much smaller scale than the actual hands that hold them. In the case of screen versions either smaller or larger than standard books, the drawn hands in ghostly non-marginal margins would call us perhaps to witness the funereal corporeality of the book, or perhaps the book's undead permanence—its new efficacy as a digital trope. In either case, our fingers become virtual as well, so that in addition to the materiality-digital divide, autography's hands bridge multiple ontological and epistemological domains: the known text and its knowing maker on the one hand, and the infinite anonymities of the unknowable reader on the other. When we place our hands where their presence has been anticipated, we become part of the text's representations and subject to its *management* in all etymological senses of the term (i.e., *manus*: hand). Haptic, participatory forms of that management turn these illustrations into minor ludic outbreaks. As such, they compare to children's books that similarly presume physical reception contexts, in which the material page (or screen) is subject to many more kinds of interaction than reading. Playing *Epileptic*'s embedded game is by no means the same as chewing the book's corners. But, as we shall see, to play the game at all we must first see the page as a manipulatable object, susceptible to myriad adjustments, markings, and excisions, each one a potential solution to the puzzle.

A Closer Look at the Example in David B.

The tone of the caption that accompanies David B.'s turn to the ludic is aptly playful. The phrase "dear reader" is ironic since, as we have been noting, it comes at the precise moment when the reader is called upon to evolve into something more. Indeed, the trope of direct address draws attention to a type of verisimilitude that graphic novels render problematic. Even for the traditional, non-illustrated novel, direct address produces—among other things—the very readerly consciousness that it seems merely to name: "The interest served by the cohabitation of textual markers like 'the reader' with the undeconstructed presencing of told space, the collusion between cited narrating and narrated site, is for classic fiction nothing short of narrative interest itself—the coalition of suspended disbelief and cued self-consciousness" (Stewart 5). In our case, the *un*-presencing of told space cued by *Epileptic*'s visual game gives rise to a coalition of suspended narration and cryptogrammic activity.

The particular cryptogram offered by the panel is an optical challenge of visual cognition and recognition. In *The Puzzle Instinct* semiotician Marcel Danesi devises a taxonomy for picture puzzles, according to which, this one by David B. primarily corresponds to the first of three subtypes defined by Danesi as *picture incongruities*: "(1) pictures that conceal disguised images; (2) pictures that contain inconsonant figures (e.g., a modern automobile in a nineteenth-century scene); and (3) pictures that hide differences in detail" (73). Pedagogical in structure—as most games are—David B.'s begins with a lesson whose application equates to playing or solving the puzzle. The caption discloses the hidden visual grammar of the yin and yang, from which we extrapolate the rule of play. We are meant to lay these image-keys, like decoding devices, over each image-object within the panel. Whatever else any of these images signify, in the realm of the puzzle they will only have one or the other meaning, and only one is correct. Although the game depends upon an aggressively restrictive hermeneutic, the rest of the graphic novel embraces the pluralities of meaning and life. During puzzle play, however, this fluidity ossifies into an either/or logic that releases us from the manifold demands of visual significance. To be conscious of solving the visual puzzle, therefore, is to witness the polarization of meaning through the prism of repetition.

Of course, attempting to solve the puzzle also brings to light other meanings and misrecognitions, which could be acceptable had we never been made privy to the hidden grammar that relentlessly binarizes meaning. In a way, the game is an inverted homage to the visual polysemy that reigns beyond its ludic borders. It is an omen of interpretative pluralities to come. Perhaps in its play with uncoupling and un-bodying, the visual puzzle nods obliquely to the byzantine structures of identification and trauma that Murray Pratt uncovers at the heart of the text's many "attempts to bring back to life (rather than explain away) the traumatic realities of coping with a condition that is characterized in the text by its unknowability, the withdrawal from presence and communicability experienced by those confronted by the epileptic" (135). Such prescience would not be uncommon for visual puzzles. Even while the optical puzzle "adds an element of surprise, bewilderment, or mischief to . . . visual texts" (73) according to Danesi, it also operates as a cautionary tale that "warns us, in effect, to be wary of our visual perception" (74). This loss of perceptual reliability brought about by the picture puzzle induces in us "a momentary feeling of discord, upsetting our inborn need for visual harmony. By identifying those differences and marking them," Danesi goes on to say, "we seem to be restoring harmony to the 'look of things,' albeit in a diminutive and inconsequential way" (74).[17]

The pleasure we take in picture puzzles, moreover, may have metaphysical implications, revealing, according to Danesi, "the presence of a peculiar duality in the human soul—an inner struggle between order and chaos" (109). And what better cipher for that definitive tension than yin and yang? "In Chinese philosophy," Danesi claims, "this duality has been encapsulated by the notion of *Yin* and *Yang*—two opposing forces that are believed to combine in various proportions to produce all the different objects in the universe, as well as the different moods in human beings" (109). How fitting that the puzzle in *Epileptic* be a universal signifier of opposition as harmony, in which perfect difference is the ideal *telos* toward which everything strives. And strive we must, for as many observers report, differentiating the yin from the yang in David B.'s visual exercise is no automatic endeavor.

Perhaps the game of the puzzle is really being played on us. Indeed, there is no simple correlation between the yin or yang as each has been visually defined in the panel. The illustrated elements strictly obey neither the isomorphism of the yin-yang symbol nor the either/or logic it contrives as a means to harmony. Certainly, we might impose that logic onto the discernible elements, "restoring harmony to the look" of the images, as Danesi might put it. We could see the pear with the face on the left to be the yin that balances the star on the right. But that logic does not hold when considering the other design elements. Indeed, the game truly begins on the other side of the tipping point of effortless decoding. What about the spotted animal on the right? What serves as its counterpart on the left? Those leaf shapes? No, or at least not satisfyingly. The playable elements do not conform to the same strictures of visual symmetry alluded to in the rules of the game.[18] Thus, the matching game we are invited to play disintegrates after so many rounds.[19]

Whether sincere or not, functional as puzzle or not, the embedded play space of *Epileptic* seems to cede authority to readers; however, it does so only by virtue of the author-artist, who casts playing as a hiatus from narrative. A textual enclave, the ludic bolsters an otherwise opaque system of narrative authority. Flaunting play is another way to parade authority before us. To be sure, control (both narrational and illustrational) is the yin to *Epileptic*'s ludic yang, and the author-artist seems intent on making us take notice. The aggression I read in the game panel is informed by Debra Malina's account of "the violent streak underlying this persistent breaching of constitutive boundaries," which causes her to "detect, even in the metaleptic joke or game, a certain aggression towards the subject, whether internal or external to the text" (3). To clarify the game's aggression, we could compare its placement in the text to the "how-to" ending of Lynda Barry's *One Hundred Demons*, which, as Hillary Chute convincingly argues, "does not enshrine or sanctify itself" (*Graphic Women* 113) and, in true populist fashion, teaches readers to take up "the responsive, dialogic creation of narration" (113). David B.'s optical puzzle, by contrast, is a less revolutionary model of interactivity. It enshrines itself and its creator by virtue of its placement near the beginning of the narrative. Rather than learning a craft at the end of a text in order to make our own, as with Barry, we learn a looking practice from David B. early on so as to better appreciate all the visual intricacies lying ahead.

Nevertheless, there are implications to this lesson that are potentially subversive to the centrality of power in the domain of the author. In addition to assuming an educable reader, one who can be prompted to change and grow, David B.'s game trains us to forestall the equivalence of juxtaposition and sequence essential to comics structure. We cannot technically be said to linger in the panel while playing the proffered game, for in becoming a field of play, the panel becomes a space unto itself. It is always on some level detached from those panels around it that make no solicitations to play. Enacting a transitory severance from narrative, the game panel transcends the sequence in which it occurs. Particularly as we solve the puzzle, the panel is no longer an accessory to narrative, but autonomous, conveying stillness and atemporality like a painting. And, as with any painting, there is visual work for us to do in the seemingly timeless space apart from narrative sequence that the ludic calls forth. It is there in that interim that the reader is expected to train and to grow, where—just as in the ending of Barry's *One Hundred Demons*—the text gives some indication of how it is to be read with lessons in seeing anew.

One effect of the puzzle's new way of seeing has to do with the representation of the body. In the puzzle, body parts promise to figuratively unite corporeality and narrative. In this regard, the puzzle is a hypostatization of the conceit of autobiography, reinforcing the discursive bonds yoking text and life, codex and corpus. Interestingly, the puzzle meets all four of Daniel Punday's criteria for the process by which bodies come to figure the texts that contain them: "[B]odies must be distinguished from other objects within the text, must be sorted into types, must be defined in relation to the world outside of themselves, and must be granted a degree of embodiment" (12). Is this not exactly the work of distinguishing and sorting required by the puzzle? And yet, so long as we're asking questions, do these illustrated bodies even count as "human" bodies? Is not the un-bodying of the text's bodies one of the implied pleasures of the game we are invited to play? Thematically, Murray Pratt reminds us that the early section of the narrative (where the game occurs) corresponds with young David B.'s development of "a nascent visual semiotic, intrinsically linked to his brother's epilepsy, but which will, as the series progresses, eventually aid him in moving beyond both this and his own illogical but psychologically formative terror of contamination" (140). Does a terror of bodily coincidence subtend our presumed delight in turning the coital body into an abstraction? Into either yin or yang? Punday considers the question of which bodies count as fundamental to contemporary narratives, "because they are anxious to police the borders upon which their storytelling depends" (59). The promiscuity of the body as a puzzle piece and the sexual body that is abstracted in it resonate in the ludic panel's central image of heterosexual genital oral sex.

The puzzle's disclosure that the image is really a pastiche, part of a visual scavenger hunt, simultaneously disappears the erotic surface of the lovers in the *soixante-neuf* position and amplifies the readerly pleasures of probing the object-space they occupy, making them game tokens on a par with the image of the pear on the left side of the panel or the smiling sun on the right. In the process, erotic corporeality facilitates totalizing absorption and figural dispersion at the same time, thus abolishing the boundary between figure and form—if only while the game mode animates the reader's imagination. The solicitation of the reader to play is thus also a summoning of the ludic more generally. Our acceptance of the offer always means acquiescence to the disappearance of the body. Bodies and the lived experiences they signify are transubstantiated in the *ludus* through pattern recognition and surrealistic hide-and-seek.

But another form of agency inheres in the puzzle. The consumer reserves the right to negate what is offered as a superfluity, an extra affordance to be enjoyed by being passed over. To bypass the game, for ludologist Gonzalo Frasca, is to ignore simulation's plea for repetition: "[Y]ou could play a game only once, but the knowledge and interpretation of simulations requires repetition" (227). The foregone simulation or game is thus also a forfeiture of knowledge, though it rarely ever feels that way. Take the cut-outs from Chris Ware's *Jimmy Corrigan*, for example—or, better yet, don't take them! By disregarding Ware's supra-textual overtures, readers activate a different kind of *ludus* with forms of play operative only when negated. In fact, by repeatedly ignoring the puzzling gifts of arts and crafts Ware's text inexhaustibly provides, we simulate the conditions of melancholic fantasy so important to the

narrative and its production of a world that refuses interactivity. The formative connections withheld from Jimmy, in other words, get reflected in our
own unreturned hospitality towards Ware's constructions.

Thus, the game that is tendered but deferred aligns the reader's agency with
the sovereignty of the commodity consumer. We partake of the commodities
we choose in the sublime knowledge that others exist different from the ones
we select—but they are just as available to us should we decide to enjoy them
and possess the funds to do so. Such a move through the ludic that we pass
over points us to the hinterlands of *jouissance*, locating us at the center of our
own recalibrated desire to read and not to play. Hence, even the decision not
to play fortifies the illusion that the text has helped us to find ourselves in its
articulate gaps and fissures. We grow under its tutelage in spite of ourselves.

Conclusion: Autography and the Game of Death

As a final perspective, it is worth mentioning that ludic gaps are also epistemological training exercises for dealing with that ultimate deviation from
an established pattern: death. Discussing the interrelation of narrative endings and the apocalyptic end of all things, Frank Kermode sees incidences of
peripeteia, or narrative reversals and unexpected narrative turns, as preparation for apocalypse: "[s]o that in assimilating the peripeteia we are enacting
that readjustment of expectations in regard to an end which is so notable a
feature of naïve apocalyptic[ism]" (18). Similarly, play spaces index an author's
confrontation with the unknowable terrain of the reader's activity. In autobiography, ludic interruptions demarcate the zone where the author's life story
transmutes into the ground for another's doing and becoming. However,
the ludic is only ever to accomplish such demarcation in a play space that is
always already haunted by the effaced author. Therefore, on the other side of
the metaphysical parentheses that the embedded game entails are epistemological terrors real and imagined. The ludic incites temporary revolution from
the universalizing impulses of narration within whose discursive jurisdiction
any breach of authorial agency signifies as death.

It is thus armed with admonitory premonitions of mortality that the autobiographer ensnares us. In hopes of achieving a pristine ambivalence (the yin
and yang), autobiographical narration surrenders to its other, giving over to
the extra-textual demands of the reader and reader-governed activity. These
demands are also recursively textual in that they involve moves of play which
respond to, traverse, and temporarily annihilate the designing consciousness

associated with the author. Hence, the supposedly alternative regimes of the ludic and the participatory reader turn out to be misleading, contingent upon the impossible abdication of a narrative authority that authorizes the play space into being. Despite their potential aggression, such turns to the ludic presume a reader willing to refine ways of looking and being, to reconfigure looking *as* being. In this regard, they point optimistically and perhaps nostalgically to a notion of the human (and of the humanities) in tandem with a transformative, progressive model of learning, which sees reading as a site of participation already, where further developments ever await reader-actors and author-artist-texts alike.

Then again, whether a ludic event happens at all in *Epileptic* remains in question. David B.'s play space is perhaps best understood *sous rature*, snatched away and crossed out by the author as soon as it is offered. Some would-be players, as noted, experience difficulty seeing absolute yin and yang patterns in the forms given. For them, the task is less puzzle than puzzlement, lacking the certainty that the solutions to most optical puzzles guarantee. Un-playability tilts the entire gesture more towards parody than puzzle, but whether it opens up forms of reception other than the ludic one limned here is for another book to determine. It suffices to say as part of our ongoing assessment of autography's pedagogical leanings that a standard reading experience is to pass on the games proposed, no matter their structure. We have better things to do than grab our scissors and cut along the dotted lines that Lynda Barry or Chris Ware have prepared for us. Playing takes time and effort, which, perhaps, is the point. The ideological forces that efface labor meet resistance in the graphic autobiography's embedded game. There, we are induced to acknowledge, upon extended and ludic review, that there is something more to see in the images after all.

Throughout, we have posed a simple but recurring question to ask about the implications of interactivity: What is produced? In the games analyzed above, is it not production itself or, at the very least, the trace of artistic labor that is produced? Because image scrutiny and the ordinary labors of reading comics tend to abbreviate complex visual information, the artistic labor that goes into the illustrations remains invisible. As David B. and other graphic novelists utilize it, the game reverses this veiling phenomenon of comics reading, revealing the mystifications of artistic labor that continue to haunt autography, a subject explored further in the following chapter.

Whether played or passed over, demystifying or enshrining, the embedded visual game forces us to see while teaching us how. Standard to its pedagogical brief: first, that images signify on many levels at once and thus abjure monolithic schemas of interpretation; and second, that we must act (play or work) to see them so rigorously. Indeed, the content of the game is incidental to its function as a reading lesson expertly disguised as an extracurricular surplus. Thus, the play spaces of autobiographical graphic novels beckon transformative agency in the field of the reader, whose actions therein are as emancipatory as they are puzzling.

4

The Work Behind the Work of Graphic *Künstlerroman*

How would the worker come to face the product of his activity as a stranger,
were it not that in the very act of production he was estranging himself from himself?
—Karl Marx "Estranged Labor" (72)

A chief principle of Marxist critique is that commodity objects obscure the labor that produces them. Estranged from the market power of their labor, workers perforce meet their work as strangers. In the process, they endure a form of alienation observed by Marx to be anticipated, if not managed, by the already dehumanizing nature of labor under capitalism. Nowhere is this tidy axiom of exploitation contested more resolutely than in the autobiographical graphic novel. Take the cover flap imagery of either volume of *Maus*; the creator, busy at his drafting table, greets us there, as do the entwined temporalities of his narrative. The crematoria of history pierce the super-present through a window, invading the self-reflexive *now* of creation. Ribbons of smoke from the smokestacks appear in that window, which, like a comics panel, frames and dissolves the narrative meaning of the images reflected therein. All the while, and with increasing significance, the smoke of history's exhaust mingles with the plume of Spiegelman's inevitable cigarette.

Metacritical flourishes abound as Spiegelman presents himself meditatively suspended from sketching the very book we read. Rather than draw himself drawing, this intermission from work allows him to evoke, as Jacques Derrida says of all self-portraits, "a drawing potency"—as if at this moment Art realizes that "[h]e invents drawing" (*Memoirs* 2). To celebrate so momentous a tautology, Art holds against his face a material version of the mouse "mask" worn by his character as a type of narrative skin. In light of its cross-time

4.1 Self-portrait of Art at his drawing table from *Maus II*. Graphic novel Excerpt from *Maus I: A Survivor's Tale: My Father Bleeds History* by Art Spiegelman. Copyright © 1973, 1980, 1981, 1982, 1983, 1984, 1985, 1986 by Art Spiegelman. Used by permission of Pantheon Books, an imprint of the Knopf Doubleday Publishing Group, a division of Random House LLS. All rights reserved.

content and its placement in the extra-diegetic space of the coverlet, the self-portrait connotes an ever-blurring edge of the story's beginning and history's end. The coverlet enfolds and opens up onto as fine a location as any for the poignant encapsulation of the "work" of *Maus*. And what grim work it is.

In a related image that opens *Maus II*, the corpses mounding at the base of Art's drawing table impel Erin McGlothlin to conclude that Spiegelman's "artistic production is thus, to a certain extent, based on their suffering and death" (*Second-Generation* 81). At the same time, McGlothlin importantly recognizes that "Art is also marked here as a victim . . . he becomes the inmate" (81) of the text and its labor of traumatic representation. This is precisely the trauma Michael G. Levine reads into Spiegelman's cigarette smoking, tying that activity to drawing and drafting: "[t]his interaction between the drafts-man's work and his drawing of smoke, between activities that sustain and contaminate one another, is further complicated by the artist's portrait of himself" (46). Having established a psychological connection between Spie-gelman's drawing in of smoke and his drawing out of history's incinerated bodies, Levine stresses the traumatic repetition that structures *Maus*: "His self-portrait is thus a *draft* in the further sense that it is but one in a series of provisional renderings, none of which may be said to constitute the final, definitive version of himself" (49).

The following chapter investigates similar *drafts* eddying along the bound-aries of the maker and the made. As it turns out, exhibits of the author-artist at work are recurring features of autography, perhaps even *de rigueur*. Several instances may be found in Chapter One to confirm my suspicion that they are: the mirroring of Lynda Barry at her drafting table at the start of *One Hun-dred Demons* or James Kochalka's elf who is psychically halted while drawing. Countless other texts and artists could be noted in this regard, such as Alison Bechdel's preoccupation with drawing herself drawing. All of these examples, though varied, echo the mysterious drafts of Spiegelman's self-portrait. No less relevant than *Maus* are the many other graphic novels that classify as autographic *künstlerroman*, or self-told comics about the artist's develop-ment. Max Saunders succinctly describes the intent of the *künstlerroman* as "the desire to present not just the artists' life, development, consciousness, but also their experience of creating" (xxxvii). Spiegelman's conscious engage-ment with the aims of the *künstlerroman* tradition is of titular concern in his autographic *Breakdowns: Portrait of the Artist as a Young%@&*!* (2008). There, as elsewhere, Spiegelman takes up the project of reflecting lived expe-rience according to the mechanics of the mirror, fashioning himself as both drawer and drawn, the reflected and the reflector, and cueing reader-viewers once again to the critical potency of the image of the artist-autobiographer at work. More than *mise en abyme*, such images reveal the extent to which autography continues to depend upon ideologies of making and production congruent with the *künstlerroman* and hint at the ways in which these ideolo-gies are imbricated within systems of value (making something in exchange for something else) and belief (making something from nothing).

Although comparatively rare among popular print autobiographies, the *künstlerroman* virtually subsumes autography.[1] Within the logic of *Blankets*, for instance, Craig's sketches of Raina, his first love, yoke the development of the maker of marks to the liberating transformations that those marks catalyze. As a result, drawing comes to encode itself and much more. No longer simply drawing, the act of illustration is hereby shown to function as a technology of the self, helping to manufacture Craig as a subject—which is to say, figuring the artist-to-be as the seat of consciousness from which all the text's narrative concerns radiate, like Spiegelman's smoke, braiding the heartbreak of first love with an escape from repressive environs and interweaving both into the story of Craig's salvific vocation as an artist.

In *Epileptic*, by contrast, David B.'s transition from the ordinary to the artistic is no singular event. The idea that drawing is a transformative act has no origin in *Epileptic*; drawing is an agent of ontological expansion from start to finish. It could even be argued that scenes of David B.'s official art education are demonstrably ineffectual. After all, it is not until David B. recounts his art school immersion in surrealism that viewers receive the clearest explanation of *Epileptic*'s aesthetic underpinnings. The full-page spread of the title banner proclaims: "Come visit the inside of David B.'s head at the end of the 70s" (277–78). But the explanatory value of that display is both tardy and disingenuous, coming as it does more than three quarters into a rather long text, which has arranged plenty of rigorous instruction for motivated viewers beforehand (as investigated in the previous chapter's analysis of *Epileptic*'s ludic aptitude). Therefore, when David B.'s protagonist officially learns to see surrealistically, we have already graduated from that curriculum. Our schedules thus misaligned, readers may experience the image of the young artist lying on a floor surrounded by influential drawings as belated, not so much a simulation of instructional seeing as it is an elapsed performance of one.

In general, tableaus of the artist at work, frequently in the process of making the exact text we hold in our hands, serve as the tantalizing supplements to comics as a medium. In addition to those ludic elements of hands in the margins from the previous chapter, tropes of drawing as work further express autography's desire to resist the obsolescence of the book. Within autographic discourses of drawing, books are talismans of a neo-Romantic investment in the *artiste* or *auteur*—shibboleths of bourgeois culture, denoting an elite art producer whose endeavors necessitate not only a special terminology but special economic considerations as well. Indeed, these terms themselves confer a mystifying exceptionalism to the bearer. Integral to the graphic novel's category of the *auteur*—most exponents of whom belong to an emergent canon of autobiography—is the generic wish to make the conceptual visible and to wring subjective and affective truths from the process. That wish lies behind autography's standard play with the reversibility of fiction and verity, an ambivalence partly achieved through a familiar set of Romantic conventions still flourishing in US popular culture.[2] Congruent with that tradition, all genuine artistic labor carries the disavowed spark of the original *poesis* (literally, making) of creation. A secular cenotaph for divinity, art permits devotees to apprehend the infinite without any of the disagreeable appurtenances of dogma or ritual.

If the historical incompatibility in this line of thought gives pause, then a bolder economic comparison to Romanticism may prove stupefying, not least because it seems to depend upon a naïve periodization of capitalism, its presumed differences at distinct evolutionary stages, and so on. From this view, it is scarcely possible to imagine parallels between our contemporary valuation of art objects or commodities and the bygone system of value for anything crafted in the late eighteenth century, a time when Romanticism and capitalism were young. Commenting upon "capitalism's youth," economic historians generally invoke a pre-corporate system founded upon the self-corrective dynamics of the market, as do Foster and McChesney here: "During the classical phase of political economy, in capitalism's youth, it was natural enough that economic theory would rest on the simple conception of a modified barter economy in which money was a mere means of exchange but did not otherwise materially affect basic economic relations" (55). From this perspective, alienation, reification, and the omnipresence of commoditization may be nothing more than the unfortunate growth spurts of economic development. Perhaps, then, it is better to say, by way of a thesis, that capitalism remains young in autography. In the following pages, we shall track how the autobiographical graphic novel's relentless view of the author-artist at work relishes just such a fantasy.[3] Next to the child, the self-regarding artist in the midst of making art is one of autography's premier masks, behind which lurks a naïve yet potent fantasy of production.

Fredric Jameson takes account of capitalism's growth during the phase of Taylorization, which organizes a world of commodity objects structurally coordinated with the physical spaces that buyers and laborers actually inhabit. In the colonial phase, however, capitalism no longer generates a world that can be mapped by its subjects, according to Jameson, because "those structural coordinates are no longer accessible to immediate lived experience and are often not even conceptualizable for most people" ("Cognitive Mapping" 349). The difficulty subjects have mapping themselves within complex economic systems pervades literature, as characters in the Bildungsroman tradition, in the words of Eric Prieto, "attempt to break out of a naïvely phenomenological perspective and enter into the more worldly 'cartographic' perspective that Jameson promotes" (190).

With their obsessive returns to moments of genesis and their *künstlerromanic* treatment of drawing as a salutary union of art and work, autographics cultivate for themselves (and implicitly for reader-viewers) a mythical immunity from Jameson's late capital diagnosis. The worlds mapped by autographic texts are spatially sensate and economically cognizable. Although autographic protagonists often characterize themselves as exemplars of social alienation, they are anything but alienated in the Marxist sense—or so it would seem. In fact, this paradox may be endemic to the *künstlerroman* as theorized by Herbert Marcuse, who, according to Charles Reitz, keenly recognized in the genre "the harsh duality of the ideal against the real, perceived by modern artists in the alienating quality of their life and activity vis-à-vis the general forms of social existence" (Reitz 31). As the autographer sees it, then, alienation occurs in life but not in labor. Inalienable labor persists in the dream-work of the genre as an unproblematic effectivity.[4] In autobiographical graphic novels, drawing constructs exacting spatial, symbolic, and relational localities that prove eminently accessible to mapping.

We should assume, then, that the ability to cognitively map is in negative proportion to economic alienation. That is, when a high degree of alienation permeates the social order, the nature of value is also obscured. In such an order, cognitive mapping likewise erodes along with other faculties by which one may interact with one's environment. The problem lies, as we all know, not at the superstructure but at its prodigious though unseen base, which, in the case of Jameson's notion of late capital, has been profoundly distorted by a substructure of disappearing and evermore dispersed bottom lines (the consequent occlusions of a global economy).[5] Even so, as Hillary Chute has argued, the visual and hybrid nature of graphic narrative "offers textured representations of mapping" (*Graphic Women* 27), making memoir comics the perfect test case for the reconsideration of the unmappable nature of self-consciousness amidst conditions of late capital and its baroque systems of exchange and value.

This chapter attempts to unveil autography's peculiar textures of visuality and capitalism in self-portraiture. Here, as nowhere else, autographics betray an exigency for dissecting the visual subject, a figure Kimberly DeFazio historicizes as "an exuberant observer of . . . capital-driven phenomenon at the level of visual culture" (84). And if, as Nicholas Mirzoeff suggests, the "ability to assemble a visualization manifests the authority of the visualizer" (2), self-portraits display a rather paradoxical assemblage of authority and objecthood. As we shall see, when artists I-conicize themselves as makers, they risk demotion to the status of objects, swapping disembodied viewing for the cryptic self-regard of drawn things.

Back to the Drawing Table: Autography's Colophonic Imaginary

To what extent are self-portraits derivative of the self-reflexivity that contemporary graphic novels have been shown to rely upon as part of their formal operation? To respond, let us return to Spiegelman's *Maus*, particularly the conversation Art has with his wife, Françoise, about the kind of animal she would be in his book. Should he represent her (in some imaginary future) according to a principle of ethno-religious affiliation—as a mouse like the other Jewish characters? Or should it be in terms of national affiliation—as a frog, in recognition of her Franco-Belgian origins? There, near the start of the second volume, the audience enjoys a window into the troplogical rationale of the first book. There, too, is the guilt-laden interior of the artist's conscience as he walks to his therapist's office after being interviewed by a throng of reporters while, more significantly, composing *Maus* at a drawing table perched atop gruesome mouse corpses. This latter is not of the same order of self-reflexivity as the debate about Françoise's animal mask, which is comparable to (and perhaps the inspiration for) the moment in *Epileptic* when the creator argues with his mother about how to portray an alcoholic grandmother. In both, temporal ambivalence links the work as an idea to its material instantiation in the reader's hands. We know the answers to these speculations as *de facto* proofs before us, though they remain hypotheses in the diegesis. A Judeo-Christian perspective prods a further implication than dramatic irony; the viewer is made audience to the postlapsarian world of fallen objects and redemptive labor (in the finished commodity, the book) as well as to a prelapsarian state of Edenic possibility: How will Artie depict Françoise? Will David B. depict the alcoholic grandmother? Rife with dramatic irony, these ambitious scenes further attempt to re-present invention.

Aside from the "drafting table" spectacle of Artie and the corpses, these self-reflexive examples do not cite the work being fabricated. They opt rather for a schizophrenic vision of labor as either cogitated or completed, an immaculate conception. However, in the coverlet image from *Maus*, Artie *is in the timespace of artisanal production*. He is visually tied to his labor and the tools of his trade, albeit transfixed in a moment of pause. Likewise, and more generally, the drawing table self-reflexivities of autographics seem to undo the process of alienation that seeks to pry artists from representation, which happens also to be their physical labor.

Of course, self-referential authorship is not limited to autobiographical comics. An interesting example occurs in Alan Moore's esoteric fantasy *Promethea* (2000), when the character of a goddess attempts to unravel the fabric of creation in parallel with Eve's transgression or Pandora's box. The fate of all creation—the fate the Real—hangs in the balance. In order to convey the gravity of the situation, both writer and illustrator enter the text awestruck by the horror of Promethea's world-shattering intention. In one panel, we see Moore aghast at his computer; in the other, the artist looks correspondingly astonished at his drawing table. Together, they assert Promethea's act to be so extraordinary that it ripples over from its own diegetic time and space— what Bakhtin would call its *chronotope*—to affect these dual spaces of authorship that are no longer able to contain it. As Annalisa Di Liddo has pointed out, Moore's "manipulation of the chronotope" in this instance "opts for fluid space and time, resulting in a ceaseless, metamorphic narrative continuum" (95). That continuum also naturalizes what has been a conventional division. No longer split, the domains of producer and product touch within the supposed fiction exactly as they would in any autobiography.

Beyond the conventions of genre and narrative, peeling back verisimilitude's chimerical surface spotlights a few intrinsic properties of comics. It is for good reason that the subtitle of McCloud's foundational study refers to "the invisible art." Comics conceal their work. Thanks to a convergence of certain protocols of art appreciation (unity within variety, symmetry, minimalism, legibility, the suppression of narrative clutter or noise, etc.), comics cover their tracks in the metaphorical camouflage of their own mimesis. Even in autography, the spectacle of narrative content is sufficient to muffle the extraneous noise of authorship. Only in the *künstlerroman* do self-reflexive revelations of work equate to narrative content without the slightest violation of any of these protocols or conventions.[6]

Hence, autographic self-portraiture is structured by antinomy, for although such images champion the material labor behind the story—the work behind the work—they simultaneously function as visual signatures, autographs of the ambivalences of authorship. The first movement of that structuring antinomy materializes the author, engendering what Elisabeth El Refaie calls "dysappearance": "Every act of self-portraiture entails a form of dys-appearance, in the sense that one's body can no longer be taken for granted as an unconscious presence" (62). What intrigues me about autographic self-portraits is that, epiphenomenal to their production of a material artisanal body, they also posit a quixotic temporality—no doubt in their eagerness to retrieve labor's lost and intersecting time zones. Their Romantic affinities for an art that would transcend the market are unmistakable, but that historical influence hardly reaches far enough.

Instead, visual autographs of self-possessive labor, such as Artie at his drawing table, resemble medieval illuminations, especially those elaborate single letters that limn the scribe at his task, making the very symbol of which

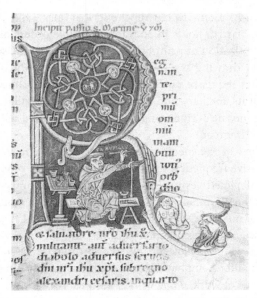

4.2 Colophon of Frater Rufillus from *The Passion of St. Martin.*

4.3 Colophon of Hugo from *Jerome's Commentary on Isaiah.*

he is now a part. As a *mise en abyme*, the scribal image, like that of the contemporary comic artist, holds in abeyance multiple orders of abstraction: a miniature concretization of print literacy, or letter drawing, self-portraiture, and, oddly, letter-drawing as a method of self-drawing. Much like the single panel of a comics sequence, the monumentality of the printed letter cannot hold. In view of its ancillary and adjacent signs, the singularity of the letter crumbles into a mosaic of signifying fragments, the scribal self-portrait being merely one such fragment.

While scholars of the medieval *colophon*—a signature-inscription—disagree on its relative frequency, there is consensus on the general meaning of the colophon's depicted gesture.[7] As with our contemporary comics artists, the presence of the illuminator sets in motion the ruptures and convergences that connect the mediated object to its actual maker and implied audience. Given the nature of the texts copied and the fact that many of the artisans were also clerics, scholars have attributed a spiritual dimension to the signature-inscription and its emphasis on generative acts of making: "[T]he image is of the craftsman at work, *doing* work, and thus, perhaps, we are to appreciate the fruits of his finished labor. If this interpretation is valid, this type of self-image would parallel many existing colophons that enjoin the reader's attention to the worthiness of the work, and recommend the scribe's soul to God" (Rejaie unpaginated).

A competing composition design of the medieval colophon concentrates less on the doing than on the cogitative suspensions that result from doing. In opposition to the first type of colophon, exemplified by Frater Rufillus of Weissenau, who is pictured hard at work on a decorative initial letter from *Passionale* (*The Passion of St. Martin*, ca. 1170–1200), there is a second type, in which meditative becoming and spiritual being overtake the scene of labor.[8] An example occurs in the self-portrait of Hugo at the end of *Jerome's Commentary on Isaiah* from the late eleventh century. Significantly, Hugo's line of sight eclipses the production-centered mindfulness of Rufillus, thereby introducing the very different kind of work that seeing does in the colophonic imaginary: Seeing links scribal activity to prayer.[9]

From its earliest expression in Western culture, therefore, the artist's self-portrait pivots on the fulcrum of the sacred and the profane, showing artistic labor to be a special kind of work, more consonant with prayer, as with Hugo. Or else art is proto-proletarian activity commensurate with the building of any table or chair, as with Rufillus. This split in the colophon corroborates Eyal Peretz's summary of the two-pronged ideological work of self-portraiture as "a defensive operation where the self either shields itself with a projected unity or constitutes itself as a unity through the luring of others' gazes"

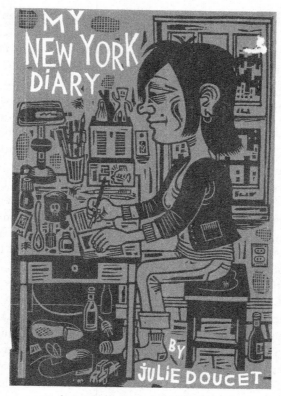

4.4 Cover of Julie Doucet's *My New York Diary*.

(173). Rufillus attains unity through the shield of laborious absorption; Hugo through an externalized optical relation. As twin visions of self-portraiture, these types alert us to the residual concerns for either the suspension of or immersion into artistic labor that ramifies autography, as seen in the coverlet image of Art from *Maus* paused at his drawing table. If, as Bakhtin theorized it, the aim of self-portraiture is more about essence than resemblance—"*[t]o purify the expression of the reflected face*" (34 italics in original)—then we might usefully track the symbols autographers use when attempting that expression, an attempt, we should hasten to add borrowing from Bakhtin, that defines autographic authority: "[A]chieved only by [an] authoritative and essentially necessary author: it is the author-artist as such" (Bakhtin 34).

Little effort is required to find colophonic analogues in Julie Doucet's delightfully gritty *My New York Diary*. With a style that combines the aesthetics of punk rock with the anxious sensibilities of a hoarder, Doucet exhibits herself on the cover in a pose as old as Hugo's from the illuminated manuscript of *Jerome's Commentary*. Like her contemplative iconic forebears, she sits in profile, writing meditatively in what looks to be more of a journal than a comic. Indeed, her pose and the instruments near her confuse drawing with writing and complicate our colophonic classification of her. While the verso page of the "diary" visible beneath her left hand is cast in shadow, the recto denotes writing more definitively, insofar as writing within the language of cartooning has enduringly been delineated by the same vertically arranged wavy lines seen here. And whereas Art's pose from the coverlet of *Maus*, like Hugo's from *Jerome's Commentary*, refuses the optic commitment to labor that we see in the eyes of the other type of colophon of Frater Rufillus, who focuses on his work, Doucet's enormous head (another sign of the cogitative type) is angled so as to avoid making eye contact with the work below.

And yet perhaps our standards of classification have been applied too hastily. For, upon closer inspection, it is clear that her pupils are downcast, trained on her stylus. But even after discovering her downward-looking eyes, we may remain skeptical that those eyes really see. She does not seem to look at the work before her the way busy Rufillus looks at his. Indeed, there is somewhat of a blindness about her image that coincides with Eyal Peretz's analysis of self-portraiture *tout court*. Following Derrida, Peretz interprets the self-portrait in terms of blindness, producing "a self that is inaccessible to itself, blind to itself, suffering a fundamental and disorienting groundlessness . . . whose main forms are the self's exposure to a gaze that emanates from nowhere specific" (173). If my own impression of Doucet's blindness leads me to reject the fact of her labor-centric sightline in order to claim the cover image as a contemplative colophon, the new principle to be deduced would have to do with that overwhelming impression (trumping all details to the contrary) of a certain blindness in the self that offers itself up as an object of scopic contemplation. The distant look required of the pensive colophonic type gives the ironic impression of an artist who has ceased to see, at least in the ordinary way, perhaps to become a seer instead.[10] In *Memoirs of the Blind*, Jacques Derrida theorizes that very impression as fundamental to drawing: "[I]n the moment proper to it, the operation of drawing would have something to do with blindness, would in some way regard blindness" (2). Therefore, although it shares features with the laboring colophon, Julie Doucet's I-con more prominently evinces a spiritual withdrawal or distractedness. As an artist, she is blind to the overflowing mundanity of the ordinary world. Hence, her contemplative colophonic posture consecrates her drawing to the unseen essences that call it forth.

If self-portraits, in part, materialize the unconscious, Doucet's self-conception gathers under the auspices of identity promiscuous *things* normally rejected from consideration. Her table heaves with clutter and diverse objects litter the room. In this way, Doucet's vision arranges its materials in a spirit of radical egalitarianism. Amidst the frenetic profusion, each object is curiously recognizable, endowed with frontality, sometimes even with faces. The shoe, hairbrush, can of pens, electric plug, coffee cup, and waving little man all contribute to a cacophony of unexpected subjectivity. A careful orchestration governs their placement. Each thing occupies its space in the panel, with all available panel spaces occupied. Visually independent, readily recognizable, and bursting with ego, Doucet's objects are dramatically impatient with their status as *mise en scene.*

The tradeoff for all this dispersed egalitarianism is a proportionately decentralized visual focus. Too much vies for attention within the panel for there to be a single focal point not besieged by iconic intercessors. And why not? The ashtray, like most every other object, has ego and thus competes with Julie for our sympathies. In a strange way, Doucet's bottles, brushes, and baubles acquire an expressive instrumentality. They are on a par with the overlarge stylus she manipulates. Unlike them, however, the stylus is a sovereign object in the artist's self-portrait, since every object owes its simulated life to that special interface between the pen or brush and the artist, an interface allegorized in the self-portrait. A distinction we might now make between Doucet's stylus and the other objects in her self-portrait derives from literary critic Max Cavitch's observations about a similar object metonymic of authorship in Thomas Smith's *Self-Portrait* (ca. 1680)—"of the skull: the instrument, as it would appear, of Smith's subjectivity. The skull, in other words, represents the ossature not of Smith-as-person but rather of Smith-as-subject" (101). Likewise, we might say that, taken as a whole, Doucet's stylus presupposes the provocative equivalence of Doucet-as-person and Doucet-as-subject. Thus, Doucet's self portrait maintains the ontological reversibility of humans and things as well as the absurdity of that proposition—as suggested by the fact that the action figure who waves to us is a Gumby doll, an established locus of humor and infinite pliability in popular culture.[11]

Winking to us all the while, Doucet's clutter is seldom taken for itself. It musters an aggressive egoification of detail, blurring foreground and background, human and thing, yet it does so always with its tongue in its objectal cheek. We know this by virtue of the abundant sight gags amidst *My New York Diary*'s charismatic junk—the cup that smiles at us from one panel to the next or the bottle that begins to do a little dance in the corner of a panel. The unexpectedly animated detritus of Doucet's unkempt existence may require us to let go of the arbitrary settlements of foreground and background, squinting away the boundaries that separate humans from hodgepodge—but only temporarily. Doucet's sympathies for an interregnum of *animata* and the *ahuman* recall Julia Watson's discussion of Bobby Baker's sketches of mental breakdown, which "could be said to disavow a humanist framework of rationality: the retrospective narrator, that is, performs the posthuman as an encounter with the limit of the human that her sequence of drawings chronicles" ("Visual Diary" 24). As with the colophon, Doucet's self-portrait disavows rationality by relocating the "limit of the human" within the domain of the object. It kindles our fascination for the tools the artist uses to recreate her sacred violation of the human limit, shedding that mortal coil to fuse with less fragile iconic materials. But it is insufficient to associate the world Doucet creates for her I-con to inhabit to be dystopic, post-human, or fallen. It is rather pan-human in effect, fulfilling a childish wish (which is to say, the wish of the comic's ghosted presence of author and reader): lending to every drawn thing a touch of drawing's magic, as it were, through the fiction of personification. To the extent that the artist's body is like any of the other drawn objects, it similarly benefits from illustration's restorative magic to make *things* democratic, articulate, and alive.

The animation of commodity surpluses in Doucet recollects Marxist notions of fetishism. To be sure, Doucet's dancing things call to mind that lively moment in *Capital* where Marx extricates commodity fetishism as the source of our fascination for bought goods, so loaded with subjectivity they generously lend us their overages. Marx's analogy for this phenomenon is the table that dances when asked to speak for itself as a commodity. The dancing table elucidates the ideological conditions of commodity fetishism, as if to prove how knowledge of the fantasy cannot dispel its magical aura. According to Marx, the table's "wooden brain" swells with "grotesque ideas" (*Capital* 163), such as the wish to dance even though it is a commodity and therefore logically empty, a thing, dead. Our unseen animation of the object and concomitant disavowal of the market's alienation make it so that the thing dances as if *it*, rather than we, desired it to. But the table's animus is itself a mask, veiling the labor that produced it. A truism of Marxist philosophy—that commodities suppress and abstract labor—coincides, then, with the supernatural effects commodities have on us.[12] As a result of that ghosting, labor is alienated, spooked from its products and recoverable only in the spirit-rapping traces of their circulation.

If all autographic *künstlerroman*, as mentioned, strive to represent their protagonists moving away from "a naïvely phenomenological perspective" in embrace of "the more worldly 'cartographic' perspective that Jameson promotes" (Prieto 190), one could positively chart a similar trajectory in Doucet's colophonic cover with its rampant object world. There, too, the artist situates herself among the raw materials of creation, not to simplify that reimagining, as dictated by neo-Romantic discourse, as a form of market-escaping mastery, but to establish Doucet-as-artist as another kind of commodity. The self-portrait glimpses the artist in a state of profound self-understanding, mappable in coordination with other commodities. However, the same pictorial narrative can just as easily be seen skeptically. Does it not fail to accomplish Jameson's cartographic perspective by continuing to insist upon the phenomenological capacities of art to supersede economic relations? It is never the cup nor the ashtray, after all, whose experiences are recounted in the center of the diary's panels. Those centers belong almost exclusively to Julie.

In general, *künstlerromanic* autographics routinely mask the phenomenological, as well as the Romantic, with the psychological.[13] To explore how the story of the making of an artist conceals and entangles neo-Romantic ideologies behind and within masks (I-cons) of personal and family trauma, let us turn now to consider a widely celebrated example of *künstlerroman* in the comics form: David Small's *Stitches* (2009).

Stitches and the Oedipal Dynamics of the Graphic *Künstlerroman*

Throughout David Small's memoir, *Stitches*, art encapsulates many of the clichés attributed to it in classic *künstlerroman*. For one thing, it provides a means of escape to young David after he flees a group of bullies. They assault him with homophobic insults for identifying with art too much, as indicated by the blond towel he wears on his head in emulation of Alice in Wonderland. If these bullies are the menace, drawing is the rabbit hole young David slides down to avoid them—literally, in panels that show him crawling into a drawing on the floor. Taking the shape of a stomach, art's escape hatch is also thoroughly visceral in *Stitches*. That it opens into the floor of David's childhood home echoes the cartographic topoi of *Fun Home* and *Blankets*, locating the domestic as the site of a psychological wound whose bandages are made of ink and panels. To be sure, in the scene of David's rabbit-hole escape, the domestic space remains hazily sketched in an upper corner. Meanwhile, numerous Davids slide into a gustatory Wonderland, analogizing a fear typical to memoir writing, in which publicizing private injury equates to becoming a commodity, a consumable ingested by the text and its voracious readers.

Despite being populated by a rowdy troupe of cartoon animals, what is most notable about art's Wonderland, as Small draws it, is its proximity to the Real. Art is always, fortunately, just below the dermal surface. Its gifts of self-expression, though tempered by family dysfunction, lend a status of exceptionality to artists. David's escape is therefore invisible to those out-side of art's magic circle. Nevertheless, drawing does not lead out of but into the Real. On the page of David's burrowing into art, where the living room remains in view, fantasy permits a new and unusual vantage on the family space without receding from it entirely. Heartbreakingly told and masterfully drawn, the artistry of *Stitches* implores us to recognize, surely at some point in the reading, the utter familiarity of its project, making the new story feel suddenly antiquated.

One would not be wrong for feeling so because, on the whole, drawing in *Stitches* dusts off the back catalogue of Romanticism's cherished stan-dards; it is an escape, a coping mechanism, a reagent of spiritual and psychic freedom, as well as a practice for domesticating the Real. The same spark of uniqueness that fuels Romanticism's artist aligns with the Promethean gift of fire, the curse of genius, which compels returning to that timespace Derrida refers to as "the origin of drawing" (3). There, the artist-autobiographer either reflects reality (as in a mirror) or refracts and thereby replaces it with lights of his own.[14]

What, then, is unique about any of these clichés of art through the lens of Romanticism when they reappear in contemporary autobiographical graphic novels? In *Stitches*, the transcendence of art acquires narrative purpose against a backdrop of sexual secrecy, gender trouble, and familial abuse. Entwining the young David's gendered humiliation when called "Fag!" "Queer!" "Homo!" and "Sissy!" by schoolyard bullies is the storyline of his irascible mother, a les-bian discovered by her son in an affair with another neighborhood mother. This revelation, disquieting to David, stands alongside the primary plot of David's sadistic father, a radiologist who subjects him as a child to clandestine treatments. Thus, David Small's confessed gender trouble in his early years and his over-identification with Alice jibe with his mother's homosexuality and his father's Munchausen's syndrome by proxy. The Oedipal anxiety that fuels the text finds resolution in drawing—a situation that generally applies to *Epileptic, Blankets, Fun Home, Persepolis, Maus,* and so many other auto-graphic *künstlerroman*.

The events leading up to David's decision to play Alice reinforce the psy-chological valence drawing possesses in *Stitches*. The young protagonist joins his more aggressive older brother, whose gendered conformity is conveyed instantly by the cowboy costume he wears. As if the visual cue were not enough, the brother ushers David to their father's medical books to peruse the sexual and diseased anatomies rendered in them. "Ugg! What is that?" the young David asks in one panel; "That's a titty!" replies the brother, exclaiming, "That's a man's thing" (53) in another. In each panel of the sequence, the older brother occupies the left side of the image space; the medical illustration, the right. In that recto display area, reader-viewers are given more than the visualized counterpart to a verbalized prompt. The small square serves as a *mise en abyme* of the larger one that contains it. As in the smaller square of the medical illustration, the larger square of the codex converts seeing into learning. But the narrative moves abruptly from the sexual to the diseased when the brother concentrates on the picture of a growth on a man's neck. That dreadful encounter with the precise wound that afflicts the adult David (a temporal collapse, as is every *prolepsis*) is what initiates young David's unwittingly dangerous game of playing Alice. The cure for the shaming he receives from homophobic bullies ironically returns him to image-making.

Thereafter, the seesaw of familial ruin and artistic growth revs the narrative to its later phase when art becomes the means by which David achieves independence "[a]t 30 . . . teaching drawing at a college in upstate New York" (303). For readers familiar with the classic *künstlerroman*, however, David's eventual embodiment of a traditional masculinity comes as no surprise. As Helena Gurfinkle has pointed out, "Inasmuch as the *Künstlerroman* follows the same pattern of competition, separation, and individuation" as the Freudian paradigm, "it promotes traditional constructions of masculinity" (96). While the plot of *Stitches* amplifies its narrative arcs of competition and separation, it represents David's individuation with such an intensity of compression that our hero turns from sixteen to thirty in a matter of eight pages. This abridgement defers the medical and emotional drama David suffers in the aftermath of debilitating surgeries on his neck. At first, he believes them to be cosmetic, but later finds out that he had cancer. An unprecedented series of revelations accompany that discovery in an ecstasy of familial exposure: It is at this time that David learns of his mother's same-sex affair, that his grandmother attempted to burn down her house and has been remanded to an insane asylum, and that his father gave him the cancer, having subjected him as a child to a battery of unnecessary X-ray treatments. Small's father confesses in a full-page panel, "I GAVE YOU CANCER" (287, emphasis in original). A full-page close-up of David stolidly taking in the confession follows as the Detroit River washes the background in grey tones. We then get a page of the young David's face overlaid onto that of the older teen assimilating these moments of memory and realization. Nearby panels picture the young child mercilessly strapped to an X-Ray table while others depict the physical rupture of the child's face, an index to the trauma. The profoundly jarring memory of these sessions comprises yet another illustrated monstrosity in the doubled face of the child and teen who realize it all together, at once, in a fugue of uncanny co-presence.

WITHOUT REALIZING
HOW PERFECTLY THEY
REPRESENTED MY
BLOCKED STATE,
I PAINTED
A BRICK WALL
AND
A CLOSED DOOR.

4.5 David and his father from *Stitches* (297). From *Stitches: A Memoir* by David Small. Copyright © 2009 by David Small. Used by permission of W. W. Norton & Company.

Throughout the wordless sequence, the father remains unfazed. His morosely grey figure lights a cigarette as David stands beside the river shocked and still. On the facing page, where this configuration is reversed, David's face is enlarged and the father stands beside the river smoking his cigarette in the middle distance. The side-by-side composition arouses a ludic commonplace in graphic novels, a visual game of deciphering the differences between two nearly identical images. Whereas white light gleams in David's eye, the father's eyes are so reflective behind glasses as to be opaque, their emotional possibilities annulled. We turn the page to see the figure of David walking into an amorphous space of darkness, an image that earlier betokens the stultifying loss of his voice—another significant image, incidentally, akin to this one, deposits David inside a prison-like version of his own cavernous mouth. Here, the void of self-expression morphs into the unknown of experience, terrifyingly uncertain on all counts except one: that it lies in a direction opposite the father. Small squeezes about fifteen years in the following eight pages that move away from the father toward a post-void space of recovery, toward life and individuation.

4.6 David at his easel from *Stitches* (302). From *Stitches: A Memoir* by David Small. Copyright © 2009 by David Small. Used by permission of W. W. Norton & Company.

The "one-room apartment in Detroit's inner city" (295) that David moves into is home to a cadre of hipsters and weirdos, whose "circumstances and behavior were, by almost any standard, bizarre, but [around whom he] felt more normal . . . and less lonely" (300). This setting also precipitates the book's most ardently *künstlerromanic* figurations of the artist learning his craft. In one sequence of panels, David shows himself painting a canvas. In the first, words seize an unbordered, unillustrated space: "Without realizing how perfectly they represented my blocked state, I painted a brick wall and a closed door" (297). The following two panels convey exactly that, a brick wall with some indication of a top molding and a glimmer of sky; to ensure that viewers properly read this expanse of lighter colored space above the wall as a sky, tiny bird shapes adorn the corner. In the second panel, we do not get a closed door as reported but a pictorial synecdoche: a close-up of a doorknob and keyhole. The keyhole, a trope of voyeurism, invites the same expanse of freedom beyond psychological blockage as the sky in the first panel or the doorknob here. Both allow for complexities that run counter to the absolutisms of the linguistic panel that precedes them. Thus, by the time we arrive at the penultimate full-panel of this eight-page montage of David's maturation from sixteen to thirty, where he draws at an easel beside three admiring girls, we are less prone to see it as an illustration of the caption's misleading finality: "Art became my home. Not only did it give me back my voice, but art has given me everything I have wanted or needed since" (302). Rather, the referent for "everything" he desires is supplied by the image, where art even seems to have increased David's sexual magnetism.

Because so little from the intervening years is narrated, the zone of the private within the public life of the artist is represented through elision. These lost years are equivalent to the screaming he does in his car in order to toughen up his vocal cords. Now, in place of the loss of voice, the fear of that loss persists, threatening the disappearance of self in traumatic repetition. Like many *künstlerromanic* protagonists, David's pictorial repetitions—the drawings themselves—are never simply representative of trauma as the content of their narratives; they often demonstrate the cuts and wounds of trauma by performing them in their structures. *Stitches* is quite explicit in aligning its own project as a narrative with the therapeutic possibilities of drawings, calling attention to these possibilities in its title. Insofar as stitches call to mind wounded skin tied shut, the title aptly metaphorizes comics closure. Comics, too, suture gaps between gashes of experience, staunching otherwise deleterious holes. At the same time, though, we would be justified in extending the analogy based on the inverse motif in *Stitches*, in which drawing is a therapeutic practice that opens up protective holes in an oppressive reality. From this perspective, the narrative affords the traumatized autobiographical subject the opportunity to close and open up wounding cuts from the past—with *trauma*, in this case, signifying a wound that exceeds the perceptual, psychological, and linguistic structures necessary to comprehend it as such.

It is therefore interesting to return to the temporal gash caused by *Stitches'* most manifestly *künstlerromanic* episodes, the jump of years between the confrontation with the father and David's actualization as a painter surrounded by approving girls. In its span, undisclosed experience constitutes self-possession, thereby reinforcing a psychological model of wellness complementary to capitalism.[15] In no way, however, is this to imply that the un-stitchable gap of withheld experience is traumatic in the same way or to the same degree as any other aporia in *Stitches*. As mentioned in the previous chapter, the literary critic Frank Kermode might classify any of these omissions as forms of *peripetea*, or departures from expected narrative patterns. For Kermode, such divergences are proleptic of two grander absences to come: on one level, the ending of a story; on a deeper level, death, the ultimate terminus, about which all narrative endings implicitly speculate. Given the *künstlerroman*'s pervasive allegory of the artist as a godlike creator (another Romantic inheritance), the gap years in *Stitches* help to stake out a terrain of experience rescinded from view by sovereign decree of the creator. That experience is expressly left for the creator to enjoy alone, a sort of seventh day of rest, to borrow from Judeo-Christian mythology, as fitting recompense for the present narrative of autogenesis.

Despite these possibilities for a cathartic and deifying privacy, the atypical plot hole in *Stitches* still demarcates a story out of bounds, not unlike the one adumbrated in the final pages of the book. There, a collection of family photos give rise to an apologia regarding the mother's sexuality: "If this had been her story, not mine, her secret life as a lesbian would certainly have been examined more closely" (327). The ghost of another story, a para-narrative, gets summoned and exorcised in these captionary lines attending the mother's photo. In the process, David's private maturation as an artist coordinates with his mother's sexuality as mutual gaps in the record. Accordingly, privacy for David turns on a form of maternal identification, in opposition to the father, a Victor Frankenstein mad with scientific ambition. That allusion plays out in the title, where stitches conjoin the lacerated child to the trademark forehead stitches of Frankenstein's monster.

To be exposed to cancerous radiation by the father is to become the grotesque object of another's agentive becoming. It is to be feminized, the hole of another's whole. In this way, David is like his mother—just as he is like Alice at the beginning—seeking reconciliatory identification as part of the stitch-work of his memoir. In other ways, however, David finds himself by the end of *Stitches* strangely replicating the paternal, as do many of his *künstlerromanic* peers by the end of their narratives. Like Craig in *Blankets*, Alison in *Fun Home*, or Artie in *Maus*, David has become a master, achieving mastery in illustration and now authorship too. He now represents some of what the law of the father has so problematically exacted from him. And it is around these irresolvable tensions between filial revolution and social reproduction that art and artists stake their most desperate claims for exceptionality. In return, perhaps, for that public struggle with consciousness glimpsed in the mirror, they seek exemption from the myriad woes of aesthetic, economic, and ontological determinism.

Conclusions in View of the Colophon

The finale of *Stitches* rehearses the climax of artistic becoming at the heart of every *künstlerroman*. David represents himself going through the transition according to a particular colophonic trajectory. He starts out as the hard-working Frater Rufillus and eventually becomes the spiritually suspended Hugo. In his final self-portrait as an artist, even the scarf that could diminish his claim to heteronormative masculinity is recharged by the panel's enlistment of one of the young women who compliments it (even as she *complements* it as both adornment and bandage). The scarf is not merely curative to a wound, whether the stitches in his neck or the Oedipal injuries to his sense of self and manhood. Rather, it is a fetish, as are the assorted girls, of the heterosexual male artist's vitality, which in turn depends upon the validity of the artist as a capitalist subject. The artist's forays into making must turn out to be profitable, both productively and reproductively so. To become an artist, then, is to become a man for David Small. But to become either, as this chapter has suggested, requires passage through the symbolic of self-portraiture, where the marriage of art and life is consummated—how else?—through conspicuous consumption.

It is important that David's most mature I-con-as-artist looks directly at us. The returned gaze establishes the figure as having agency tantamount to that of the reader. Inducing *mise en abyme*, the I-con is not solely a character in a book but a maker of books and characters. This material paradox is how *Stitches* responds to the question, posed earlier as a statement: What are the "naively phenomenological" (which is to say, Romantic) perspectives that the artist breaks from in his *künstlerroman*? One provisional answer hinted at here is that resolution, no more than meaning, remains self-contained, autotelic, or monological. The book and the real-world experiences it relates cannot do all the work; a reader-viewer is both assumed and required, and anything we might ascertain as having signifying value proceeds from systems of exchange. The look returned from the artist at his easel limns his evolution towards this "more worldly 'cartographic' perspective" (Prieto 190) of the necessarily dialectic economy of art.

More than motif, the visual trope of the comics author-artist at his or her drafting table, at work on the exact text we happen to be reading, is a signature feature of autography. As has been shown, it ramifies the sexual and Oedipal subject formation of David in *Stitches*, the colophonic implications of Julie Doucet's object affiliations in *My New York Diary*, and the traumatic drafts of Art atop the mouse corpses from *Maus*. In many ways, the *künstlerromanic* in each case provides a narrative structure and a visual grammar for agonizing over the representational and ethical burdens of self-creation.

And that visual language is nothing if not precise. Creators constantly peek out from graphic *künstlerroman* in surprisingly invariant poses—as artists at work or, more accurately, at *this very* work. We could press on to mine even more of the self-portrait's meanings, but we would soon find ourselves not only at the limits of the verbalizable in any image, but thwarted as well by the conceptual impasses of *"this"* work—whose materiality we are called upon to verify as we hold the book.[16] Enigmatically, *this* book also solidifies the story's equally necessary intangibility. All of these obscurations coincide with the blurring of past and present that Charles Hatfield and others have noted as central to *Maus'* artist-at-work motif in the "Time Flies" section, but which, as it turns out, is essential to the artisanal self-portrait more generally.[17] Standard inventory of such an image includes: the artist, some indication of the stylus (the brush, pencil, or pen), and the paper on which the artist invents something far more materially grand—either the collection of images that readers hold or the mental catalog of the same. Together, these features comprise a cartoonal, self-contained unity of self-portraiture that is evacuated from the site of its realization like ghosted labor from commodities.

For the image, these processes of *mise en abyme* and recursive synecdoche hinge upon the inclusion of a visual reference to the panel that the artist in the self-portrait is making. That the image is always being made in an embedded square of paper (within the larger "square of paper" of the panel or page) exacerbates confusions of made and maker, object and subject, the present temporality of the object and the past temporality of production—not to mention issues of seriality (in which this image is simply one of many other potentially stand-alone images) and sequentiality (in which this image is central to understanding how all the other images next to it cohere as a legible narrative). In spite of these categorical breakdowns, the self-portrait guarantees all three aspects of Philippe Lejeune's "autobiographical pact," as it emblematizes author, protagonist, and narrator.[18] Only in *künstlerromanic* self-portraiture does the trinity appear as one, becoming an icon in the truest sense of the term (and raising theological implications about artists and incarnation too complex to pursue here).

And, finally, that a deictic exigency governs the effectivity of the colophonic self-portrait is a principle best explained by returning to the title of the present chapter. For it is not so much the work behind the work that matters, but rather the work behind *this* work, *this* very object, be it this book (at the macro level) or this picture (at the micro). And all that matters more than that textual solipsism is that the act of engaging with the text's immediacy, its physically tenable form as media, be conducted in a space of instructional viewing and reading. That space is commensurate with the ludic of the previous chapter, where textual activity seems to belong to the reader exclusively. Graphic novels strive in general to deify the reader-viewer as part of their ideological charms. It is in making viewers feel like gods that graphic novels dance on their heads like Marx's table, grotesque ambition swelling their wooden brains. We witness that implied panegyric in Marji's turn from the mirror to the panel to ask us where we have gone, we readers—her abandoned gods. We see that deification again in the final colophonic self-portrait of David Small, the psychically mature artist still seeking confirmation from his audience.

Unlike Hugo, whose gaze drifts to find that mysterious addressee in the presence of whom all work is prayer and supplication, David cues the artist's transcendence by interminably seeking out our gaze in the endless textual relay of the self-portrait's Grecian Urn-like proclivities. Caroline Edwards pointedly summarizes the theory of ceaseless becoming that underwrites the *künstlerroman* as advanced by Ernst Bloch, for whom "the artist-protagonists of the *Künstlerroman* are exemplary figures of an erotic and poetic expression oriented towards the Not Yet of utopian futurity in their ceaseless desire for creative expression" (197).[19] The community sought there in the Not Yet of the presumed reader-viewer everywhere deified by the graphic novel may be an impossible one, a "utopian fantasy," but it is also always the same intimacy, immediacy, and immanence that every pictorial encounter solicits. Such is the case even when that encounter is an eruption of the traumatic Real, as in the next and final chapter's exploration of deified viewers of race history, who are permitted reprieve from the trauma of that history by virtue of the superheroic race leaders who incarnate it.

5

Visual Pedagogies of Impossible Community
in *Incognegro* and *March*

There can be no comprehension of black theology without realizing that its existence comes from a community which looks back on its unique past, visualizes
the future, and then makes decisions about possibilities in the present.
—James Cone, *A Black Liberation Theology* (28)

A review of graphic novels written or drawn by black authors in
recent years reveals a preponderance of revisionist histories. The
same animus James Cone discovers in black liberation discourse,
to visualize the future through the past, activates the pages of Kyle Baker's
Nat Turner (2008), Ho Che Anderson's *King* (2005), Mat Johnson and Warren Pleece's *Incognegro* (2008), Jeremy Love's *Bayou* (2009), and John Lewis's
acclaimed memoir, *March* (2013). All revisit black history deliberately. In the
process, and as part of the inherent necessity for any comics text to teach its
viewers how to process its under-language, many of these works also create
formal pockets within their narrative and pictorial textures that re-enact the
oceanic suspensions Hortense Spillers detects at the pre-personhood sub-
strate of African American consciousness:

Those African persons in the Middle Passage were literally suspended in the
"oceanic," if we think of the latter in its Freudian orientation as an analogy for
undifferentiated identity; removed from the indigenous land and culture, and
not-yet "American" either, these captive persons, without names that their cap-
tors would recognize, were in movement across the Atlantic, but they were also
nowhere at all."[1]

To be sure, it makes sense to culminate our study of embedded lessons in comics with African American graphic novels—graphic memoir by and about African Americans. Just as we first had to understand masking before interrogating the comics child, we are now prepared by our exploration of the ludic and the labor of comics to return to the form's potential to depict consciousness. If one problem of autography is the obdurate objecthood of drawings meant to signify as subjects, consider how much greater the issue is for subjects once classified as objects par excellence. Centuries of European representation have reinforced the association. And the picture (thought of here in the abstract) suffers a comparable denigration. Seen but never to see in return, pictures are not subjects but objects. As such, they are passive to the sensoria that circumscribe them. They seldom (by definition as objects, never) instantiate anything on their own.

Comics readily avail themselves of the objectal status of their images to make readers not only active participants in the meaning-making process but also subjects who impart significance, through affect, to otherwise inert, insensible images. So, while examining how authors imbue images, avatars, or icons with consciousness, we must also mind the work that such devices do by prioritizing a determinatively optic notion of the subject. All protagonists in autobiographical graphic novels are both pictorial objects and subjects of consciousness. This is emphatically so in graphic memoir, especially that of minoritized subjects. For the marginalized, the formal space where pictorial objects undergo humanization is not simply defined by alienation (alienation from narrative, as with the puzzle, or of labor, as with artist self-portraits at the drawing table). Rather, that space is also one of illumination in minority discourse, bringing out into the open the usually unseen parameters by which racialized subjects have been and continue to be deprived of agency.

In what follows, we shall investigate what happens when race history is the authorial subject of graphic life writing. As we shall see, *Incognegro* renovates traumatic black history via comic book conventions of the superhero and the form's potential to situate its viewing subjects within a politics of space—that is, as subject to spatial arrangements that accord power in terms of distance. Readers of *Incognegro* must negotiate affective allegiances towards categories of identity (of race and duality, interior essences and appearance in the mirror) in terms of time (then and now) and space (foregrounds and backgrounds). Ultimately, *Incognegro* locates its protagonist and viewers at the dissolving edges of community, where identification with the all-important object of historical trauma (the lynch victim in *Incognegro*; the chickens in *March*) becomes narratively urgent but formally inoperative.

March also revisits historical trauma by personifying it in the protagonist. Background becomes foreground as speech balloons of illegible writing and an extended metaphor of a young John Lewis's sense of duty towards his first flock, barnyard chickens, all give voice to subjective intensities lost to history. When scrawl and brute empathy converge in an image of young Lewis's body written upon by the very Bible scriptures he declaims to his "flock," *March* accomplishes what *Incognegro* obsessively fails to do; it visualizes precarious identification with the mute and illegible objects of traumatic history. Operating under the principle that identification salvages history, *March* and *Incognegro* construe race history's graphic lessons through graphic subjects. Both texts attempt to re-see diasporic trauma and the communities constituted by it, and in so doing, help us to see anew the relationships between visuality or visibility and history.

Incognegro as Comic Book Hero and the Mirror Scene of Race Trauma

The Warner Bros. Bugs Bunny cartoon *Southern Fried Rabbit* (1953) commits a heresy common to representations of slave history. Unlike the cartoon's original audience, contemporary viewers can freeze-frame the cotton bales that shadow the distant horizon, those verdant, rolling hills across which our trickster hero and his ever-furious antagonist chase each other. Aside from Yosemite Sam's rebel uniform and the now-deleted scenes of Bugs in blackface, these background images of the raw material of history—the locus of the labor that slaves and their sharecropping descendants inherited (along with a culture of lynching)—seem all the more freighted with oppression for being so conspicuously backgrounded. It is as if the very fact of their positioning as scenery or framework within the hand-drawn universe of the cartoon confirms once again both the normalization and the invisibility of historic America's black and injured bodies.

Incognegro: A Graphic Novel (2008), drawn by Warren Pleece and written by noted African American author Mat Johnson, confronts these tendencies to miniaturize black labor and embodiment and to render the violence of black history ghostly. It is the mission of *Incognegro*'s fictional protagonist, Zane Pinchback, to go undercover for a New York newspaper in order to expose the lynching epidemic infecting the South in the early 1930s. The book's setting represents a slight deviation from most historical retellings that place the acme of lynching in the 1920s, a deviation the graphic novel establishes in the

5.1 Mirror scene from *Incognegro* (18).

opening captions of its first panels: "Between 1889 and 1918, 2,522 Negroes were murdered by lynch mobs in America. That we know of" (7).

Loosely based upon incidents from the autobiography of famed anti-lynching crusader Walter White, *A Man Called White* (1948), *Incognegro* bor-rows many of its visual tropes and character templates from superhero comic books. It would be an understatement to say that the superhero's unlikely influence makes ideological trouble for Pleece and Johnson. Even the name, Zane Pinchback, recalls Western gunfighters, noir films, and golden-age comics, genres whose naming preferences blend the cutesy and the grandiose in equal measure. In light of *Incognegro*'s plot, Pinchback connotes the very act of going back, pinging back to an inimical archetype of historical injury. But, as is the case for many comic book heroes, Pinchback is only an official name and thus a misnomer. The hero's public name—the one that matters—is the eponymous Incognegro. In the mystifying guise of Incognegro, Pinchback is part Dick Tracy and part Shadow, using his passably light complexion, as did Walter White, to inch dangerously close to the primal scenes of Southern lynching. His aim is salvific journalism, inscribing lynch victims and perpetrators into a revised history so that racial injustice may finally meet its match. Like Kyle Baker's temporary flirtation in *Nat Turner* with the comic book's visual tropes of masculine strength—as when the behemoth slave, Will, takes on poses reminiscent of the Incredible Hulk—the comic book references in *Incognegro* strive for similar recognition in a visual idiom historically reserved for white avengers.

If the superhero's inevitable alter ego is but one characteristic of the fascination for hybridity inherent to the genre, we might not be surprised to find the superheroic here as well.[2] There is even a gratuitous transformation panel (fig. 5.1), in which Pinchback stands in front of a mirror to declare: "I am Incognegro." Is it not crucial that the explication of his identity take place in front of a mirror? Once again, the mirror seals the character of Pinchback/Incognegro to the material index of that abstraction in the comic drawing. A failed encounter with the Real ensues, relating racial trauma to historical trauma through a series of negations. In the mirror, we picture him in the costume he claims not to possess as he negatively compares himself to other contemporary heroes: "I don't wear a mask like Zorro or a cape like the Shadow but I don a disguise nonetheless" (18). The next two panels replicate with little variation the outer figure who looks at himself heroically transformed in the mirror. The second panel contains a panel—a mirror image and now also a projection screen. There, Pinchback's Incognegro body becomes the revelatory surface on which one of those unmentionables of Southern tradition—"Slavery. Rape. Hypocrisy" (18)—achieves visual articulation.

The image offered is a pictorial abbreviation of miscegenation. An older white man overbears a black woman supine in shadow. Both figures wrestle transparently over the otherwise invariant body of Incognegro in the mirror—a projected heroic body that is itself a magic surface on which things normally unseen become cathartically visible. And, in keeping with the redundancies of golden- and silver-age heroes who identify themselves and their powers at the start of every issue, Pinchback elaborates on his status as Incognegro over the next several panels. He becomes the projection screen for a transparent American flag in the next mirror panel, making himself "invisible" so that he may "step outside of history," a strategy he dubs "assimilation as revolution" (18). Taken together, these images produce Incognegro, in the words of Tim Caron, as "the unacknowledged but literal embodiment of America's racist past" (158). The final image of the sequence yields a fully suited Pinchback. He stands looking at himself in the mirror, hat in hand, with the tool of his trade (the typewriter) for the first time in the transformation space he occupies.

And yet, as we replay the incessant doubling of the split identity made whole for our viewing by the end of the scene, we perforce return to the underlying imagery for which the surface of Incognegro functions as both screen and veil—the dyadic rape and the flag; the one grossly particular, the other, an icon, generality in the absolute. A central ambivalence structures the origin story of *Incognegro*'s conventionally split comic book hero. Insofar as that ambivalence humanizes the hero, it does so in part by drawing upon the potential threat in any depiction of miscegenative rape. Linking reproduction to violation under the sign of nation, these mirror scenes declare that, in America, what generates violates. Of course, from a psychoanalytic point of view, violation is integral to the formation of any identity, even for divine personhood, as Žižek has demonstrated in his discussion of the incarnation:

> In order for (human) subjectivity to emerge out of the substantial personality of the human animal, cutting links with it and positing itself as the I = I disposed of all substantial content, as the self-relating negativity of an empty singularity, God himself, the universal Substance, has to "humiliate" himself, to fall into his own creation, "objectivize" himself, to appear as a singular miserable human individual, in all its abjection, i.e., abandoned by God." (*God in Pain* 169)

Žižek's notion of humanity forged in the cauldron of humiliation recurs in graphic novel autobiography, whose I-cons typically undergo the same agonistic crisis of alienation Žižek ascribes to divinity. Whether in *American Elf* or *Incognegro*, mirror moments furnish character and identity as scopic totalities. Identity is whatever we see it as and we are enabled to see it in the comics both serially and all at once. While we do not continue to see the flag or the rape projected onto Incognegro, for example, the visual impermanence of that scopic totality implicates reader-viewers nonetheless. We must project those grey-scale interiorities from the mirror onto images of Pinchback-Incognegro that circulate beyond it. As a result, we are reminded of our viewing labors and the unfinished business of incarnating forms we may only be decoding, merely looking at. To see history through Pinchback's de-objectifying eyes is to limn the polyvalent slippages of race (and time) that passers exacerbate.

The Temporalities of *Incognegro* and the Image-Ghosts of History

A staple of American fiction, passers like Pinchback often serve as tropes of racial mediation and its challenges, as Hazel Carby and others have argued.[3] Referring to historical incidents of passing, Joseph Roach points out how passers frustrate not only Jim Crow logics but also a range of social and representative substitutions integral to twentieth-century democracy: "[M]ulattoes of any kind might be expected to induce crises of surrogation, but even more so when the marks of mixture were ambiguous or invisible" (182). *Incognegro* wastes little time establishing Pinchback's capacity for surrogacies—of and between bodies, races, temporalities, and genres, to name just a few.

Incognegro is preoccupied with splitting. It cleaves its heroic identity and its narrative timescape. The opening panels evince the desire to be in two racial eras at once, depicting a lynching scene familiar to us through photographs, such as the one taken in Marion, Indiana (1930). Oddly, though—and we shall say more about this—the illustration style chosen for *Incognegro* portrays everyone as white. Only the darkest of shadows in any given scene are black. Halftones seldom occur, receiving a minimum of crosshatching when they do. Visual searching and sorting eventuates the figure to be lynched amidst a crowd of whitewashed bodies where another surreptitious figure lurks—our hero, Zane Pinchback, who polls the audience gathered for the lynching as though he were the cameraman's assistant, busily querying them for their addresses.

Rectangular captions accompanying Zane's antics elucidate the situation. During most lynchings, "pictures are taken to remember the special day" (9). The unseen interlocutor in the captions, whom we learn to be Zane's girlfriend Mildred, doubts the veracity of the postcards we see Zane collecting. A different Zane, who "recollects" the event in conversation with Mildred, manifests in the captions to clarify: "Personalized postcards, Mildred. It's part of the ritual" (9). Like a postcard that travels to adjoin disparate places and times, these scenes complicate the visual dominance of Pinchback's past time heroics. The traumatic past, the narrative implies, may be inscrutable apart from its recapitulation of it in the present, from an imaginary North: an Ur-space of freedom via authorship in African American literature since the slave narrative.

These incongruities of caption and depiction at the beginning of *Incognegro* emphasize duality. No theme is more crucial to narratives of either superheroes or race passers, two wildly different archetypes that Johnson and Pleece meld together. The critical problem raised by that melding, however, is less about commensurability than it is about affect. To explain, let us return to the rhetorical force of the opening panels. Pinchback is not there to save the lynch victim, who remains confined to a domain of pictoriality, which further demarcates the space of historical death that he occupies. Pinchback nears that space first to get the story and then to get away. But just how are we supposed to feel about his bravado as he makes his death-defying escape?

A survey of the top two panels of a later page shows Pinchback returning the gaze of the viewer. He is standing in front of a suspicious mob. Everyone looks frozen, as if in a tableau or posing for a picture. All (including Pinchback) are in composition analogous to the customary assembly below the lynched body of historical photographs, save for one detail: the mob looks menacingly at him as he looks out at us. His expression, verging on a smile, intensifies with telling beads of sweat in the following close-up panel: "How y'all doing? Let me say this is a lovely lynching you're throwing here" (11). Pinchback's remark may ring awkwardly to viewers raised up on the denunciations of Klan-era racism typical in such films as *Mississippi Burning* (1988). Pinchback's tone is comedic; his remark, a punch line. Later, when Pinchback concludes with another pun, declaring himself to have run "like beige lightening" (not black lightening given his complexion), we witness the intrusion of the comedic onto a scene usually sequestered behind affective protocols of silence, condolence, and solemnity.

Were it not for the doubled timescapes of narration, it would be difficult to accept, let alone appreciate, the humor of the occasion. The two present-tense scenes unfolding before us include that of the pictorial during the lynching and that of the oral, in which the lynching is recounted and from which any such thing as an affectively viable humor derives. The opening sequence of the lynched person's desecration ensures that reader-viewers receive the pivotal scene of Pinchback's (super)heroic escape with the proper affective calibration. After a "ritual—de-masculation," the lynch victim, who is also a soldier, is made to wear a uniform less offensive to the racist mob. He is dressed as a harlequin clown and suspended from a tree branch by a noose around the neck. The leitmotif of inappropriate joking finalizes the escape. In a panel where a car driven by sidekick Carl rescues Zane on the other side of a train that divides them from the mob, Mildred proclaims in the caption, "Joking aside Zane, what you do is a great service to our people. You're not just passing for white to get a table at the Waldorf-Astoria" (12). Of course, a comment like this returns us to the controlling gesture of retributive justice animating *Incognegro*. What service can such a story provide today? What service does the daring hero provide, propped up as he is with an alias, a sidekick, and what passes for an Olympian emotional distance from the violent spectacles he bravely researches but refuses to witness?

While it is fair for us to ask these questions of *Incognegro*, it is perhaps asking too much of the text to supply us with clear answers. Provocations, on the other hand, come in generous supply. To begin with, the opening hails us as familiar readers of comic books. It invites us to expand upon presumably well-established superhero reading knowledges in order to reread the history of racism. It pits the abject historical content of the lynched and desecrated body against a weirdly revamped hero archetype, fusing the two together. The question of how to *serve* traumatic history resounds in Pinchback's description of his own superpower. Perhaps like its protagonist, *Incognegro* hopes to be "stupidly, impossibly lucky" (12) in its attempt to voice historical wrong in the timber of the ever-righteous superhero.

The pedagogical upshot of *Incognegro*'s tropological mixtures is conservative in the sense that readers need not abandon the superhero genre as a dominant template of comics storytelling in order to appreciate a "supposedly" revisionist history. I qualify here because for most revisionist paradigms, dominant narratives are shown to be ideologically responsible for drowning out or distorting minority experience. But that critique assumes too simplistic an account of the role dominant (superhero) culture plays within the text. Perhaps the lesson is not that we must un-see dominance (to eschew the dominant superhero narrative) but that we must continue to extract new American heroes and villains from a once-fixed notion of history. However, doing so requires a more radical embrace of hybridity than the average reader is likely to muster.

Evidence for a hybrid vision of history may be found in the book's dichotomous timescapes, phantom bodies, and ghosted visual source texts. These tactics center on the politics of the seen and the unseen, which Johnson and Pleece, like their speculative hero, wish to make visible. As with the visual anomalies of Kyle Baker's *Nat Turner*—the dead slave body that is spoken for in designatory images that vacillate, impossibly, as speech balloons—the ghost imaging of *Incognegro* works in part to resurrect the dead as surpluses of past injustices that refuse erasure.

The first instance of image-ghosting takes place in front of the mirror. There, a dynamic common to both cinema and psychoanalysis transforms the body of Incognegro into the screen on which the normally eclipsed primal scene of interracial rape is projected. Interestingly, the narrative made possible by the mirror is Pinchback's origin story, *de rigueur* for the super-hero. It blends the archetypical account of the hero's assumption of super-heroic status with the standard scene of his transformation. In other words, the mirror is both Krypton and telephone booth for Pinchback: both the diachronic and synchronic reason for his superheroic difference. To be the screen of violent amalgamation as well as the icon (the American flag) which occludes that violence is to flicker between revelation and cooptation, history and its illegibility in the present. More than a palimpsestic capacity to embody the invisible, Incognegro has a feel for it. He possesses literacy for things unseen: the violent past and its palpable erasures. In this way, Pinch-back/Incognegro sees and feels, undertaking both in dramatic fashion—perhaps in surrogacy, so that we do not have to. And the text manages its dynamic of sight and feeling spatially.

The Politics of Viewer Positioning in Plenary Scenes of Lynching

If, as Robyn Wiegman has compellingly argued, lynching may be seen "as a disciplinary activity that communalizes white power while territorializing the black body and its movement through social space" (13), *Incognegro*'s permutations of the lynched body not only de-territorialize it but do so through the specular image of its tormentors. Thus, the lynched body is a type of abstraction. And the most durable embodiment of abstraction in visual culture is whiteness. According to Wiegman, the lynch mob disciplines in two ways: through physical torture, frequently castration, and through its "function as a panoptic mode of surveillance," whose power is dispersed (through photographic souvenirs, newspaper publicity, etc.) to impose upon black bodies "the threat of always being seen" (13).

By seeking to undo the logics of racist spectacle, *Incognegro* obscures the black lynched body as well as the photographic architectures of its symbolic subjection. What results, of course, is not the fantasy (or even the wish for a fantasy) of retrospective liberation in the vein of Octavia Butler's *Kindred*, but rather the traumatic deflection of that fantasy. A hysterical response to the historical is produced, in other words, which peeks through in visualizations that are often pathetic, sometimes even ludicrous. In this regard, I take issue with Tim Caron's otherwise astute reading of *Incognegro*, particularly the claim that "Pleece's drawing succeeds in re-humanizing the lynch victim" (152). For how can Pleece's lynched body articulate the redress Johnson in the Author's Note claims to want for it if its terms of address are muddled, muted?—precisely the question raised by *March*, as we shall soon see. We cannot know how to feel about the violated body or its spectral history if we cannot see either one.[4] Far easier to make out is the ritual community that the lynched body convenes, a *communitas* that now includes us as unwilling spectators.[5] Similar to Foucault's conception of public punishment, the event we are made to witness confers a disciplining role to its audience automatically. In light of such potential implication, we may be quite relieved to find just how difficult the lynched body of *Incognegro* is to discern. To be sure, while playing the "Where's Waldo" game that Pleece's mob compositions routinely embed, we might conclude that it is the lynched body rather than Pinchback's that is the real Incognegro. Zane is merely its proxy and, more troublingly, its failed witness.

The deliberately aerial view that obscures the lynched body reflects the graphic novelists' retreat from the burdens of historical representation into fictive enclosures. The *story* of lynching, complete with motive, drama, iconography (lynching tree, gathered mob, the photographer, etc.), allows reprieve from the traumatic *spectacle* of lynching and the tyrannical singularity of historical lynching photography. Moreover, the perspectival structure of the plenary or mob scenes of *Incognegro* appropriates the "panoptic mode of surveillance" (13) that Wiegman aligns with the "terror" of the white lynch mob. Evidence for this appropriation comes in the very first panel of the book, a splash page in which the lynched figure is easier to spot by virtue of the triangulating sight lines of the rope that hangs him. Even a cursory analysis of the opening image and these two subsequent scenes demonstrates a shared manipulation of perspective. All of these scenes are plenary, moreover, meaning that they are organized around a concept of the mob in which a white *communitas* is brought about through ritual violence against the black body. As viewers of this image—as well as the one that finalizes Part II, in which Carl is about to be mistakenly lynched for being Incognegro—we are elevated by the text. In both images, perspective lifts us up and slightly away from an imminent violation.

Our aerial view precipitates a flooding of indiscernible bodies. One is reminded of the dizzyingly plural composition of weird frolic in paintings by Hieronymus Bosch or the peasant figures whose activities across Breughel's canvases lend human depth and variety to depictions of social collectivity. As here, the motive behind these totalizing perspectives seems to be merely technical; that is, to afford the singular space of the removed spectator an expanse equal to the human vista to be perceived. As Tim Caron has argued, Pleece's repeated use of the "elevated perspective. . . . allows the viewer to gain a critical and moral distance from the lynching" (151). More particularly, the landscape view treats human agents as organic masses, so that the assembled

5.2 First plenary lynch scene from *Incognegro* (7).

are reduced to discrete bits, each one divorced from the totality of which it is a part. The distance afforded the viewer to apprehend these parts in their panoptic totality revises privilege, redefining it as a comforting, unifying distance from spectacle.[6] Distance thus intimates the same accommodationist politics that traditional passing narratives betray. As Valerie Smith contends, passing narratives rely "upon the association of blackness with self-denial

5.3 Second plenary lynch scene from *Incognegro* (104).

and suffering, and of whiteness with selfishness and material comfort" (44), a differentiation *Incognegro* perpetuates by elevating its deified, compulsorily white(ned) viewer subtly away from lynch scenes.

Furthermore, these two scenes articulate *Incognegro*'s curricular unconscious. They are complementary studies in racist social formation—snapshots of the social order at the limit of its visual horizons, where the discriminations necessary to its stratification are most in question. That the first plenary scene is organized as the chromatic inverse of the second is interesting for reasons beyond aesthetic variety or contrast. The opening is pitched in a chromatic key of whiteness. The clubs and children differentiate the first lynch from the second and adjoin the social reproduction of white privilege to violent black subjection. The most significant difference, of course, is that the people in the first image are nearly universally rendered in the lightest tones, as is the central figure of the tree. The opposite is true in the second scene where human plurality and misery are conspicuously darker. Here, the bottles, crates, and food connect lynching to festivals and consumption more generally. Despite these obvious differences, the stark contrast in the brightness of the plenary moment signals the savvy viewer to look beyond the surface to underlying compositional linkages, where the elevated perspective, the centrality of the tree, the obscuration of the victim amidst human plurality, *communitas* itself—all predicate history and trauma as repetition.

To press our comparative analysis further, we might turn to consider how these plenary scenes differ from the average moment-to-moment or action-to-action panels of the text. Looking through the majority of its pages, we soon notice that the standard for panels in *Incognegro* is to contain one or two figures. Only rarely do three appear in a single panel. In fact, the usual capacity for a panel is two figures and these are almost never full bodies, but close-ups of faces or bust shots. Because most panels exhibit a preference for limited faces, shifts to plenary scenes of lynching, controlled and rare as they are, are designed to shock.

However, the corollary effect of that shock is to load up with secondary meanings the negative space of the lynching, by which I mean the opposite of what is shown: the average facially prominent, one- or two-person panel. Thus, faces in *Incognegro* are tantamount to persons. Faces are relatively more benign than bodies, and exponentially less inimical than a gathering of bodies (whatever their color). We could tweak the lesson further to note that it is more particularly the speaking face that equates to a classical notion of the human in this text, complete with fallacious presumptions of humanity and humaneness in tow. By contrast, no great feats of speculation are required to observe a contrapuntal force in *Incognegro* playing out in the field of the sadistic viewer.

The Sadistic Pleasure of Responding to History and the Final Lynching Scene

We are most powerless, affectively, as elevated viewers totalizing the scenes that spread out before us. However, we are presumed to be most affectively

5.4 Final lynch scene of Carl with Pinchback in distance *Incognegro* (110).

responsive in the scene where Pinchback arrives too late to rescue Carl from the mob. Here, a different but no less dynamic perspective—a zoom effect— orchestrates the scene. Rather than elevate the viewer abruptly as with the preceding scenes of racial violence, the final lynching of Carl presents a lateral view. The kids and the clubs from the first scene and the bottles from the second combine to enmesh racial violence with consumption and social reproduction. No longer plenary, the audience is cropped. As an image, this scene comes closest to citing its photographic referent. It minimizes the artifice of distance common to *Incognegro* but rarely seen in historical lynching photographs, which preserve a mid-ground distance between spectator and spectacle. The final lynch scene of *Incognegro* insists on a similar middle ground. For, unlike the other plenary images, the page here is not devoted to the lynching. Two panels flank the scene, re-containing its citational and traumatic energies. Although sadistically and suddenly closer than the rest, the final lynching yet upholds *Incognegro*'s pattern of distancing as a means of regulating spectatorial responses to the trauma of racist brutality.

As with the emotionally charged bails of cotton that dart the background of the Bugs Bunny cartoon, the background close-ups of Pinchback are to be sutured by the historically traumatized viewer. His two faces traverse the mid-ground lynch scene. Because of this panel arrangement, the sensitive viewer will move from the violence to its sublimation in sequentiality. In particular, Pinchback's initial horror at the scene in the upper panel reflects our presumed disturbance. Having established a circuit of identification, that face then passes through (and passes us through) the terrible interim of the lynched body (a body now narratively known to us; not just a figure but a character, named and fully human). The paneling then routes us to a space of affective finality. Pinchback's "Nooo!!!" seems engineered to draw upon his reflective superpowers earlier established before a mirror and later maintained by his sensitivity for reanimating that which has been suppressed or made invisible. As an affective mirror for viewers, Pinchback's magnified facial horror *gives vent* to an unchangeable historical *event*. In this regard, it depends upon a rather naïve view of history. Indeed, a sentimentalization of history follows in the wake of Pinchback's facial relay between excitation and exclamation that prods the reader toward an identification no better than Harriet Beecher Stowe's notorious recommendation at the end of *Uncle Tom's Cabin*: "There is one thing that every individual can do,—they can see to it that they feel right" (389).

Despite its use of the middle ground, *Incognegro*'s unusually non-plenary final lynch scene produces a distancing of the lynched body, facilitating our efforts to "feel right" about it. To consider the facial drama enacted by the final lynching as being pedagogical is to notice how the viewing pleasures we are instructed to mirror—Pinchback's zooming in and away—enable a withdrawal from history's traumatic body. Therefore, Pinchback's "Nooo!!!" is consolatory in more ways than one. On one level, it invokes sympathy as the mask of resignation for past and ongoing racial violence. But, on the other, the negation it demands depends upon a sadistic viewing pleasure that would seem to negate the negation. The psychic terrain for such an utterance unfolds in the distancing relay space of the "Nooo!!!" Even typographically, that negation doubles and triples back on itself (the three o's and three exclamation points are less hyperbole than hypostatization). The diacritical excesses suggest the impossibility of the task—to allow present-tense readers to scream defiantly back to a traumatic history and for that affective exhaust to operate as a type of closure in all senses of the term.

The inevitable failure of negation as a type of closure recalls the mirror scene in *American Elf*. Both connote symbolic castration, in which, according to Žižek, "the loss of something that one never possessed, i.e., the object-cause of desire is an object which emerges through the very gesture of its loss/withdrawal" (*God in Pain* 58). The pattern established in earlier panels—to occlude the lynched body as "the object-cause of desire" and to literalize the viewer's constitutive remove from it—teaches us the vicarious joys of re-experiencing an indulgence as its opposite, as a deprivation of symbolic access to the loss object. While access to an abject history motivates the topics, tropes, and timescapes of *Incognegro*, it also creates a counter-logic of symbolic castration, which covers the tracks of the pleasures it affords. The panel, by extension, epitomizes Žižek's account of psychic entries into the symbolic order and the *jouissance* one experiences at such moments—the transgressive joy that suspends the tyranny of the superego: "Insofar as the Other of the symbolic Law prohibits *jouissance*, the only way for the subject to enjoy is to feign that he lacks the object that provides *jouisssance*, i.e., to conceal from the Other's gaze its possession by way of staging the spectacle of the desperate search for it" (*God in Pain* 58).

In *Incognegro*, the "desperate search for" the lynched body is not just integral to the narrative but crucial to its form. Visual devices of obscuration and distancing structure the panels to bring the fetish object of trauma close and far simultaneously. If we were to experience a transgressive joy in the paradox of indistinguishability that surrounds the lynched body, the *sine qua non* of traumatic race history, such a feeling may be amplified by the permissivity of the comics form. The unmistakably drawn effect of comics equips them with ready mitigation, an affordance Hillary Chute cogently describes: "With comics, images carry an immediacy and proximity, while the form overall is deeply, self-consciously artificial, composed in discrete frames; it thus necessarily flags a certain aesthetic distance, an interpretation of depicted events" (*Graphic Women* 92). In consequence, depiction may deny what narration claims, making comics analogous to the passer in that both inveterately decouple knowledge from visual perception. Interestingly, both passers and comics also launch their various interventions into notions of optic truth while insisting, in one way or another, upon the centrality of the visual field.

Incognegro shares its concerns with John Lewis's *March*. Both circle around traumatic ciphers of history (of dubious optic truth) along currents Hortense Spillers might associate with the "oceanic suspensions" (72) of diasporic consciousness. What each graphic history discovers there is a way of seeing the invisible and the erased (true optic untruths). What each deposits there is a means of entering into an impossible relation with those visualizations—a means of entering into community, in other words.

Impersonating History and the Unintelligible Words of *March*

As the only living member of that legendary group of Civil Rights leaders who spoke during the 1963 March on Washington, John Lewis received widespread plaudits for the 2013 publication of his autobiography, *March*, in the form of a graphic novel. Written by Lewis and his aide, Andrew Aydin, and drawn by Nate Powell, *March* narrates a success story of black Christian vocation: The farm-raised young minister rises to national prominence in defiance of Jim Crow segregation. Never simply saccharine but in no way cynical, the ideological underpinnings of the narrative fuse at key moments with the book's visual strategies to convey an exceptional life amidst the volatile backdrop of a larger history.

But how should that history be told? If it is to signify as personal, it must risk specificities disastrously incongruous to the essence of the Civil Rights movement as it has been distilled in countless narratives that bring its milieu and character into textual being. Lewis's story must be particular enough to be personal, but sufficiently legible as a standard history as well, and therefore beholden to established media constructs. Once this balance has been struck between the personal and the public, there is still a politics of style to be negotiated. How can a graphic novel rekindle a time that has been racially inflected by distortion and miniaturization via a language of images? These are the questions that instigate the opening panels of *March* and, not surprisingly, they are the very questions with which Ho Che Anderson's *King* grapples.

A biography told in long-form comics, Anderson's *King* is constrained by a mounting archive of newspaper photographs, documentaries, films, and digital clips that precede it and simultaneously threaten to invalidate its claims to historical accuracy. Anderson circumvents this problem by making his engagement with the photographic archive that competes to depict MLK one of the defining features of the text. Conventional (*studium*) snapshots

5.5 Opening standoff with inscrutable speech on bridge from *March* (3). Work copyright John Lewis and Andrew Aydin.

of MLK appear in *King* with *punctum*-ous makeovers.[7] When the surface of famous photos are drawn over, scratched up, or marked up and down, the ubiquitous presence of Anderson's hand integrates the historical source materials, and any Bloomian anxieties of originality affecting the multilayered site of biographical authorship dissipate in the process.[8]

Like Anderson's biography, *March* registers its struggle with history more through anomaly than generic conformity. Interestingly, both graphic novels reflect the weight of their slightly different historical burdens in their use of text. Both evince a form of national ambivalence astutely described by Rebecca Wanzo as "melancholic patriotism," in which an affective relation to the US on the part of African Americans must balance "investment in democratic principles promised by the state and mourning at the impossibility of having full access to the rights guaranteed by the state or the mythology of the American Dream" (341). Perhaps brought about by an anxiety of patriotic affiliation described by Wanzo, *King* registers its melancholic burdens in assigning speech balloons to MLK that are unusually ponderous, and at times in such close proximity to other balloons that it is not until later chapters, when the race leader's balloons are tinted blue, that readers are able to distinguish them from the words of others at a glance (the way red letter editions of the Bible visually encode the utterances of Jesus). *March* marks the weight of its words in another way, delivering its lessons in word trouble punctually.

The very fist images of *March* recreate a historic standoff on the Edmund Pettus Bridge while enacting tensions of lexical representation. The image on the first page, in fact, radiates contradiction. Whereas the italicized epigraph is perfectly legible above the uncertain and decontextualized image of framing material (whether of windows or patio doors; whether in front of a flooded room or not), the words in the first speech balloon are anything but legible. They are swirls of mute fish, at first glance, swimming futilely toward a scale of typographic clarity that they, as stubborn curls where words should be, shall never reach. These are not just flourishes of an artistry demonstrating itself to be capable of presencing those words that pass by unheard in a naturalistic rendering of volatile history—the oaths, muffled shouts, and the stifled cries of the human flattened into its animalistic other. This is purposeful, the entire mumbled affair packaged in a small though recognizable speech balloon attached to a larger one addressing an as yet unspecified "John?" (3).

It is not until we turn the page that we see a repeated and enlarged version of the scrawl that blooms into words. We can now discern the address to John, the protagonist of the narrative, in the question, "Can you swim?" The query operates retroactively as an implied caption, identifying the swirling forms taking shape in the first image as water. Diegetically, the question lends humor to an impending confrontation with police on the bridge. The standoff escalates from peaceful protest to police violence as the viewer dives into the rough visual waters of the Civil Rights era. Characterized by a sudden transfer from rational language to onomatopoeia, the bridge riot leads readers to the interior title page (10–11) where the tranquil Potomac sparkles at dusk and the Washington Monument looms in high contrast against the horizon. That the riot leads to this new beginning in a panoramic idyll endorses the assumption that history is progress. Of course, the book's epigraph complicates that assumption with an image of temporal fluidity: "to the past and future children of the movement" (3).

Symbolically, Lewis as autographer re-enacts the epigraph, projecting the past forward and back again. The depicted riot and its plural referents in black history give rise to Lewis's redemptive leadership. They indirectly authorize his status both as history and as icon. In them, the racial strife that beleaguers a nation only hardens John Lewis in its cauldrons. The initial unintelligibility of the first speech of the narrative, however, tells a different story. And we would be justified in lingering over this initial unreadable speech balloon, which regulates the reading and viewing pace, as Groensteen attests: "[A] piece of dialogue is frequently introduced into a panel as a way to slow down the reading" and ultimately to "prolong our participation in this eminently dramatic moment" (133).

The drama of the balloon's unreadability creates an incredibly slow reveal of the logophobia haunting the edges of *March*. That a speech too incidental and too small for any clear transmission initiates our entry into the narrative only underscores the book's formative lessons in textual suspicion. We might compare the symptomatic nature of *March*'s word trouble to the unreadable density of language in Ho Che Anderson's *King* or to the wordless structure of Kyle Baker's *Nat Turner*. These parallels raise questions about the generic anxieties that attend language in African American graphic histories. Are these similarities merely orthographic anomalies or do they signal the imbalance Lindon Barrett has diagnosed regarding the oversubscription of acoustic culture among people of color vis–à–vis their overwhelmingly hostile treatment in dominant culture's words and pictures?[9]

The opening of *March* would seem to affirm as much. For, after the illegibilities of the words (and imagery) of the first page, the riot that erupts on the bridge maps the toxic exchange routes of the words that shuttle between white police and black demonstrators. The upper left quadrant of the page illustrating the encounter is divided into two small panels of Lewis with his hand outstretched at his open mouth, as if to help his words along. The speech balloon significantly reads: "May we have a word with the mayor?" The second square just below this one inches further in on Lewis's face. Because relatively little changes in the composition, save for a greater focus on the concerned eyes of Lewis's confidante, the second panel is nearly automatically decoded with its upper partner. The other difference occurs in the jagged framing around the balloon, which emanates from the gutter space beyond the second panel to report the police's megaphonic response: "There is no word to be had." The closed circuit of stultifying dialogue is repeated again in the third panel located in the upper right-hand quadrant of the page. With the silhouette of Lewis's body in the foreground and the police taking up extreme postures of diagonal encroachment in the background, the word balloons occupy much

5.6 Riot on the bridge from *March* (7). Work copyright John Lewis and Andrew Aydin.

of the active space of the panel. "May we have a word with," Lewis's speech balloon begins, now with the jagged-edged megaphonic reply superimposed upon it: "There *is* no word to be *had*" (7, emphasis in original). Evocative and graphic, the placement of words about words makes the historic logophobia that plagues black history succinctly pictorial. The police officer's response dwarfs Lewis's humble plea for a word, drowning one requested word in the torrent of another's enunciation. The two-word command uttered by authority is among the largest text of the book: "Troopers Advance!"

Form and content coalesce in these prological exchanges, training readers to accept a certain measure of unbridgeable distance in moments of dialogue.

5.7 Fade to black from *March* (9). Work copyright John Lewis and Andrew Aydin.

Even when characters are brought close, as in the last panel of the protestors, their prayers are conveyed by speech balloons containing little more than private hieroglyphs—marks of speech denied, precisely like the "word" Lewis is not permitted to have with the mayor. In addition to introducing readers to Lewis and his plight, the prologue of *March: Book One* prepares us for a unique form of readerly desire, one that unites with spectatorial desire to bewitch us into scanning the scrawl for a lexical meaning that cannot be divulged. Instead, the words in these panels bear a meaningful presence for being so tangibly hushed and evacuated of alphabetic substance. They remind us, also, of the metonymic and hieroglyphic signifying properties that, according to Qiana Whitted, recirculate in African American autogra-phy in order to "trigger the readers' awareness of their own subject positions as observers. . . . [and] to undermine the alterity of the colonial gaze" (81).

And while scrawl is the common speech of the protestors, it is not theirs alone. That police are shown speaking in an illegible miniature script opens up the device to suggest something unifying about speech amidst histori-cal rupture. At the very least, inconsequential language is not a marker of isolation, but rather the means for producing a new kind of community, as Jared Gardner claims in a different context: "The question for the tradition of autography has long been, and remains, not whether the act of graphic mem-oir will set the autobiographical subject free [. . .] but whether it will release him into a chain of common suffering and whether that chain can be made to communicate and bind one to the other" (130). To be unheard despite invest-ing in the power of speech is to be conscripted into a historical community of American Civil Rights remembrance—particularly in view of the Christian context of that narrative, in which the word or Word doubles for the Bible as well as for Jesus. It is that phantasmatic community that *March* engenders for its reader-viewers in commemoration of a history that is here equated to the muting of redress.

One image from the prologue in particular stands in for all those protesta-tions forever muted in history. After the riot erupts, Lewis first loses himself in the fray and then loses consciousness. The loss of his view (as the focalizer of the narrative) and our view of him (as the protagonist of the action) suddenly give way to a panel of pure blackness. It hovers above a chaotic background of black and white that competes for sovereignty. The panel of blackness thus resolves chromatic tension by blurring consciousness and perspective. Like the tiny scrawl we can see but not decipher, it is a hyperbole of absence. The black panel and the scrawl hypostatize erasures of history for which the text seeks redress.

The oblivion of the panel complicates the comics' established pattern of focalization, or "the subjective filtering of characters' or narrators' minds" which help to "cue the reader to reconstruct the storyworld under the aspec-tuality of a specific fictional mind" (Horstkotte and Pedri, 335). Best under-stood, as Hannah Miodrag would have it, as "contextual utterance not system, of *parole* not *langue*" (178), the blackened panel unveils the political valences of focalization in *March*, for it stages a collapse of presentation. As a *prolepsis* of later narrative strategies, it makes re-presentation possible. It becomes, in other words, a space that reflects on its own production, or, as George Hart-ley might theorize it: "This space of incommensurability—the gap or abyss opened up between the figure and the concept—this space of impossibility, is at the same time the space of possibility of representation as such" (4). The black-out invokes nescience, of course, or cognitive blankness, but it does so narratively as the starting place for eventual illumination. Blackness thus operates unconventionally in *March*, flickering as both knowledge and absence. By catalyzing a postmodern sublime, the blackened panel reconfigures African American history into a form of mnemopoetics, which Valérie Bada defines as: "[A] symbolic dramatization of the African American experience that comes out of the darkness of history and overcomes social invisibility (even erasure) through the ceaseless production of words, sounds, and songs" (43). Out of that defining darkness, *March* circles back to an ahistorical figurative time before cognitive erasure and political conflict.

Mirrors, Chickens, and Messianic History: The Visual Curricula of *March*

Words and invisibility, protest and prostrated words—all are implicated in *March*'s retelling of an epochal demand for black civil rights. As part of that retelling, the narrative structure presents John Lewis as messianic or, as Wilson Jeremiah Moses puts it, "as having a manifest destiny or a God-given role to assert the providential goals of history" (4). Allusions to the deluge further link Lewis's story to its eschatological templates in the Bible. In an astute reading of lyrics from James Baldwin to Ice Cube, Allen Dwight Callahan connects the trope of the flood to a politics of violence: "In traditions of the African-American vernacular, the rainbow is not so much promise as threat. The violence of the deluge is invoked against the violence of the present world order: the violence of human beings is overcome by the violence of God" (197). The flood discourse of *March*, therefore, suggests how swimming (and marching) against the retributive floodwaters of history is the only viable response to racist violence—a sure target of deific correction.[10]

In its historiographic orientations, *March* represents a hybrid approach to Civil Rights. It riffs off of the traditional "King-centric" biographical treatments of the era, which, according to Kevern Verney, posit a "traditional 'Montgomery to Memphis' chronology" of the movement in order to highlight "the emergence of Martin Luther King in the 1955 Montgomery Bus Boycott" (93). However, by focusing on a relatively lesser-known figure, *March* aligns with more recent Civil Rights historiography to explore "broader long-term historical processes as the key catalyst for the emergence of the post-war Civil Rights Movement" (94). Nevertheless, the myopia that results from a repeated application of the "great man" theory of history sacrifices the possibilities for a politics of collectivity in favor of triumphalist individualism. Uplift ideologies based upon singular heroes are not simply illusory but socially damaging, as Robert J. Patterson argues in his critique of exodus politics: "[I]nvestment in the idea of one male messianic leader inhibits communities' abilities to act on their own behalf and generate indigenous leaders" (8).

Except for the presidency, singular leadership is never more incarnate in American politics than in the figure of MLK. Lewis and Powell are not slow in paying their debts to the Reverend Doctor nor to his representation in the comics. There are two mirror scenes in *March* that pay graphic homage to Ho Che Anderson (whether intentionally or not), particularly his manner of introducing MLK at the beginning of *King*. After refusing an uninterrupted view of King's photorealistic face on the cover and in the prologue, Anderson opens the story proper at Boston University in 1952, as MLK readies himself for a party. He is in a bathroom but lines from Nat King Cole's "Sweet Lorraine" thread through the visual space like classical phylacteries. Over nine panels, King appears only through visual synecdoche. The historical whole of the man is reduced to iconic constituent parts reflected in a mirror— a cross, a watch, shirt buttons, shined shoes. He becomes a series of units, in other words, emblematic of the comics form, which await closure from reader-viewers.

Just like Anderson's hero, Lewis is shown grooming himself in preparation for his public obligations (including his role as the protagonist of *March*). He sings along to a blues tune whose apt lyrics wind across panels—"but you cannot take my dignity" (15). As with Anderson's MLK, Lewis sings to his reflection, and although his figure possesses a greater degree of completeness than Anderson's atomized protagonist, the fullest view we get of Lewis in these panels is in the mirror where he is little more than a sketch of loose grey swaths adjusting its tie. A later image of Lewis bracing himself for the new anti-segregationist challenges of his ministerial work returns to the mirror. This time, the inspiration Lewis (as historical figure) receives from King seems to blend with the inspiration Lewis and Powell (as authors) may have received from Anderson. Below a montage of media sources reporting on the boycotts, Lewis again adjusts his tie before a mirror; to the left of that image— now iconically charged from the opening of *March* to echo Anderson's *King*— a borderless caption explains Lewis's reverence for King's precedence: "Dr. King's example showed me that it was possible to do more as a minister . . . I was inspired" (59).

These mirror scenes in *March* combine to claim a citational logic for Lewis's public face, both his historical face of leadership as well as the face his character and text wear in relation to the singular One that has come before—the ineluctable face of King. As a cognate sign of MLK, Lewis is both obscured and paradoxically envisaged. Whether or not there is an intentional influence passing from Anderson to Powell and/or Lewis, there is nevertheless textual evidence for the significant *effect* of such influence. In that effect lies the possibility of a textual community, wherein literary signs of graphic black history seem to speak to one another, to recognize one another, and to thereby realize a tradition. Nevertheless, the iconic—that is to say, the public—John Lewis that the opening mirror scene in *March* builds toward is repeatedly deferred. Instead, we get a more personal version of the man, or at least, the effect of one.

When Lewis goes to his office, a black mother who is in town for Barack Obama's inauguration arrives unexpectedly with her two sons, Jacob and Esau (their names furthering the book's union of eschatology and biography). After mistaking the solicitous Lewis for an aide, the mother expresses her desire for "my boys to see their history" (18). Her utterance also transfers that desire to the image of Lewis, which must convey not only his person but also his literal impersonation of Civil Rights history. The good congressman immediately consents, inviting the conspicuously single mother and her sons into an office whose walls teem with photographic snapshots of Lewis embodying history. Significantly, his walls resemble a comics page, gridded with rectangular image-frames, each one bordered by gutters.

Even so, the page that transmutes Lewis's wall of history into a comics-like photomontage never accedes clarity to the photos. They are scrumbled and as loosely sketched as his earlier reflection in the mirror. And although Lewis begins to attach momentous captions to them—"Here I am when I was 23 years old, meeting with President Kennedy" (19)—the page places greater visual stress on the paddle or oar that he removes from its mount among the photos. The oar participates in a Biblical discourse of the flood by not being spoken of at all. We surmise its symbolic importance by virtue of its singular unmentionability as an object within the visual field. The evident but unmentioned oar thus waylays the anticipated focus of the photographs in a manner not unlike the indecipherable speeches found throughout *March*. Both function rather like the chickens the young boys interrupt Lewis to ask about. All are inexplicable emblems of Lewis's personal yet publicly undisclosed relation to history. They are ciphers of his burden to embody a history that calls out for re-vision and re-membering.

The question "why do you have so many chickens?" unveils the memoir's proper chronological structure, momentarily belied by the sudden un-timeliness of the prologue. Based on these multiple points of re-entry into the past, we might surmise that *March* will not be like any of the stories already

5.8 Lewis inscribed by scripture and his flock of chickens (27).
Work copyright John Lewis and Andrew Aydin.

framed by the photographs on Lewis's wall. It will not be, in other words, another glimpse from a veritable *studium* (to borrow from Barthes) of posed and invariant public history, but rather a *punctum* of anomalous, subjectifying iconography, which (as Barthes says of *puncta*) "rises from the scene, shoots out of it like an arrow, and pierces me" (*Camera Lucida* 56). At the very least, this is precisely the effect Lewis's *statua* of chickens has on Jacob, one of the boys from the outer diegetic ring of *March's* temporarily framed narrative (the frame of Lewis telling his story to the mother and her two boys is abandoned midway through in exchange for a disembodied voice of reminiscence). Jacob cuts Lewis short of his prepared history and forces him to tell a different one rooted in an agricultural black past where the separation between animals and humans dissolves. Whether rekindled sentimentally or not, as is the case with young Lewis's proleptic and no doubt sincere empathy for the family chickens, such vivid deployments of animal metaphors in the context of a storied African American life can hardly bear meaning without conjuring slavery.

The animalization of African Americans is at least as old as the slavocratic practice "of naming, branding and even pricing slaves according to their equivalent in cows, horses, camels, pigs, and chickens" (D. B. Davis 13). Doubtless that beastly history of association would inform any account of anti-segregation, which seeks redress for the persistent social and racial logics of apartheid naturalized by slavery. The fact that Lewis must go back to a farm to tell his whole story performs diaspora by gathering into the backward glance of personal memory the larger and longer history of a people. In casting his past as a proud but impoverished site of agrarian labor, where animals and humans commingle, Lewis exhibits confidence in his representativity. Despite connections to slavery, perhaps even because of them, Lewis embodies Manning Marable's claim that "[t]he black freedom movement had permitted Negroes to perceive themselves as real actors in their own living history" (190).

And yet Lewis's chicken anecdote may also be a means of enlarging the politics of his memoir beyond race, using the greater chasm between species to promulgate sympathy not only between the races but between all "real actors" with a "living history" to either claim or lose under erasure. As a result, the text proposes a foundational ethic of trans-species relation. Lewis's involvement with their plight, as chickens rather than human-like chickens, refutes the long-standing predilection in comics for the anthropomorphic animal. The bottom panels that capture close-ups of the chickens portray their human-like attentions ironically. They are portrayed as animals whose gaze configures only an abyss of ethical relation—except to Lewis, who is preternaturally attuned to the human frequencies of the chickens. He pretends they are his first ministerial flock, the pun on which renders the young Lewis's earnestness both solemn and glancingly comedic. A conflict between image and text arises when *March* delineates Lewis as a young boy, arranging flowers for an elaborate funeral he is to conduct for a bird. The text claims: "This was not child's play. I was genuinely grief-stricken, and the services were painstakingly precise" (30). We are called upon to infuse the image of the child with the consciousness of the adult voice of narration. As with Satrapi's Marji, it is only through the image of Lewis as child that an authorial myth of impossible origin forms around the suggestion that the greatest space of authorship—a divine one—has foreordained the author's right to tell such a story and to have such a life in the first place.

However supernaturally inflected, Lewis's eventual successes at overturning Alabama segregation are shown to derive from a politics of super-species kinship. The emblem for the space across which that kinship must traverse, between the human, would-be minister and his all-too bestial flock, is the Middle Passage or diaspora. That space of irrecoverable origin encompasses a racial ontology of traumatized relation, where chickens and chasms, chiasmus and the territory that "middles" the very term "African American" collide. *March*'s strangely protracted detour through the chickens that come home to ethically roost also furnishes an origin story for the crusader Lewis is destined to become. The chickens are as unlikely as slaves in their role as the starting place for an historic triumph against oppression. And, in an American context, few registers are as evocative for telling such a story as the rags-to-riches discourse, which is summoned by the chickens. Up from chickens a great man wends his way toward greater sympathies. But, importantly, it is through them that he receives his blessed calling, a vocation of improbable spiritual kinship. It is from the doomed but sympathetic chickens of Pike County, Alabama, that *March* intensifies its plot arc: Lewis's providential rise from his meeting with Dr. King in Montgomery in 1958 to his lunch-counter protests in Nashville that victoriously close the book: "[A]t 3:15 on May 10, 1960, those six downtown Nashville stores served food to black customers for the first time in the city's history" (120). Without them, Lewis's history would be less legible as a sacred one.

Interestingly, that the chickens are more realistic than the cartoony animal-human hybrids of "funny animal" comics plays up the sincerity of young Lewis, whose ethical precocity obeys several of Linda Vance's cautions regarding the human-animal bond: "We want to avoid anthropomorphizing animals even though that has proven itself an effective tactic for mobilizing public sympathy toward them. We need to be faithful to their stories, not our own" (185). The successful sympathetic encounter with another species entails an expanded sense of community, as Donna Haraway contends: "As ordinary knotted beings, they [animals] are also always meaning-making figures that gather up those who respond to them into unpredictable kinds of 'we'" (5). The new "we" that Lewis's chickens congregate is ethical, historical, and textual. It is a community of feeling and redress that opens onto what Jean-Luc Nancy deems the *inoperative*.

In *Incognegro* and *March*, the racializing mirror of traumatic history unmasks the individual as an impossible I-con of a community that cannot be realized. The history that would collectivize race trauma, which each graphic novel imagines, is a futility to Jean-Luc Nancy, who claims that "community has never taken place along the lines of our projections of it" (11). Rather, Nancy locates community within the experience of its loss: "[T]he thought of community or the desire for it might well be nothing other than a belated invention that tried to respond to the harsh reality of modern experience: namely, that divinity was withdrawing infinitely from immanence" (10). *Incognegro*'s relentless search for a consolatory space, from which to divinely excoriate and thereby redeem history, finds its theoretical reflection in Nancy's diagnoses of modernity's anomic response to godhood's infinite withdrawal. How similar to the engineered recessions in space that attend *Incognegro*'s lynched body or *March*'s unintelligible words. Both seek out spaces of empathy to achieve what Nancy might refer to as "pure immanence"—a relationship with history (as psychically formative trauma) in confirmation of Nancy's axiom that "[c]ommunity is revealed in the death of others; hence it is always revealed to others" (15). However, for the muted words and massacred bodies of diasporic history, notions of community founded upon the unaccountable dead are neither exceptional nor so permanently inoperative. Nor should we hasten to concur with Nancy when he minimizes the difference that diasporic community makes in his global theory: "[t]he emergence and our increasing consciousness of decolonized communities has not profoundly modified this state of affairs" (22).

The African American graphic histories under review here teach us to consider the opposite. They create looking and learning environments that depend upon our notice of the dead amidst the semiotic detritus of history and language. And although both texts seem to concur with Nancy that "the genuine community of mortal beings, or death as community, establishes their impossible communion" (15), neither may be said to support his notion that "the exigency of community is still unheard and remains to be discovered and thought" (23). These texts evince that exigency. By making readers parse visual systems that frustrate dominant standards of optical clarity, legibility, and immediacy, *Incognegro* and *March* likewise teach their reader-viewers how to think community—as a way of thinking towards impossibility, or as Nancy puts it, towards that space "where consciousness *of* self turns out to be outside the self of consciousness" (19).

CODA

Richard McGuire's *Here* as an Autography of Place

Soon after entering the window of the textual house Richard McGuire builds for us in *Here*, we may recognize just how profoundly the architecture of place pervades our reading and seeing. In many ways, *Here* offers an alternative to the autographies studied throughout *Reading Lessons in Seeing*. McGuire's premise enables a departure from the tyranny of the human altogether, presenting instead a series of images representing various moments of time. The year each image is taken from is dutifully reported in accompanying captions. The year comes to figure as a reading anchor, stabilizing our navigation through vastly disconnected images. Most grounding of all is the image of a corner within a house, the very spot from which all the scenes of the graphic novel are taken. That corner undergoes momentous change over the decades, witnessing history remixed, as visual mélange. By reducing humanity as well as history to so many discreet units of possibility, *Here* presents captivating alternatives not only to comics narrative but also to the presumed subjects of autography. In its pages, place seems able to possess a life worth recounting, but not always according to the same standards of human reason or emotion common to autobiography.

According to *Here*, the non-human consciousness of locality makes possible new ways of understanding time and our all-too fleeting relation to it, particularly when compared to the fanciful snippets of human experience recollected by the narration. In the mirror that every graphic novel imagines within its panels, the persistent place of *Here* takes on an I-conic value. The image of the place's sense of itself (or its view of itself) surely corresponds to the corner of the house. Because it is represented most often, the domestic interior or corner with chimney in turn becomes I-conic of the work's governing design. Despite trafficking, then, in the deep past of geological time,

Here establishes the twentieth-century place of bourgeois home ownership as its essential pictorial personality.

The possibilities the book suggests for rethinking the primacy of the human in terms of place are likewise biased, eventually giving way to a decidedly human preference, not to mention a specific regional affiliation—New England and colonial history. This should come as no surprise as McGuire is from Perth Amboy, New Jersey; the house used as a model for the illustrations, he has admitted in interviews, is his childhood home. Thus, what seems to be the autobiography of a place turns out to be a mask for autographic business as usual. But what remains intriguing about *Here*'s fictive decentralization of authorship is the way in which the pictorial narrative prepares readers for the book's eventual retreat from ahistoricism and liberating anachronism.

Indeed, *Here* makes use of temporality as if it were the only logic able to make sense of place, with its non-human ontic timelessness. Even though a spot in the landscape may be said to occupy a different order of time than finite or mortal organisms do, the very structure of the narrative relies upon a deliberate rigidity of time. We see similar manipulations of time—compressions of temporal experience—in lyric poetry, a connection, which may lead some to classify *Here* as graphic lyricism rather than graphic prose or narration. Contemplating the model of selfhood emerging from Alice Oswald's poetry, the critic and poet Deryn Rees-Jones notes how entangled the coordinates of self, object, and place become in lyric modes, producing "a collective version of a historical moment in which biography and autobiography, which become our histories, are scrutinized in relation to nature and thus redefine it as they coalesce into a dramatized autobiography of place" (234). Armed with this critical fragment, we might leap to the conclusion that *Here* is up to a similar lyrical commingling of autobiography and biography, conjoining a subject-less view of the invariant place in order to reconcile the human and the object world of locale. Collectivity is certainly implied, if not produced, by the graphic novel, since by eschewing the individual-centered narrative (punctuated by protagonists and narrators) in favor of multiplicity—the panoply that defines even a single place when seen across the vast eons of its ontological situatedness—the text gives us no single entity with which to identify. Rather, we are assumed to become in the process of reading more like places than people ourselves.

This mirroring is not dramatized in *Here* as occurring between narrated subjects but across them. Across the threshold of the page, the reader is constituted by the text to experience an assumed stasis, mirroring the unchanging point of view, whose stasis becomes the focal premise of *Here*'s unruly narrative design. Indeed, while scrutinizing the text we may become increasingly aware of our own positionality. We may notice that we occupy a similarly immovable position relative to the views presented and re-presented. That affect in all its human variation (jokes, curses, boredom, laughter) manifests as an organizing principle of the text only heightens the underlying impression that there is something rather inhuman about experiencing time with the same cosmic indifference one may expect from a corner of a room. This is not to say that such a perspective is ahistorical or apolitical. To be sure, the very appeal of such a narrative means little outside of our current ecological urgencies. And yet, this is precisely the appeal of the mask in many graphic novels, particularly autobiographical ones. The autobiographical mask attenuates the human to anthroposcenic or hyperbolic extremes, while conferring to it nevertheless a tincture of the divine—whether through affect, reclaimable experience in participatory games, storytelling, or memory. What sets the graphic novel version of *Here* apart from the original black and white comic published in *Raw* vol. 2, no. 1 in 1989 is its borderless placement of ex-tempo panels, whose colors bleed seamlessly into one another. Freed from the hard outline of the earlier comic design, which drew upon a visual analogy between comics panels and windows on an early computer screen, the graphic novel version of *Here* crowds its temporal miscellany onto single page-panels that seem to go on forever. Fictive, seemingly authorless, and narrator-less, *Here* is an admittedly imperfect example of autography, but its use of the mirror shatters our misconceptions about either subjectivities or the devices that reflect and produce them.

The same could be said of *Here*'s inherent juvenility. Its cheeky, witty play, with its mirroring and the underlying humor of the text in general, aids readers in breaking from another misconception about the separateness of the personal past and the planetary one. The narrative opens by indulging in the fantasy of a return to childhood—and even further back to the recesses of recorded time. In 1957, a woman walks into the living room that serves as the graphic novel's protagonist. She wonders, "Now why did I come in here again?" as a cat crosses her path in an interposed panel with the caption, 1999. Within several page-turns, *Here* thus initiates its narrative game. And there is more than simply a childlike reception at work in this game. We turn the pages forward and back again, returning like the initial woman to the same room to pick up on linear backstories of mini-dramas that play out as the story advances. Significantly, there is a stable group of children who get their picture taken over the course of many years; though they age as individuals, they are arranged in the same way as a group, always in answer to a voice off-panel urging them to "smile." Their unfolding lives compress many decades of existence into a series of photo portraits set in the same room. We may presume the old man who dies while telling a bad joke about dying is their father; at the very least, he is their father figure. The coincidence calibrates the world of *Here* so as to accord with that of the bad joke. A juvenile presentiment reigns as we are encouraged by the architecture of the text to mock death repeatedly. It is interesting to note, therefore, that a politics associated with the picaro initiates our entry into the text, mooring our reception of an anthroposcene, which manifests as a series of temporally disconnected but meaningfully rearranged intersections of life and landscape.

The analogy between *Here*'s play with deep time and the picaro's jaunt through the social order is apt. Consider not just the many scenes of childhood glee depicted in the graphic novel, but also the implication that these scenes in particular are riven with loss. Perhaps this is why the boy from the first dozen or so pages, who finally accomplishes the headstand begun pages earlier, implores us: "Don't look at me." It will be childhood that humanity shall miss the most after submitting to the ineluctable ravages of time, the impending ecological end that hangs about at the narrative edges of *Here*. That end is less about nuclear annihilation or climatic apocalypse than it is about timelessness, the deconstructed meaningless (and potential transposability) of times lost, past, and passing. Overwhelmingly, the consciousness behind the narrative suggests a complementary ambivalence towards order that the picaro harbors. Recapitulating Joseph Meeker's *The Comedy of Survival*, Dana Phillips notes how urban space, an analogue for the social order more generally, is always represented as an effect of the picaro's unabashed subjectivity: "the incipient chaos that the picaro senses and celebrates wherever he goes" (146). The insight leads Phillips to speculate about the possibility of anything striking a picaro as being wild, like the uncollected strips of lived experience that *Here* re-orchestrates out of a wilderness of meaning: "Thus the alternatives of wilderness versus civilization and of country versus city have no meaning for the picaro: in his eyes, even the city is a wilderness." If picaros are useful harbingers of capitalism and modernity, then their introjection or immanence within graphic novels may be seen as continuing this important work of deconstructing the terms by which our reality is made to appear visible. *Here* mitigates the suggestion of climatological disaster by drawing a central equivalence between the urban landscape and new formations of capital (value) according to a celebration of temporal whimsy. Reader-viewers are thus inculcated by the text to take up the same perspective associated with the "knights errant" topos that the picaro has been said to replace, as Ginacarlo Maiorino claims, so that "the picaro's wanderings give readers access to modernity's new kinds of urban knowledge" (296). In this way, *Here* achieves a perspective on time similar to the one Jared Gardner

6.1 Native couple from *Here*. Graphic novel excerpt from *Here* by Richard McGuire. Copyright © 2014 by Richard McGuire. Used by permission of Pantheon Books, an imprint of the Knopf Doubleday Publishing Group, a division of Random House LLS. All rights reserved.

ascribes to newspaper comic strips. Both present new prospects for experiencing history by rigorously sketching out for readers the "soon-to-be-past traces of the living present" ("Archives" 804).

It goes without saying that the narrative design of *Here* proposes temporal simultaneity or juxtaposition as a type of play for readers to enjoy. But to what deeper purpose are we presented with this ecocritically provocative matching exercise? *Here* is structured like a game in more ways than one. On the one hand, it eschews linear unity and the focality of human protagonists and characters; on the other, it makes reading and viewing comparable to interpretive practices of decoding and puzzle-solving. Conceptually, readers must bring together at least two disparate units of visual information in order to grasp the first level of the text's insinuations of plot: Ben Franklin with grandson visiting his estranged son; the 1950s housewife who is widowed and visited by archeologists, whose sons grow up to play a futuristic board game together; and the Native American couple who hear an alarming sound in the woods in 1609. These narrative connections can never be confirmed by the text, existing on what could be classified as a first level of signification and corresponding to the text's creation of a *ludus* or play space. The game we play with the images is rarely contrastive. So long as we read for narrative continuities, we are bound to encounter two panels facing one another as being in spatial dialogue, and contiguity is synonymous with dialogue in *Here*. Two proximate panels are often shown to have narratively proximate timescapes, their content symbolically touching one another. For example, in two facing panels on a background captioned "1970," the panel on the left from 1959 shows a housewife asking her husband for his "Keys? Watch? Wallet?" The panel on the right from 1954 shows the back of someone unseen in a lounge chair, who offers a sociological interpretation for the conjugal behavior just witnessed: "It's a symbiotic relationship. It's a little ritual they do, a little performance." Readers are hereby solicited by the text to fold the diagnosis onto the symptom—the content of the counterpoised image—in a coordinative matching game across the axis of the book's spine.

Once initiated, the game plays out across many more capacious gaps in time and space, over many more page-turns. Indeed, during play the page swells with renewed formal meanings. It encodes planetary time-space as an insuperable distance, separating the Native American couple, for example, lying in the woods in 1609 from the archeology students who come to search for their remains several pages later. But the page also encodes a contrary metric of distance. It stages the bridgeable collapse of difference that makes the Natives seem to inhabit the same present, according to the same rules of presence, as the archeologists or any other figure in the book. This collapse occurs so long as we endeavor to read one step beyond the matching game's reliance on narrative coherence, which is the game's point, after all. Narrative connection, *Here*'s game seems to suggest, makes sympathy possible—not to mention humor, irony, and epiphanic moments of coincidence. But narrative also forecloses other kinds of connection more crucial to the book's less-than-subtle ecocriticisms. In our games, as with our readings, we are prone to confront the cosmological fact of our eventual demise—as when we notice the archeology student in 1986 wearing a yellow T-shirt that says (in morbid echo of the Yellow Kid perhaps) "Future Transitional Fossil." This image appears across the page from another image of two elderly men in 2050 playing a game with floating colored rectangles. How like the reading of a comic this game is. And how much like the comics mirror this game looks. As one player pushes his face through the panel, becoming a younger version of himself, we observe the transformative, youth-giving powers of the imagination, of reading as play. At this moment, however, game-playing turns ominous. Like reading and seeing, playing is shown once again to be a unifying practice that creates identification across chasms of difference, planes of experience, or eons of geological time. But in *Here*, all these practices are bound to snap under the duress of their fictive impossibility—their impossibility, in other words, beyond the ineluctable fictions of the pictorial. That impossibility is even more salient perhaps when the pictorial is materialized as witnessed by viewers of a recent three-dimensional installation of McGuire's pictures in Frankfurt, Germany, in February of 2016.

Finding the game mechanics of *Here* is relatively easy; teasing out the text's autobiographical effects, less so. It is also at this point in the application that one struggles to fit the narrowest of generic definitions onto *Here*'s patently fictional design. Neither *Künstlerroman* nor autography in the traditional sense, McGuire's text seems indifferent to the gospel of self-reflection espoused in most of the memoirs discussed in comics scholarship. The fact that *Here* is not a self-announced autobiography helps to conceal the apprenticeship strategies in reading and viewing that structure it. *Here* is thus ideal for identifying how autobiography operates when it is not a generic paradigm but a mode.

What I mean to say is that although *Here* is not an autobiography in the strictest sense, it is autobiographical. Traces of that ambivalence may even be read into the front matter. There, McGuire spells out some of the legalistic intentions and indemnifications typical to autobiography: "This is a work of fiction. All incidents and dialogue, and all characters with the exception of some well-known historical and public figures, are products of the author's imagination and are not to be construed as real." On the facing page, we are given an image to accompany the truth disclaimers and copyright information—the I-con of the fireplace, which anchors our foray into McGuire's imaginary through lines of time. More text in the form of a dedication appears above the I-con in the same bold style as the disclaimer: "To My Family." Interestingly, like the loophole into verity that the presence of Ben Franklin suggests in an otherwise fictional work of art, the dedication seeks to gift the art not to "public figures" but to private ones. That these particular receivers of the work are cited there, at that precise spot, takes on further significance when we notice that the dedication rests on the same site as other important object-symbols: a mirror, a wall-mounted TV, a star-shaped clock, and sometimes a landscape painting, which not coincidentally resembles the "actual" landscapes that fill those pages meant to depict the area before its domestication by way of farming, European settlement, and the building of the house.

Thus, while there are no recognizable self-portraits of the artist hard at work—no indications of the metafictional exigencies crucial to the *künstlerroman*—*Here* still conjures the work behind the work and the creator who both carries out and covers over that labor. The *künstlerroman* petitions us to heed two related ideologies, commingling themes of Oedipal competition—in which rebellious sons combat bourgeois fathers and all they stand for by acquiring the métier of the artist—and themes of art's resistance to commerce. In the latter, art's position somehow apart from the market parallels the dream in the former of the privileged but somehow un-co-opted son. And although these themes are stretched through the graphic novel's prism of metaphor, both of them resonate in *Here*.

Paternal anxiety enshrouds the text's strange fascination with its singularly recognizable historical figure, Ben Franklin, a forefather who in McGuire's hands is more of a literal father than he is the great politician or inventor. Franklin's presence amplifies the temporal conceit of *Here*'s embedded game to include history. Franklin is less a fixed or sacred icon than game token, an image we as reader-viewers are enjoined to figuralize in unexpectedly imaginative or ludic terms—as mere costume or one fleck of human experience among many. Thus, the text nods to the work behind its work. This labor is neither about self-portraits nor seeing McGuire drawing a panel from *Here*. It is about the reading we must do to see and to un-see Franklin according to these ludic terms. It is fitting for a text that dreams itself to be subject-less (and perhaps author-less as well) to concomitantly fantasize its readers to be decoders who must lose themselves in the colored panels before them, like the old man who becomes temporarily young while pushing his head through the abstract squares of color floating before him. This is perhaps the real self-portrait of the work behind *Here*'s work: an image of reading as playing and transformation, as a movement through the text's transformation-granting pages.

Ultimately, however, these exercises in reading, playing, and laboring bring us to the brink of an impossible community. A tantalizing community dangles before us as a result of the graphic novel's prosoponic play with masks. While attempting to figuratively push our heads through the panels of *Here*, we are inevitably moved to cogitate an elsewhere, not a here but a there—a back there of irretrievable history. Although supplied with ample training, Western reader-viewers may be less inclined to grow in fresh directions when confronted with one of the text's few narrative situations, such as the Native couple engaged either in consensual or non-consensual intimacy. The very flicker of their situation arouses disturbing connections between ambivalence and denunciation, genocide and something far more complicated. In addition to creating uncertainty about the couple's motivations, *Here* creates uncertainty about an impending danger they sense but cannot confront or name. At times, the text suggests it may be an animal in the forest drawing near; at others, as mentioned, the panel arrangements encourage us to locate that danger in the archeologists who knock at the house now marking their remains. It would be no great leap for us to imagine at least three other possible sources for their alarm: a subsequent history of Native removal and genocide, a future-oriented projection of anthroposcenic destruction, and us. We are thus uncomfortably gathered into the graphic novel's construction of a colonial gaze and made to play along in its dream of time as a Tower of Babel.

It has been one of the aims of this study to show how we are automatically and often unconsciously put to work repairing the linguistic fissures of that Tower in the comics. Through acts of closure and a largely unexamined predilection for narrativity, the comics form conscripts readers to suture the gaps even when they represent tumultuous ruptures of history—traumas in all senses. Perhaps this is why *Here*'s lightness, its insouciant play with deep time, is solemn as well as ironic. Each trivial exchange draws us further and further towards the end. Though enlarged by our need for connection even in the face of catastrophic rupture, each lost moment points us to the next rupture, the final closure, so that every reading engenders a community of remembrance. *Here* summons a community of mourning for an end that has not yet happened. The contradictions in such a formation mirror those of the text's potentially obscene play with Native extinction, in which one intolerable demise (or not-yet demise) is figured in terms of another, more tolerable demise. In other words, the certainty with which we are induced to read the not-yet demise of the Native couple mirrors, produces, and thus encourages us to suture the not-yet demise of the planet.

Like many so-called graphic novels *Here* prods us to contemplate the inverse of its central conceit. Instead of glorying in the caprice of place as an enduring construct, we are solicited to see place as timely, perishable. Place is not the unkillable other to subjectivity as *Here* inadvertently teaches us at the start of our game play of reading. Place is already dead in the text; it has been killed off long ago by time. Years and dates, as well as seasons and other metrics of passing experience and lost time, get stamped onto every panel for a reason. Few graphic novels are as coordinative as *Here*, which time-stamps its imaged places with strict regularity as if to hide the absorption of even the creaturely into the realm of human abstraction. What is the underlying message of panels showing blurry creatures at a shadowy time before human consciousness existed with legible dates crisply attached in captions? Just as there was a mathematics of the human at work estimating the vanishing origins of lived existence—the logic of the graphic novel seems to argue—so too will a human consciousness endure the final vanishing, outliving the materiality of that greatest of husks in the planet. Like the chickens in *March*, the Natives in *Here* cipher an impossible relation to history as rupture. But they also represent a placeholder for a desire for community, which is the same as a desire for unity, relation, and narrative coherence. It is that desire which all graphic narratives perpetuate, flouting it at times, serving it at others, but always in anticipation of a reader who will change and grow in response to instabilities essential to the form—of figure and concept, drawing and reality, selves and communities, there and here, here and then.

NOTES

Introduction

1. The term "autography" has been promoted persuasively by Gillian Whitlock (2006 and 2008) to name the subgenre or mode of autographical comics. Her term stresses the self-written and self-illustrated nature of pictorial life narratives and allows for leaner grammatical articulations than the bulkier terms "autobiographical graphic novel," as opposed to *autographics*, or "graphic memoirist," as opposed to *autographer*. Alternate terms include "autobiographix," used by comic artist Mary Fleener, "autobiocomics," or "autobioBD"—the latter an abbreviation of *Bandes Desinee*, the French term for comics. Throughout, I shall use the term "graphic memoir" interchangeably with its longer cognate, "autobiographical graphic novel." I shall continue to use "graphic memoir" or the longer construct, "autobiographical graphic novel"; although lengthy, the latter is more precise than other neologisms. Also, it should here be conceded, the term coined by Will Eisner of "graphic novel" is somewhat of a misnomer. Fictional or not, a graphic novel may be any long-form story told in the comics form, comprised of images or drawings arranged sequentially in panels or strips and often incorporating words as speech balloons or captions. Even though many comics scholars are wary of the term, the "graphic novel" is typically approached as a form or a medium, not as a genre. Rather than thinking of comics as a type or subgenre of fiction, as with the detective novel, most comics scholars think of comics as a particular means of storytelling, on a par with grander literary categories like fiction and poetry. Furthermore, graphic novels are best distinguished from comic books physically. A comic book is a pamphlet, whereas a graphic novel is bound either in hardcover or softcover like any other book able to be shelved in stores or libraries (unlike most comic books).

2. Beyond the prison, Foucault applies that panoptic concept of authorial surveillance in *Discipline and Punish* to everyday social interactions, asserting that the machinery of panopticism—systems of surveillance or display based on the panopticon—"automatizes and disindividualizes power" (202). In addition to the theorists and critics mentioned here,

I would also point to the foundational work in visual studies advanced by Jonathon Crary (1990), Martin Jay (1996), and Mieke Bal (1999).

3. For more on the contradictions that this entails, see Robin Varnum and Christina T. Gibbons's "Introduction" from *The Language of Comics: Word and Image* (xiv–xv).

4. In my approach to the division between comics form and content, I am informed by Dylan Horrocks's well-known critique of McCloud. For Horrocks, McCloud's prescriptive definition of comics as a visual medium constituted by sequentiality is a buried polemic: "McCloud uses the form as vessel metaphor primarily to suppress the perception of comics as 'a cultural idiom' (i.e. a collection of cultural conventions, styles, genres, publishing formats etc.). It allows him to separate comics from their 'content'—or history—which, as we have seen, is a primary cause of their 'ghettoization.' But it also allows him to select one element of comics ('Sequential Art') and to identify it as the 'form.' It becomes the *essential* element (the 'vessel'), and all others are merely *contingent* (things which we have the option of putting into the vessel)." See Horrocks, *Comics Journal*, no. 234 (June 2001).

5. The "pact" solicited by every autobiography, according to Lejeune, "supposes that there is *identity of name* between the author (such as he figures, by his name, on the cover), the narrator of the story, and the character who is being talked about" (12).

Chapter 1

1. This sovereign space of difference is partly influenced by Jean Baudrillard's notion of the simulacrum, since in this chapter I shall argue that some sequential relationships between panels suggest the gutter to behave as a kind of mirror, replicating as well as relating images in narrative time and space. In Baudrillard's usage, a representation ultimately preserves the "sovereign difference" between itself and its referent between the concept of a thing and the thing in reality. Simulacra, on the other hand, call both this difference and its sovereignty into question. Jean Baudrillard, *Selected Writings* (170).

2. *Mise en abyme*, French for "put into the abyss," is the miniature replication of the whole within some portion of it, a device that therefore reveals the constructedness of mediation (visual or textual). Clichéd uses of it include the picture of someone holding a picture depicting the same scene *ad infinitum.*

3. Throughout, I shall continue to use Gillian Whitlock's term (2006; 2008) "autography" to name the subgenre or sub-field of the comics known as "graphic memoir" or "graphic novel autobiography" or an even longer and less manageable cognate, "autobiographical graphic novel."

4. The phrase is Lacan's and shall be elaborated later in this chapter as a "failure" that crucially structures consciousness; for more, see Harari (84).

5. My use of the term "caricature" draws on the general distinction that "[c]aricature is not the same as cartoon. Caricature is the image, cartoon the space where figures brush up against other figures engaged in social situations" (Banta 52).

6. For a slightly different view of many of the same concerns discussed here, see Elisabeth El Refaie's *Autobiographic Comics*, which complements my notion of the I-con; in particular, El Refaie's view of autographic authority manifests most prominently through its routine multiplication as a form of "pictorial embodiment" (51).

7. For image-word relationships in comics, see McCloud; also, Carrier (61–74).

8. Ann Miller and Murray Pratt, "Transgressive Bodies in the Work of Julie Doucet, Fabrice Neaud and Jean-Christophe Menu," *Belphégor* 4.1 (2004): unpaginated.

9. See also Lucien Dällenbach, who explores the many ways in which the mirror trope signals the literary or artistic self-consciousness of the work.

10. The interpretive dilemmas arising from this unfinished business of the self and the real in comics relates to Lacan's notion of the mirror stage, which has produced surprisingly few illuminations for scholarly commentary on comics—essays cited here by Don Ault (2000), Ann Miller and Murray Pratt (2004), and Marc Singer (2008) being only a few of the notable exceptions. Neither space nor scope permit a detailed account of Jacques Lacan's famously slippery thesis on the mirror stage, but later discussions of the terror of the mirror in autobiographical graphic novels depend upon a few key points. According to Lacan, the developing child sees in the mirror a fantastically integrated object-version of the self that exists, on the other side of the mirror, in a subjective state open to all the fragmentation, disunity, and resistance to synthesis of lived reality. Anything we can communicate as identity, then, becomes a function of this dialectic between the specular image of an integrated self available only in the mirror and the desire to embody a totalizing ideal of iconic self-coherence. This desire for the integrated mirror self maps onto a familiar constellation of Oedipal prohibitions and drives: castration anxiety, the scopic drive that situates subjects within the gaze of the other, and entry into the symbolic order (see Gallop, "Lacan's 'Mirror Stage': Where to Begin"). Less a scientific explanation of identity than a phenomenology of selfhood, Lacan's theory stresses subject formation as a trade off between the ideal self of image and the one that sees and desires to be that image. This bargain is also an initiation into the symbolic order of language and time—a temporality of narrativized existence revealed as historical consciousness. A "temporal dialectic" results from the self in the mirror seeming to occupy an ideal future that therefore bears the trace of prior self-disunity (Lacan, *Ecrits* 4).

11. For a related and quite formidable study of identity and mirrors in *Persepolis*, which employs an Althusserian model of subject formation based on interpellation and ideology, see Babak Elahi, "Frames and Mirrors in Marjane Satrapi's *Persepolis*."

12. Groensteen uses the proliferation of autobiographical comics in America to argue for the centrality of considering the form a language unto itself, but in the process, suggests that this is so because just about anyone can begin to make meaning using the form, not just artists, but autobiographers. He thus undermines the aesthetic value of autobiographical comics while elevating the form: "[T]he proliferation of autobiographical comics is a remarkable phenomenon of recent years, stemming from America, where the works of Robert Crumb, Art Spiegelman, and Harvey Pekar, notably, have opened the door. This plasticity of comics, which allows them to put in place messages of every order and narrations other than the fictional, demonstrates that before being an art, comics are well and truly a language" (19).

13. To further explore the formalistic divisions invoked between these two panels from *Persepolis*, we could borrow from Thierry Groensteen's categories related to the multiplex author-function of autography from his essay "The Monstrator, the Recitant, and the Shadow of the Narrator." Applying Groensteen, we might posit that the authorial personae of the *recitant* narrates certain propositions that are radically revised by its corresponding but in no way subordinate personae of the monstrator, the one "responsible for the *putting into drawing* [mise en dessin] of the story" (4).

14. Satrapi charges parts of the iconic body with particular meanings throughout *Persepolis*, but these meanings also enfold iconic relations and oppositions. For example, the uniformity of the girls' hands at rest, their arms entwined close to the body, is obviously symbolic of social proscription; less obvious, however, is the way that later panels of Marji's self-aggrandizing authorial address inevitably show her with one finger upraised, making the upraised finger—like the eye that pierces through the veil—a metonym for voice in contrapuntal relation to this early scene of the restrained agency of the hand.

15. In *Understanding Comics*, McCloud defines closure as "the phenomenon of observing the parts but perceiving the whole" (63). Although indebted to his groundbreaking analysis of the process, I am less optimistic than his statement would suggest that a transhistorical "whole" is always universally perceived.

16. Davis's claim about Satrapi's control being intensified because her "life writing act involves actual, though stylized, self-portraiture" (271) hinges on a debatable, albeit implicit, distinction between actual and stylized self-portraiture. Is a stylized self-portrait less actual? What would a non-stylized self-portrait look like? Davis goes on to refer to two particular panels in *Persepolis* in which the self as portrait is most manifest, where "the child literally finds herself caught between the religious and the secular worlds; between tradition and technology" (272). The first occurs in the opening chapter, where the ten-year-old Marji admits, "I really didn't know what to think about the veil" (6), standing in a panel that splits her in half: one half showing a black background with gears, a ruler, and a hammer; the other, a white background with Persian adornments. The second self-portrait is of a veiled fourteen-year-old Marji wearing a denim jacket with Michael Jackson buttons (131). As with most readers, I too find these panels to be explicit acts of self-portraiture; however, I also see them as models for similar engagements performed throughout the text, where every panel that includes the author-narrator becomes the occasion for self-portraiture, actual *because* stylized.

17. Ann Miller and Murray Pratt, "Transgressive Bodies" (unpaginated).

18. *Prosopon*, Greek for "face," is the mask produced by hypostasis.

19. At this point in the argument, I wish the term "mask" to conjure many of the same foundational anxieties of represenatation Benjamin discusses in an explanatory prelude to his thesis that "[a]rt teaches us to see into things," while "[f]olk art and kitsch allow us to see outward from within things"; Benjamin goes on to claim that folk or popular arts provoke a kind of *déjà vu* in beholders that leads to a recognition of what he calls "the primal fact of the mask"—"the primitive, with all its devices and pictures, opens us to an endless arsenal of masks—the masks of our fate—by means of which we stand apart from moments and situations that have been lived through unconsciously but that are here finally reintegrated" ("Some Remarks on Folk Art" 255).

20. Barthes defines the *punctum* as a detail in a photograph "which rises from the scene, shoots out of it like an arrow, and pierces me" (*Camera Lucida* 56).

21. Obsessional behavior may illustrate this lack of the Other. According to Slavoj Žižek, the act of hiding inconsistencies in the symbolic order transfixes obsessional subjects, who "must be active all the time so that [such inconsistency] does not come to light that 'the Other does not exist'" (Žižek 1992, 35).

22. The realistic face also configures the concept Lacan refers to as *objet a*, which "in the field of the visible is the gaze" (*Four Fundamental* 105). The implications of this designation are illuminating in the context of Kochalka's work, since as *objet a*, the normative face masks even as it marks unconscious desire in the visual field. The fantasy elf-face at this moment cannot presume scopic autonomy. It is no longer the sole presence viewing its world from the self-constituting perspective of the sovereign subject.

23. In this way, comics memoirs often serve as radical exceptions to the rule, whereby the subject who speaks (the subject of enunciation) remains distinct from those spoken about (subjects of énonce). In addition to a linguistic or poststructural perspective, we could also approach this obliteration of distinctions phenomenologically, as creating an unsettling conflation of subject and object, where it is the very notion of relation or of the systematic relatedness of persons to things that is everywhere called into question in the panels of autobiographical graphic novels.

24. I am, of course, referencing Harold Bloom's classic thesis, *The Anxiety of Influence: A Theory of Poetry*.

Chapter 2

1. Because the focus of the chapter is primarily on imaginary rather than actual children, there is little need to specify age markers for the iconic child under investigation here as is sometimes done in literary analyses associated with childhood studies, which make necessary distinctions between the child (birth to twelve years old) and the youth (roughly twelve to mid-teens).

2. Erin McGlothlin uses the term "super present" to reference those exchanges in Spiegelman's *Maus* where Art and Vladek discuss the making of the comic and the process used to carry out the interviews. See McGlothlin, "No Time Like the Present" (177–98).

3. Two strong essays, in particular, inform my reading of *Persepolis*'s word-image patterning: Rocío Davis, "A Graphic Self: Comics as Autobiography in Marjane Satrapi's *Persepolis*," *Prose Studies* 27.3 (2005): 264–79; and Gillian Whitlock, "Autographics: The Seeing 'I' of the Comics," *Modern Fiction Studies* 52.4 (2006): 965–79.

4. For a thorough history of children in early comic strips, see Ian Gordon, *Comic Strips and Consumer Culture, 1890–1945*.

5. For more on the history of the Comics Code Authority, see Amy Kiste Nyberg, *Seal of Approval: The History of the Comics Code*.

6. The difficulty with which viewers may parse Arabic designs from Western indications of the avant-garde rehearses the global transmission of Islamic art by European traders that Doris Behrens-Abouseif narrates in *Beauty in Arab Culture*; ironically, this process of cultural adoption intensified "[o]nce the design was on paper, [so that] its diffusion across geographical borders and its application in a variety of materials and techniques was easy" (158). One can hardly think of an easier transmission for these design elements than Satrapi's graphic novel. Also, the breakdown of the image to fulfill so strict a division verbalized in the caption initiates a type of game mode for readers while "solving" the puzzle of this panel,

a system of comics reading related to children's activity books discussed at length in the following chapter.

7. In *Simulacra and Simulation*, Jean Baudrillard defines simulation in relation to the "cartographer's mad project of the ideal coextensivity of map and territory" (2). Here, too, as in all autobiographical graphic novels the viewer is prompted to equate image and actuality, representation and the real. Panels like this one, which function more in the style of the chart, blueprint, or map of identity, highlight this tendency for an ideal coextensivity in comics memoir.

8. My use of the term "synapsis" is informed by Giorgio Agamben's discussion in *Stanzas: Word and Phantasm in Western Culture* of Aristotle's notion of the *synapsis*, in which Agamben conceptualizes the work of metaphor (as well as caricatures, fetishes, and emblems, by the way) as containing a barrier to signification linked to the classical idea of enigma. Applying Agamben, we might see the comics' production of the space between—for which the child serves as mask—as "a connection of impossibles—not a relation of manifestations, in itself nonproblematic, between signifier and signified, but a pure barrier" (*Stanzas* 149).

9. I do not mean to suggest that the streetwise kid begins with American comics. In her landmark study of caricature, *Barbaric Intercourse: Caricature and the Culture of Conduct, 1841–1936*, Martha Banta narrates the ascendency of Victorian middle-class taste through the evolution of caricature, one proponent of which was *Punch* artist John Leech, whose work in the 1850s would "alternate charming sketches of the domestic vicissitudes of the middle class with equally charming vignettes of tattered urchins mimicking rituals of middle-and upper-class social protocol" (253). It is also in Banta where interested readers may find the most comprehensive summary of the intermingling of a nascent form of the comics and the establishment of the bourgeois; as Banta argues: "[C]omic periodicals create 'representations' in the name of the bourgeois individual of a late Habermasian world" (2).

10. I am, of course, referring here to Susan Buck-Morss's landmark essay on the function of these archetypical figures of urban modernity in the work of Walter Benjamin, particularly *The Arcades Project*, "The Flaneur, the Sandwichman and the Whore: The Politics of Loitering."

11. For an insightful reassessment of the role of the child in Benjamin's analyses, see Nicola Gess, "Gaining Sovereignty: On the Figure of the Child in Walter Benjamin's Writing."

12. An alternate type of elevated view of deific, panoptic totality takes place in *Incognegro*'s lynch scenes discussed in Chapter Five.

13. To extricate the nugget of wit from the visual chaos of the comics' page would doubtless offer at least as much satisfaction as solving a crossword puzzle, which incidentally made its debut in the exact same newspaper some fifteen years after the first appearance of the Kid. For a concise history of puzzles in US newspapers, see Coral Amende, *The Crossword Obsession: The History and Love of the World's Most Popular Pastime* (2001). For a history of the *New York World* and Joseph Pulitzer's editorial agenda, see Michael Schudson, *Discovering The News: A Social History Of American Newspapers* (91–106).

14. Although N. C. Christopher Couch's interpretations of early *Yellow Kid* strips overemphasize their mockery of the poor, Couch helpfully sums up the underlying principle of social incongruity that consistently forms the humorous basis of Outcault's work: "As with all of Outcault's cartoons in this genre, the humor, such as it is, comes not so much from

the improbability of children engaging in adult activities, but from the impossibility of such poor children ever engaging in activities of the upper classes" (70).

15. Robert S. Petersen, *Comics, Manga, and Graphic Novels: A History of Graphic Narratives* (97). Furthermore, N. C. Christopher Couch claims that the renovation of text into blocks allows for the architectural structuring of the page in *Yellow Kid* and informs the contemporary comic strip: "Recurring, recognizable characters are held within a tectonic structure formed in part by the architectural setting, but which receives its most important definition from blocks of text" (Couch, "The Yellow Kid and the Comics Page" 70).

16. Critic Jens Balzer arrives at a similar analogy between the challenge of parsing the page of the Yellow Kid and that of navigating the city, putting this relation in dialogue with Walter Benjamin's notion of becoming distracted (*zerstreut*): "The gaze of the observer trying to view a newspaper page as a whole is irritated by the seemingly incompatible expectations it finds itself confronted with" (Balzer, "'Hully Gee, I'm a Hieroglyphe'" 26).

17. While Bukatman arrives at his study via phenomenology, his point resonates with my own conclusions about the effect of contemporary graphic novels, which make ample use of a similar dynamic of the child space. With Bukatman, rather than seeing these figures and figurations as visual reflections of anything, we would do well to read them for the spaces of being that they configure, for the spaces they occupy and those they permit readers to inhabit.

18. One example may be found in Darby Orcutt, "Comics and Religion: Theoretical Connections."

19. For more on the way *Tom and Jerry* was criticized for dramatizing violence, see John Culshawm "Violence and the Cartoon," *Fortnightly*, no. 1020 (December 1951): 830–35.

20. The now-classic essay that theorizes Speigelman's circumvention of the disabling logics of mimesis is Andreas Huyssen's "Of Mice and Mimesis: Reading Spiegelman with Adorno," *New German Critique* 81 (2000): 65–82.

21. Orit Ichilov summarizes these ethnographies of the games played by Palestinian children in *Political Learning and Citizenship Education Under Conflict: The Political Socialization of Israeli and Palestinian Youngsters* (London: Routledge, 2004), 84–85.

22. The term "childish" is preferred over one with less negative connotations such as "childlike" since it retains a barbed reminder of our culture's devaluing of particular knowledges and practices over others. And it is precisely this hierarchical logic, privileging maturity over childishness, adults over children, and reality over fantasy, that Sacco's perspective disrupts.

23. Nicola Gess describes one version of Walter Benjamin's theory of the child as the positive barbarian whose dialectical play always involves the destruction of the mythic order so as to create the conditions for that which is purely new: ". . . children are the mere creatures remaining after the destruction of previous humanity: not only survivors of a humanity-devouring war, but themselves devourers of human beings in that they affirm that destruction and drive it even further. For after all, devouring humans is part of their nature. Hence, in comparison with the humanity-devouring order of war, what is present here is not an instrumental but rather a pure form of destruction: one that is only a manifestation of a drive—here both the death drive and the life drive—to the extent that what is at stake is survival of creation" (Nicola Gess, "Gaining Sovereignty" 686).

24. The woodcut novels of Masereel—*Passionate Journey* (1919)—and Ward—*God's Man* (1929)—have been discussed as forerunners of the graphic novel in David Berona, *Wordless Books: The Original Graphic Novels* (New York: Abrams, 2008). Given Baker's theme, however, a more appropriate influence may be seen in Tom Feelings's *Middle Passage: White Ships/Black Cargo* (New York: Dial, 1995).

25. My use of the lowercase "i-con" is a reference to the earlier defined term from Chapter One, where it signified a convergence of the autobiographical "I" and the visual avatar repeatedly attached to that grammatical authority. As this is a biography, I want to retain the generic and modal similarities with more personal forms of life writing, while respecting the differences as well. Nevertheless, a stronger case could be made for the possible coincidence of Baker's "I" and Turner's, which I take up in the longer essay from which this section on Baker derives: Chaney, "Slave Memory Without Words" (*Callaloo* 2013).

26. Baker directly borrows the language of Turner's inculcation of literacy from Gray in captions that float apart from the pictorial sequences in a font style reminiscent of a nineteenth-century text.

27. This is not to suggest, of course, that Baker upholds Gray's textual inscriptions of Turner. Quite to the contrary, in fact, as Andrew Kunka and Qiana Whitted have ably shown. For Whitted, Baker's recreation of Thomas Gray's pen-snapping interview at the end of the graphic novel takes to an extreme W. J. T. Mitchell's notion of ekphrastic fear or the fear of the merger of images and words: "[I]n Baker's illustration, the black figure uses his startling exegetical knowledge of the Bible to seize rhetorical control and for a fleeting moment, to rebuff the colonial gaze" (89). For Kunka, "[t]he juxtaposition of Baker's images and Gray's text is often complementary, but more often, Baker's visual narrative expands or even contradicts Gray's verbal narrative, creating a kind of antagonistic relationship between word and picture" (171).

28. We shall revisit this observation in Chapter Five with respect to *Incognegro*'s culminating scene of lynching. There, too, a traumatic but constitutive scene of race history (lynching) appears within a panel (for the first and final time in the text) alongside the image of the protagonist's face. By seeking to personalize a point of identification for readers, exuding horror for the scene, the text deploys affect as a means by which traumatic history may seem to find resolution, albeit an impossible, ineffectual one.

29. I borrow this term and the conceptual orientation towards the Middle Passage that the logic here presupposes from Daphne Brooks's *Bodies in Dissent*.

30. The unnarrated state of raw experience, which is mnemonic in this case but perceptual in the previous chapter, corresponds to the imaginary as described in Chapter One's discussion of mirrors.

31. I intend this erotics in a way analogous to the dialectical play with desire famously documented by Roland Barthes in the *Pleasures of the Text*. In Barthes's dialectic, critical readers move against the grains of desire that the plot of any fiction postulates. But here, too, is the seductive call that every text emits for the reader. In this sense, the willing reader is a desiring subject awaiting union with another desiring subject (in this case, the text—an object that becomes subject through its dialectical instrumentality in the field of desire).

32. Schrag's narrative presents a critique of the erotics of reading theorized by Jane Marcus as Sapphistry, a form of lesbian seduction that assumes a desiring female reader who

engages with a text that increasingly excludes the male from the scene of desire. *Awkward* is interesting in this light as it covers a phase of pre-labeled sexuality, where all of Ariel's represented sex involves males and much of her unexamined desire involves females. Given the fact that the first graphic image of genitalia exposes the erect penis of one of Ariel's male partners whose presence in a ménage a trois buffers Ariel's affection for another girl, the text seems to equate the gross, rough, awkward physicality of sex with masculine desire, but not necessarily with the male body, as evidenced by these opening tableaux of the bathroom and the "emotional lady." Schrag corroborates Marcus's notion of Sapphistry in her consistent equation of heartfelt, crushing love with female desire. As opposed to *Awkward*, which is adamantly queer without being politically gay, *Definition* works to "seduce us into sister-hood"—as Marcus says of Virginia Woolf—by exorcising and eventually excluding male sex altogether from the textual space of love and desire in prelude to the more graphic lesbian encounters depicted in *Potential* (Marcus, "Sapphistry" 176).

33. Not coincidentally, the same may be said of other long-running lesbian comics that parody the picaresque, such as Alison Bechdel's *Dykes to Watch Out For* and Diane DiMassa's *Hot Head Paisan: Homocidal Lesbian Terrorist*.

34. A term borrowed from Chapter One, "i-con," is hyphenated to indicate its resemblance to the mask of autography or I-con, and lowercased to respect the different contract with verisimilitude Ware's text brokers with its reader-viewers thanks to its status as fiction.

35. Ware, *Jimmy Corrigan* (unpaginated, inside front cover).

36. While *Jimmy Corrigan* is not autobiography, it possesses generic markers of life writing: the mirror scene that loads up the titular I-con, elements of family chronicle, even hints in the prefatory material of supposedly hypothetical experiences that grow hilariously specific to the author's life.

37. Using the terminology of the prior chapter, we might read the vacated father figure as a critical perspective of the symbolic dimension of reality, with the truthful masks (like caricature) functioning in the idiom of the imaginary. Therefore, while it may be said of early picaresque comic strips that they constitute an ideal reader indifferent to the symbolic order, the ideal reader here is not simply a viewer of the imaginary but actively trapped by it, without recourse to any other face of the real other than those provided by the realm of fantasy.

Chapter 3

1. *Epileptic* first appeared in French as the comic book miniseries *L'Ascension du haut mal* (1996–2003) by L'Association.

2. My analysis departs from Murray Pratt's less anxious acceptance of David B.'s art as an operative yin-yang system of balance: "Just as yang contains a memory, shadow, seed of yin, his white art contains within it a horror that perhaps comes close to his brother's degeneration into brutality" (145). Though we arrive at a similar conclusion regarding the unstable therapy that drawing provides, my focus zeroes in on the inoperative qualities of this game (which Pratt does not consider) and the model of yin-yang that is supposed to allegorize it.

3. The cryptic notion of a puzzle without a solution builds on a definitional tension in game studies between puzzles and games. In *Critical Play*, Mary Flanagan succinctly

paraphrases that tension as it is invoked in the work of Chris Crawford: "Puzzles are static; they present the player with a logical puzzle to be solved with the assistance of clues. Games, however, can evolve, and rules may shift at certain points in a game and can change with the player's actions" (6). With Flanagan and the critical gamers she studies, I approach this tension as a locus for critical intervention, since, as will be shown, David B.'s puzzle soon reveals itself to have been more of a game all along. In anticipation of that evolution of the puzzle, I shall use the terms "puzzle" and "game" somewhat interchangeably.

4. My use of the term "ludic" thus finds some accord with G. Thomas Couser's use of it in *Altered Egos: Authority in American Autobiography* to account for an "impulse" (in Mark Twain and Ben Franklin) that "seems more burlesque than autobiography: its apparent purpose is not to recount the life . . . but rather to mock certain conventions of genteel autobiographical discourse" (72). Implied in Couser's logic is the perforce dialectical and frequently reactionary nature of the ludic, which is called upon to stand insistently against a reigning discourse or an established order. It is this distinction that explains my reluctance to banish the "ludic" or the opposition it necessarily represents even after discovering many of its properties (participation, activity, interactivity, play) in its counterpart—more or less ordinary forms of reading and narration.

5. What I am here describing as an effect of narrative coherence and causality, Murray Pratt envisions—in a rousing and rich exegesis—as the carrying forward of the autobiographical subject: "[T]he auto/biographical comic, generically characterized by sequentiality (in the play of same and difference, *fort* and *da*), the iconic charge of the repeatedly (re-) drawn figure, and the interplay of the visual and verbal, permits a self-embodiment that carries forward into the present, rather than delimits and measures in the past the traces of conflict, trauma, antagonism and change across generations" (134).

6. In *Graphic Women*, Chute insightfully analyzes the gender politics and form of *Naked Ladies*, demonstrating how the book "involves but decentralizes the self" (104) and uses its coloring book structure, "which implies interactivity and participation, [as] a metaphor for the book's central suggestion: its readers 'fill in' the narrative with their own experience" (105).

7. My argument about the materiality of the embedded play spaces in graphic novels as well as my inclusion of Shiga's *Meanwhile* are inspired by Aaron Kashtan's short essays and conference talks on Shiga, digital comics, and materiality. See Kashtan's "Digital Comics and Material Richness," *Comic Forum*, July 12, 2013, in which he briefly touches on the e-book version of *Meanwhile* and its use "of the touchscreen interface to create a new and distinctive version of the 'choose your own adventure' mechanic that was the primary selling point of the book on which it was based."

8. Julia Round observes how the infectious symmetry of *Watchmen*'s fifth chapter combines "signifying possibility . . . with regularity" in order to present "page layout . . . in terms of ornamentation, function, and scaffolding" (66).

9. Many contemporary games studies critics opt for a less vehement treatment of narrative and narratologists than was practiced during the so-called ludology-narratology debates of the first decade of the twenty-first century. Many of the key participants on the side of the ludologists (Frasca, Espen Aarseth) are prone to downplay or even deny that there ever was a debate. Nevertheless, ludologist scholarship earnestly defends the signifying properties as

well as the significance of the game (the *ludus*) from the perceived encroachments of nar-ratologists, who seemed equally eager to colonize games under the banner of narration and textuality. For an overview, see Jan Simons, "Narrative, Games, and Theory" (2007).

10. In her discussion of the same issue, Hannah Miodrag takes gentle issue with Hat-field's complementary reaction to McCloud's celebration of comics' "demand for active interpretation" and "participation" (McCloud 1993, 136) over and above Iser's claims for read-ing more generally: ". . . Hatfield does so with characteristic hyperbole, stating that comics are intrinsically *more* fractured and thus inherently *more* demanding of active participation than prose (Hatfield 2005, xiv)" (67, emphasis in original). This chapter dwells at the extreme edge of this argument, where the degree of participation demanded is unquestionably greater than for reading traditional print narrative. And considering my subsequent analysis of the comics trope of the reader's hands in the margins, it seems clear that forays into the ludic are not so much about venturing away from or outside of the form as they are about returning to its core.

11. It is at this point that some may wonder about the inherent puzzle-solving properties of certain non-narrative literature. In *Literary Fiction: The Ways We Read Narrative Litera-ture*, Geir Farner runs into more trouble when attempting to differentiate the "the precise boundary between literary and non-literary cognitive activity" (293), which, in his example, concerns the puzzle-solving aspects of "reading" the incomprehensibility of modernist texts: "This process-oriented cognitive function [what some would associate with the *ludus*] cor-responds to puzzle-solving in general, like crossword puzzles, mathematical problems or chess problems, and is not literary in the traditional sense of the word. However, there is a gradual transition from pure puzzle-solving to the analysis of causality and ethical, psycho-logical, sociological, political, philosophical and religious problems . . ." (293). One wonders just how many other parameters of significance could be added to this list, predicated as it is not on any observation of intrinsic modalities but rather on a principle of negation, so that the non-literary space of the puzzle is defined in relation to all the types of thinking it is presupposed to lack. Graphic novels routinely flout this standard prejudice.

12. In addition to Auerbach's classic study, my notion of mimesis in this context departs from Andreas Huyssen's use of the term, in relation to Speigelman's negotiation of Adornian mimesis, which Huyssen describes with striking resemblances to my category of the ludic, as "a becoming or making similar, a movement toward, never a reaching of a goal" (127). While this discrepancy exists at the level of definition, in practice my use of the ludic as the unfinished super-interior of pure mimesis stresses physical extremes of "becoming" that remain abstractions for Huyssen. My use of the term "mimesis," by contrast, is more in line with that of Karin Kukkonen: "the experiential and referential 'reality' [a text] projects" (43); and is especially informed by Isaac Cates's important consideration of the different Aristo-telian applicability of comics images compared to captions: "The visual aspect of a comic is straightforward mimesis or imitation, in the Aristotelian sense. As Aristotle uses these terms, the only diegetic element of a comic would be its narrative captions" (102 n.1).

13. In *Graphic Women*, Chute further explores the meaning of hands in the work of Lynda Barry, where "attention to the hand represents Barry's obvious respect for handcraft—and also a passionate project of demystification; she not only wants to call our attention to the body in the text as it writes, but she also wants to *show* us that act of writing" (121).

14. See Katalin Orban's *Ethical Diversions* for a brief but brilliant interpretation of the psychoanalytic effects of Spiegelman's use of hands (which shapes my own analysis): "The visual motif of hands potentially connects the reader's 'carnal' hand—holding *Maus* just as Art is seen holding 'Prisoner'—with Anja's then warm palm touching Art in 1958, but only through the tenuous abysmal recession, the laughing cow effect of the intervening hands" (63). Also, in "Shaking Hands with Other People's Pain," Rebecca Scherr reads the handshake in Joe Sacco's *Palestine* "as a visual metonym for the process of haptic readership" (21). Scherr persuasively argues that Sacco's preoccupation with oversized hands demonstrate "how bodily gestures can have primacy over text" (23). For more on comics and handwriting, see Gene Kannenberg, Jr.'s "Graphic Text, Graphic Context," which demonstrates how lettering in autography—what he calls the "'alternative' or 'small press' marketplace"—allows artists to "mark such comics as unique, personal creations produced by a single hand" (177).

15. These claims grow out of the energizing linkages Svetlana Alpers makes between touch and vision in light of Rembrandt's fascination with depicted hands "as the embodiment of sight" (25).

16. Few critics are as theoretically astute nor as lucid on the subject of witnessing in autobiography as Leigh Gilmore, who, in *The Limits of Autobiography*, emphasizes the co-implication of psychological and juridical forces at work in such generic moments of confession and testimonial: "Because testimonial projects require subjects to confess, to bear witness, to make public and shareable a private and intolerable pain, they enter into a legalistic frame in which their efforts can move quickly beyond their interpretation and control, become exposed as ambiguous, and therefore subject to judgments about their veracity and worth . . ." (7). The illustrated hands increase the material registration of the reader-viewer's presence relative to the testimony being given. These hands are ludic, in part, because that juridical and psychological work that the reader's presence, by way of the drawings, is invited to perform is rendered extra-narrational by their appearance. Hands and lifelike fingers in the margins thus reveal the essential activity of witnessing over and beyond reading.

17. Denasi's observations anticipate Michael Leja's claims connecting US newspaper picture puzzles of the early twentieth century to an increasing emphasis on visual skepticism, in which "every participant in the new mass culture, every beneficiary of modern science and technology . . . had to process visual experience with some measure of suspicion, caution, and guile" (1).

18. In this way, David B.'s picture puzzle fits Linda Haverty Rugg's concept of the *Vexierbild* or rebus, the picture that puzzles, which she reads through Walter Benjamin: "Such picture puzzles thus demand a revocation of accustomed systems of reference between the written and signified, the written and spoken" (138). Although David B.'s puzzle is not a rebus and therefore less focused on the blurring of the phonetic and the indexical, it strives nevertheless for a similar destabilization of signification. We might, in fact, read it as a version of a reverse rebus, as Rugg defines it, with "words meant to be read as images" (138) or, in the case of David B.'s picture puzzle, images schematized as oppositions. Interestingly, Rugg arrives at the conclusion that Benjamin's penchant for textual fragmentation "pushes" the autobiographical text "toward the surreal" (149), linking it further to David B. and his effort to use "the fragments of the past [to] find reactivation . . ." (Rugg 149–50).

19. Gonzalo Frasca's evolved distinction between games that include more open-ended forms of play, what he calls *paidia*, and those that are more rule-based, *ludus*, seems applicable here. According to Frasca, "the difference between *paidia* and *ludus* is that the latter incorporates rules that define a winner and a loser, whereas the former does not" (230). This means that David B.'s game announces itself as *ludus*, in which "the player's goals are clear: you must do X in order to reach Y and therefore become a winner" (230). But after a few rounds of attempted play, the gamer transforms into a player and the puzzle is revealed to be *paidia*, in the sense that it—in Frasca's words—"leaves its main goal up to the player" (231).

Chapter 4

1. The seeming dearth of *künstlerroman* may be due to a categorical shift in the terms of classification. That is to say, the *künstlerroman* or artist's story of development—subgenre of the standard coming-of-age model in the *Bildungsroman*—may still be seen as a vital subgenre of life writing by known figures, those possessing celebrity status to some degree.

2. I use the terms "Romantic" and "neo-Romantic" interchangeably to name a cluster of aesthetic, literary, political, and ideological tendencies and convictions, predominantly associated with the early nineteenth century but in no way limited to that period. The Romantic principle I want to conjure, in particular, has to do with the transformative powers of texts, as expounded by Carmen Casaliggi and Paul March-Russell in their introduction to *Legacies of Romanticism*, which identifies a sensibility of paradox as the first legacy of Romanticism; the second legacy points to mixed media and textual transformability: "The variability of the text—in the case of the self-sufficient fragment or the mixed media of word and image in the example of William Blake—is a second legacy that potentially may be described as Romantic. Such spontaneity expressed the alleged vitality of literary construction: the organic metaphor . . ." (6). Autography's applicable investments include a formal plasticity and a fascination for texts so rooted in organicity that they everywhere dissolve boundaries between authors and works, work and life.

3. The thesis of Chapter Two on the inherent juvenility of comics is also at play here, motivating my conception of capitalism as youth and of an equally fantastic possibility of viewing the artist as *the* artist, as a master or maestro, a maker in a naively absolute sense.

4. The context for "effectivity" in this case also conforms with Terry Eagleton's discussion of speech act theory, which assumes the "effectivity" or reality effects of utterances as "as actions in their own right" (103). The connection helps to explain the effectivity of literature: "[L]iterature restores to us this sense of linguistic performance in the most dramatic way, for whether what it asserts as existing actually exists or not is unimportant" (103).

5. There is indeed a quantitative basis for the connection between *künstlerroman* and fluctuations in national economies. Tobias Boes analyzes the frequency of artist novels published in Germany throughout the nineteenth and twentieth centuries, noting that works featuring "characters [who] withdraw from social pressures into the essentially spiritual sphere of the arts" decline during periods of increased economic or nationalizing activity, "surg[ing] in frequency whenever the general trajectory of modernization was disrupted by economic, political, or military events" (275).

6. This observation alone is worth further study—why the *künstlerroman* received relatively less scholarly consideration than other genres? My curiosity is bolstered by the fact that the 1922 thesis of celebrated Frankfurt School theorist Herbert Marcuse on the *künstlerroman* is not widely available in an English translation.

7. The designation "colophon" once indicated merely the scribe's identification of the place or date of production, but its usage has expanded—thanks to an increase in scholarly interest for images "of the scribe or author when they are the same individual wherever such images appear in" medieval manuscripts (Rejaie n.2).

8. This differentiation into types is not intended to claim appreciable differences in the meaning of the poses relative to the spiritual value the scribes depicted. Rather, I want to suggest that a greater degree of self-reflexivity does inhere in the colophon of the working scribe. This view is in line with Jonathan J. G. Alexander's asseverations in *Medieval Illuminators and Their Methods of Work* regarding Isidorus, a scribe of Padua, who shows himself at work: "His pen is once again on the letter 'x' of 'finxit,' in a clever conceit which draws attention both to his making of the manuscript ('finxit'—he made it) and shows him as if in the process of actually writing it" (18).

9. Although she does not consider the colophon, Elisabeth El Refaie comments on medieval art in another context, corroborating the significance I place on line of sight in such representations: "Medieval painters were particularly creative in developing new ways of conveying consecutive moments, including the orientation of figures so that each one is looking towards the next event in a series . . ." (117).

10. The pensive version of the colophon may be understood, following Jacques Derrida's interpretation of drawn self-portraiture in general, as an extroversion of drawing: ". . . the origin of drawing. Or, if you prefer, *the thought of drawing,* a certain pensive pose . . ." (3, italics in original).

11. Summarizing the work of Peter Zima, John David Pizer notes the shift in *künstlerroman,* from the early twentieth century "utopian and idealist dimension of the genre . . . where art can still be articulated as a weapon against the bourgeois utilitarianism of the father's generation" (8) to the contemporary moment, which embraces parody as the vehicle for a "broad critique of aesthetic idealism" (9). We can see the latter in effect throughout Doucet's autography.

12. J. Hillis Miller in *The Medium is the Maker* clarifies the issue with remarkable lucidity: "When tables stand on their heads, they conceive grotesque ideas, presumably Marx's name here for the ideological mystifications of commodity fetishism. These ideas, says Marx, are far more wonderful and 'transcendent' than what spiritualist mediums were claiming to make or to allow tables to do, under the guidance of the spirits" (20).

13. This is "phenomenology" in the classical sense, which ensures the coherence and centrality of the perceiving subject, as noted by Terry Eagleton when he complains of "the old 'intending subject' of phenomenology" (*Literary Theory* 103).

14. To consider how the self-portrait specifically abridges the psychoanalytic concerns of the mirror from the first chapter, I am most indebted to Young-Paik Chun's interpretation of Cézanne; specifically, her theorization of the way the self-portrait "allows us to face a moment of the capitation of the mirror phase through a suspension of its mechanism, and visualizes an internalized form of alienation. This is staged in the wide gap between the specular image and the represented image" (119).

15. These plot anomalies in *Stitches* may also be indicative of the ways in which the *künstlerroman* disavows its own ideological investments in competition and labor, veiling them behind themes of family, individuality, and education. In *Upward Mobility and the Common Good*, Bruce Robbins argues that most narratives of artists and writers finding their vocations deny their own patently economic ambitions, even in "the most reflexive or inward-looking treatments of the writer's formation [which] are often oblique treatments of upward mobility" (128).

16. For a slightly different discussion of the meaning of the autographic text's materiality, Elisabeth El Refaie reasons that the "action of turning the page may also be associated with temporal meaning" (132) in comics, insinuating that authorial labor may be part of the "different phases [that] leave traces in the finished product, which can be exploited by those comics creators who, for whatever reason, want to draw attention to the creative process" (132). For our purposes, the personal motivations for self-portraiture are less significant than their symbolization. Our question is not why individual artists would "want to draw attention to the creative process" but rather what the effect is of such an act and what cultural and material discourses does that act invoke, depend upon, and disavow?

17. The "cartoonal simplification" of the drawing style helps Spiegelman to accomplish a number of narrative effects, according to Charles Hatfield: first, it contrasts the aesthetic and epistemological priorities of documentary photorealism (which appear throughout *Maus* in verbal, aural, and diagrammatic historical details); second, it abstracts characters into "collective rather than individual identities"; and third, it helps Spiegelman to "avoid making the material banal" (145)

18. For more on Philippe Lejeune and the autobiographical pact in autography, see Elisabeth El Refaie's *Autobiographic Comics*, which offers a slightly different view of the ways graphic memoir exceed Lejeune's theories about the juridical identicality of the three domains of author, narrator, and protagonist being unified, noting that "a few graphic memoirists use pseudonyms or give their autobiographical alter egos a different name" (146). Although strictly true, the real trouble comics add to Lejeune's notion of the bargain stems from the property of the I-con to operate, always on some level, as an obvious fiction. It is precisely those founding generic assumptions of self-coherence and self-consciousness that autobiographical comics—at least at the level of their pictoriality—necessarily reject.

19. A complement to Bloch's thesis, which locates the represented community for the artist of the *künstlerroman* at an unreachable endpoint, is Jonathan Goldman's view of the *künstlerroman* as a genre that "understands experience as continual, uninterrupted, and cumulative, revisited only in memory" (70).

Chapter 5

1. Hortense J. Spillers, "Mama's Baby, Papa's Maybe: An American Grammar Book," *Diacritics* 17.2 (1987): 72.

2. Greg M. Smith observes the economic assumptions concerning professional privilege that inform the classic trope of the superhero's secret identity, a splitting that is "not necessarily a monstrous amalgamation or a simple fantasy split or an irreconcilable difference

between two orientations [. . . but an] interconnection between two necessary modes of her-
oism" ("The Superhero as Labor" 135). For Smith, this split encompasses that of the outlaw
hero, who defies dominant mores, and that of the Organization Man, who upholds them.

3. For more on passing, see Hazel Carby's *Reconstructing Womanhood*.

4. Caron's more optimistic claim is that Pleece's deliberate obfuscation of the visual
markers of race aver how images "can be just as indeterminate as language" (149), and that
even where "recognizable manifestations of racial difference" occur, Pleece includes them
"without placing value judgments upon them" (155).

5. By *communitas*, I mean to invoke Esposito's new etymological theory of the term:
"From here it emerges that *communitas* is the totality of persons united not by a 'property'
but precisely by an obligation or a debt; not by an 'addition' *[piii]* but by a 'substraction' \
meno: by a lack, a limit that is configured as an onus, or even as a defective modality for
him who is 'affected,' unlike for him who is instead 'exempt' *[esente]* or 'exempted'" (6).

6. My understanding of the significance of the viewer's perspectival recession is informed
by James Porter's notion, developed in a different context, that "the farther one's perspective
recedes from material reality, the more sublime does that perspective appear to be" (59).

7. I borrow these terms from Barthes's *Camera Lucida*, in which *studium* refers to con-
ventionalized and impersonal photography common to newspapers (25–28), while *punctum*
names the detail that cuts through the generic properties of a photography to move, wound,
or arrest the viewer (27; 43–56).

8. Elsewhere, I take this point further, arguing that Anderson's strategy of literally drawing on the photos that he must *draw from* as historical references "posits value based on
a fundamental codependence between the archival images comprising King's life and the
graphic novel's mechanics for recirculating, re-framing, and re-animating them. *King* not
only recollects the photographic "facts" of King's life, it also lays bare the processes of public memory and hagiographic memorialization that constitute these images as facts at all"
(Chaney, "Drawing on History" 180).

9. In an analysis of the historical legacies of the minstrel show and other derogatory
visualizations of black embodiment, Lindon Barrett reasons that a countervailing priori-
tization of music predominates African American cultural production: "Given this situation—because African Americans are in this disbarred from meaningful participation in
the sense-making activity of vision, are confronted with vision as a hostile realm of significance—one might argue that the priority of a musical legacy attests to African American
populations' turning earnestly, ingeniously, and with marked success to the less privileged
sense-making medium of sound" (217).

10. In addition to sanctifying black nonviolence and celebrating deliverance, the Great
Flood in an African American context necessarily invokes Noah's vituperative castigation
of Ham, a scriptural curse that could be readily called upon by those would essentialize
or bedevil the meaning of African American embodiment for centuries. And yet, as Craig
Prentiss has argued, by the time of the Harlem Renaissance, "African Americans had suc-
cessfully inverted the stigma associated with the mythology and transformed their imagined
link to Ham into a source of racial pride" (154).

WORKS CITED

Adams, Timothy Dow. *Light Writing and Life Writing: Photography in Autobiography*. Chapel Hill: University of North Carolina Press, 1999.

Adorno, Theodor W. *Aesthetic Theory*. 1970. New York: A&C Black, 2013.

Agamben, Giorgio. *Stanzas: Word and Phantasm in Western Culture*. Trans. Ronald Martinez. Minneapolis: University of Minnesota Press, 1993.

Alexander, Jonathan J. G. *Medieval Illuminators and Their Methods of Work*. New Haven: Yale University Press, 1992.

Alpers, Svetlana. *Rembrandt's Enterprise: The Studio and the Market*. Chicago: University of Chicago Press, 1988.

Amende, Coral. *The Crossword Obsession: The History and Love of the World's Most Popular Pastime*. New York: Berkley Trade, 2001.

Anderson, Ho Che. *King*. Seattle: Fantagraphics Books, 2005.

Aristotle, *Poetics*. Trans. S. H. Butcher. New York: Hill and Wang, 1961.

Asante, Molefi Kete. *Afrocentricity: The Theory of Social Change (Revised and Expanded)*. Chicago: African American Images, 2003.

Ault, Don. "'Cutting Up' Again Part II: Lacan on Barks on Lacan." In *Comics and Culture*, eds. Anne Magnussen and Hans-Christian Christiansen. Copenhagen: Museum Tusculanum Press, 2000.

B., David. *Epileptic*. Trans. Kim Thompson. New York: Pantheon, 2005.

Bada, Valérie. *Mnemopoetics: Memory and Slavery in African American Drama*. New York: Peter Lang, 2008.

Baker, Kyle. *Nat Turner*. New York: Abrams, 2008.

Bakhtin, M. M. *Art and Answerability: Early Philosophical Essays*. 1919. Eds. Michael Holquist and Vadim Liapunov. Austin: University of Texas Press, 1990.

Bal, Mieke. *Quoting Caravaggio: Contemporary Art, Preposterous History*. Chicago: University of Chicago Press, 1999.

Balzer, Jens. "'Hully Gee, I'm a Hieroglyphe'—Mobilizing the Gaze and the Invention of Comics in New York City, 1895." In *Comics and the City: Urban Space in Print, Picture and Sequence*, eds. Jörn Ahrens and Arno Meteling. New York: Continuum, 2010. 19–31.

Banta, Martha. *Barbaric Intercourse: Caricature and the Culture of Conduct, 1841–1936*. Chicago: University of Chicago Press, 2003.

Barrett, Lindon. *Blackness and Value: Seeing Double*. Cambridge: Cambridge University Press, 1999.

Barry, Lynda. *One Hundred Demons*. Seattle: Sasquatch Books, 2002.

Barthes, Roland. *Camera Lucida: Reflections on Photography*. Trans. Richard Howard. New York: Hill and Wang, 1981.

——. *Image Music Text*. Trans. Stephen Heath. New York: Hill and Wang, 1977.

Baudrillard, Jean. *Selected Writings*. Ed. Mark Poster. Stanford: Stanford University Press, 1988.

——. *Simulacra and Simulation*. Trans. Sheila Faria Glaser. Ann Arbor: University of Michigan Press, 1994.

——. *The Transparency of Evil: Essays on Extreme Phenomena*. Trans. J. Benedict. London: Verso, 1993.

Bechdel, Alison. *Fun Home: A Family Tragicomic*. New York: Houghton Mifflin Harcourt, 2006.

Behrens-Abouseif, Doris. *Beauty in Arab Culture*. Princeton, NJ: Markus Wiener Publishers, 1999.

Benjamin, Walter. *The Arcades Project*. Trans. Howard Eiland and Kevin McLaughlin. Cambridge: Belknap/Harvard University Press, 1999.

——. "Some Remarks on Folk Art." (1929) In *Work of Art in the Age of its Technological Reproducibility and Other Writings on Media*. Cambridge: Belknap/Harvard University Press, 2008. 254–56.

——. "Theses on the Philosophy of History." *Illuminations*. Ed. Hannah Arendt. Trans. Harry Zohn. New York: Schocken, 1969. 253–64.

Berger, John. *Ways of Seeing*. London: Penguin, 1972.

Bloom, Harold. *The Anxiety of Influence: A Theory of Poetry*. New York: Oxford University Press, 1973.

Boes, Tobias. "Vocations of the Novel: Distant Reading Occupational Change in Nineteenth-Century German Literature." In *Distant Readings: Topologies of German Culture in the Long Nineteenth Century*, eds. Matt Erlin, et al. New York: Camden House, 2014. 259–84.

Brathwaite, Kamau. *The Zea Mexican Diary: 7 September 1926–7 September 1986*. Madison: University of Wisconsin Press, 1993.

Brooks, Daphne. *Bodies in Dissent: Spectacular Performances of Race and Freedom, 1850–1910*. Durham: Duke University Press, 2006.

Buck-Morss, Susan. "Dream Worlds of Mass Culture: Walter Benjamin's Theory of Modernity and the Dialectics of Seeing." In *Modernity and the Hegemony of Vision*, ed. David Michael Levin. Berkeley: University of California Press, 1993. 309–338.

——. "The Flaneur, the Sandwichman and the Whore: The Politics of Loitering." *New German Critique* 39 (1986): 99–140.

Bukatman, Scott. *The Poetics of Slumberland: Animated Spirits and the Animating Spirit*. Berkeley: University of California Press, 2012.

Butler, Judith. "The Force of Fantasy: Feminism, Mapplethorpe, and Discursive Excess." *Differences* 2 (1990): 105–106.

Callahan, Allen Dwight. *The Talking Book: African Americans and the Bible.* New Haven: Yale University Press, 2006.

Carby, Hazel. *Reconstructing Womanhood: The Emergence of the Afro-American Woman Novelist.* New York: Oxford University Press, 1987.

Caron, Tim. "'Black and White and Read All Over': Representing Race in Mat Johnson and Warren Pleece's *Incognegro: A Graphic Mystery.*" In *Comics and the U.S. South,* eds. Qiana J. Whitted and Brannon Costello. Jackson: University Press of Mississippi, 2012. 138–60.

Carrier, David. *The Aesthetics of Comics.* University Park: University of Pennsylvania Press, 2000.

Casaliggi, Carmen, and Paul March-Russell. "Introduction." In *Legacies of Romanticism: Literature, Culture, Aesthetics,* eds., Carmen Casaliggi and Paul March-Russell. New York: Routledge, 2012. 1–14.

Cates, Isaac. "Comics and the Grammar of Diagrams." In *The Comics of Chris Ware: Drawing is a Way of Thinking,* eds. David M. Ball and Martha B. Kuhlman. Jackson: University Press of Mississippi, 2010. 90–104.

———. "The Diary Comic." In *Graphic Subjects: Critical Essays on Graphic Novels and Autobiography,* ed. Michael A. Chaney. Madison: University of Wisconsin Press, 2010. 209–226.

Cavitch, Max. "Interiority and Artifact: Death and Self-Inscription in Thomas Smith's *Self-Portrait.*" *Early American Literature* 37.1 (2002): 89–117.

Chaney, Michael A. "Drawing on History in Recent African American Graphic Novels." *MELUS: The Journal of the Society for the Study of the Multi-Ethnic Literature of the United States.* 32.3 (2007): 175–200.

———. "Slave Memory Without Words in Kyle Baker's *Nat Turner.*" *Callaloo* 36.2 (2013): 279–97.

Chun, Young-Paik. "Melancholia and Cézanne's Portraits: Faces Beyond the Mirror." In *Psychoanalysis and the Image: Transdisciplinary Perspectives,* ed. Griselda Pollock. Malden, MA: Blackwell Publishing, 2006. 94–126.

Chute, Hillary L. *Graphic Women: Life Narrative and Contemporary Comics.* New York: Columbia University Press, 2010.

———. "Materializing Memory: Lynda Barry's *One Hundred Demons.*" In *Graphic Subjects: Critical Essays on Autobiography and Graphic Novels,* ed. Michael A. Chaney. Madison: University of Wisconsin Press, 2011. 282–309.

Cole, Phillip. *The Myth of Evil: Demonizing the Enemy.* New York: Praeger, 2006.

Cone, James. *A Black Liberation Theology.* 1986. New York: Orbis, 2010.

Couser, G. Thomas. *Altered Egos: Authority in American Autobiography.* New York: Oxford University Press, 1989.

Couch, N. C. Christopher. "The Yellow Kid and the Comics Page." In *The Language of Comics: Word and Image,* eds. Robin Varnum and Christina T. Gibbons. Jackson: University Press of Mississippi, 2001. 60–74.

Cruz, Anne J. *Discourses of Poverty: Social Reform and the Picaresque Novel in Early Modern Spain.* Toronto: University of Toronto Press, 1999.

Cumming, Robert. *Art: The World's Greatest Paintings Explored and Explained.* London: ADK Publishing Book, 1995.

Dällenbach, Lucien. *The Mirror in the Text*. Trans. Jeremy Whitley with Emma Hughes. Chicago: University of Chicago Press, 1989.

Danesi, Marcel. *The Puzzle Instinct: The Meaning of Puzzles in Human Life*. Bloomington: Indiana University Press, 2002.

Davis, David Brion. *Slavery and Human Progress*. Oxford: Oxford University Press, 1984.

Davis, Rocío G. "A Graphic Self: Comics as Autobiography in Marjane Satrapi's *Persepolis*." *Prose Studies* 27.3 (2005): 264–79.

DeFazio, Kimberly. *The City of the Senses: Urban Culture and Urban Space*. New York: Palgrave Macmillan, 2011.

De Man, Paul. "Autobiography as De-facement." *Modern Language Notes* 94 (1979): 919–30.

Derrida, Jacques. *Memoirs of the Blind: The Self-Portrait and Other Ruins*. Chicago: University of Chicago Press, 1993.

Di Liddo, Annalisa. *Alan Moore: Comics as Performance, Fiction as Scalpel*. Jackson: University Press of Mississippi, 2009.

Doolan, Patrick. *Recovering the Icon: The Life & Work of Leonid Ouspensky*. Crestwood, NY: St. Vladimir's Seminary Press, 2008.

Doucet, Julie. *My New York Diary*. Montreal: Drawn & Quarterly Publications, 1999.

Dunn, Sydni. "The Amazing Adventures of the Comic-Book Dissertator." *Chronicle of Higher Education*, February 28, 2014.

Eagleton, Terry. *Literary Theory: An Introduction*. New York: John Wiley & Sons, 2011.

Eakin, Paul John. *How Our Lives Become Stories: Making Selves*. Ithaca: Cornell University Press, 1999.

Eberstadt, Fernanda. "God Looked Like Marx." *New York Times*, May 11, 2003.

Edwards, Caroline. "Uncovering the 'Gold-Bearing Rubble': Ernst Bloch's Literary Criticism." In *Utopianism, Modernism, and Literature in the Twentieth Century*, eds. Alice Reeve-Tucker and Nathan Waddell. New York: Palgrave MacMillan, 2013. 182–203.

Egan, Susanna. *Mirror Talk: Genres of Crisis in Contemporary Autobiography*. Chapel Hill: University of North Carolina Press, 1999.

Eisner, Will. *Comics as Sequential Art*. Tamarac, FL: Poorhouse Press, 2003.

Elahi, Babak. "Frames and Mirrors in Marjane Satrapi's *Persepolis*." *Symploke* 15.1-2 (2008): 312–25.

El Refaie, Elisabeth. *Autobiographical Comics: Life Writing in Pictures*. Jackson: University Press of Mississippi, 2012.

Esposito, Roberto. *Communitas: The Origin and Destiny of Community*. Trans. Timothy Campbell. Stanford: Stanford University Press, 2010.

Farner, Geir. *Literary Fiction: The Ways We Read Narrative Literature*. London: Bloomsbury, 2014.

Fass, Paula. *Children of a New World: Society, Culture, and Globalization*. New York: New York University Press, 2007.

Flanagan, Mary. *Critical Play: Radical Game Design*. Boston: MIT Press, 2009.

Foster, John Bellamy, and Robert W. McChesney. *The Endless Crisis: How Monopoly-Finance Capital Produces Stagnation and Upheaval from the U.S.A. to China*. New York: New York University Press, 2012.

Frasca, Gonzalo. "Simulation Versus Narrative: Introduction to Ludology." In *The Video Game Theory Reader*, eds. Mark J. P. Wolf, et al. New York, Routledge, 2003. 221–35.

Fuery, Kelli. *New Media: Culture and Image*. New York: Palgrave MacMillan, 2009.

Galavaris, George. *The Icon in the Life of the Church: Doctrine, Liturgy, Devotion*. Leiden: E. J. Brill, 1981.

Gallop, Jane. "Lacan's 'Mirror Stage': Where to Begin." *SubStance* 37–38 (1983): 118–28.

Garcia, Christopher. "James Kochalka: Trans Media Superstar, An Interview with a Cutesy Elf at Heart." *Fanboy Planet*, July 12, 2008. <http://www.fanboyplanet.com/interviews/cg-jameskochalka.php>.

Gardner, Jared. "Archives, Collectors, and the New Media Work of Comics." *Modern Fiction Studies* 52 (2006): 787–806.

———. *Projections: Comics and the History of Twenty-First-Century Storytelling*. Stanford: Stanford University Press, 2012.

Genette, Gérard. *Narrative Discourse: An Essay in Method*. Trans. Jane E. Lewin. Ithaca: Cornell University Press, 1980.

Gess, Nicola. "Gaining Sovereignty: On the Figure of the Child in Walter Benjamin's Writing." *Modern Language Notes* 125.3 (2010): 682–708.

Gilmore, Leigh. *The Limits of Autobiography: Trauma and Testimony*. Ithaca: Cornell University Press, 2001.

Goldberg, Michelle. "Who's Afraid of Virginia Woolf? The Ayatollahs Are." *Salon.com*, May 5, 2003.

Goldman, Jonathan. *Modernism Is the Literature of Celebrity*. Austin: University of Texas Press, 2011.

Gordon, Ian. *Comic Strips and Consumer Culture, 1890–1945*. Washington, DC: Smithsonian Institution Press, 1998.

Groensteen, Thierry. "The Monstrator, the Recitant, and the Shadow of the Narrator." *European Comic Art* 3.1 (2010): 1–21.

———. *The System of Comics*. Trans. Bart Beaty and Nick Nguyen. Jackson: University Press of Mississippi, 2007.

Gurfinkle, Helena. *Outlaw Fathers in Victorian and Modern British Literature: Queering Patriarchy*. New York: Rowman and Littlefield, 2014.

Halberstam, Judith. *In A Queer Time and Place: Transgender Bodies, Subcultural Lives*. New York: New York University Press, 2005.

Harari, Roberto. *Lacan's Four Fundamental Concepts of Psychoanalysis: An Introduction*. Trans. Judith Filc. New York: Other Press, 2004.

Haraway, Donna Jeanne. *When Species Meet*. Minneapolis: University of Minnesota Press, 2007.

Harris, William Conley. *Queer Externalities: Hazardous Encounters in American Culture*. Albany: State University of New York Press, 2009.

Hartley, George. *The Abyss of Representation: Marxism and the Postmodern Sublime*. Durham: Duke University Press, 2003.

Hatfield, Charles. *Alternative Comics: An Emerging Literature*. Jackson: University Press of Mississippi, 2005.

Haverty, Linda Rugg. *Picturing Ourselves: Photography and Autobiography*. Chicago: University of Chicago Press, 1997.

Heater, Brian. "Interview: James Kochalka Pt. 2 (of 3)." *Daily Cross Hatch*, February 22, 2007. <http://www.thedailycrosshatch.com/2007/02/22/interview-james-kochalka-pt-2-of-3/>.

Horstkotte, Silke, and Nancy Pedri. "Focalization in Graphic Narrative." *Narrative* 19.3 (2011): 330–57.

Hutcheon, Linda. "Postmodern Provocation: History and 'Graphic' Literature." *Torre: Revista de la Universitad de Puerto Rico* 2.4–5 (1997): 299–308.

Huyssen, Andreas. *Present Pasts: Urban Palimpsests and the Politics of Memory*. Stanford: Stanford University Press, 2003.

Inge, M. Thomas. *Comics as Culture*. Jackson: University Press of Mississippi, 1990.

Iser, Wolfgang. *The Act of Reading: A Theory of Aesthetic Response*. London: Routledge, 1978.

———. *The Implied Reader*. Baltimore: Johns Hopkins University Press, 1974.

Jacobs, Dale. *Graphic Encounters: Comics and the Sponsorship of Multimodal Literacy*. New York: Bloomsbury Academic, 2013.

Jameson, Fredric. "Cognitive Mapping." In *Marxism and the Interpretation of Culture*, eds. Cary Nelson and Lawrence Grossberg. Urbana: University of Illinois Press, 1988. 347–60.

———. "Imaginary and Symbolic in Lacan: Marxism, Psychoanalytic Criticism, and the Problem of the Subject." *Yale French Studies* 55/56 (1977): 338–95.

Johnson, Mat, and Warren Pleece. *Incognegro: A Graphic Mystery*. New York: DC Comics, 2008.

Kannenberg, Gene, Jr. "Graphic Text, Graphic Context: Interpreting Custom Fonts and Hands in Contemporary Comics." In *Illuminating Letters: Typography and Literary Interpretation*, eds. Paul Gutjahr and Megan Benton. Amherst: University of Massachusetts Press, 2001. 163–92.

Kermode, Frank. *The Sense of an Ending*. New York: Oxford University Press, 1968.

Kline, Stephen. *Out of the Garden: Toys, TV, and Children's Culture in the Age of Marketing*. New York: Verso, 1993.

Kochalka, James. *American Elf: The Collected Sketchbook Diaries*. 2 vols. Marietta, GA: Top Shelf Productions, 2004.

Kress, Gunther, and Theo van Leeuwen. *Multimodal Discourse: The Modes and Media of Contemporary Communication*. Oxford: Oxford University Press, 2001.

Krips, Valerie. *The Presence of the Past: Memory, Heritage, and Childhood in Postwar Britain* New York: Garland, 2000.

Kukkonen, Karin. *Contemporary Comics Storytelling*. Lincoln: University of Nebraska Press, 2013.

Kunka, Andrew J. "Intertextuality and the Historical Graphic Narrative: Kyle Baker's *Nat Turner* and the Styron Controversy." *College Literature* 38.3 (2011): 168–93.

Lacan, Jacques. *Ecrits: A Selection*. Trans. Alan Sheridan. New York: Norton, 1977.

———. *The Four Fundamental Concepts of Psychoanalysis*. Trans. Alan Sheridan. New York: Norton, 1978.

Landsberg, Alison. *Prosthetic Memory: The Transformation of American Remembrance in the Age of Mass Culture*. New York: Columbia, 2004.

Leibowitz, Marvin. *Interpreting Projective Drawings: A Self Psychological Approach*. New York: Psychology Press, 1999.

Leja, Michael. *Looking Askance: Skepticism and American Art from Eakins to Duchamp*. Berkeley: University of California Press, 2004.

Lejeune, Philippe. "The Autobiographical Pact." In *On Autobiography*, ed. Paul John Eakin, trans. Katherine M. Leary. Minneapolis: University of Minnesota Press, 1989. 3–30.

Levine, Michael G. *The Belated Witness: Literature, Testimony, and the Question of Holocaust Survival*. Stanford: Stanford University Press, 2006.

Lewis, John, Andrew Aydin, and Nate Powell. *March: Book One*. Marietta, GA: Top Shelf Productions, 2013.

Lukács, Georg. *The Theory of the Novel: A Historico-Philosophical Essay on the Forms of Great Epic Literature*. Trans. Anna Bostock. Cambridge: MIT Press, 1971.

Lyotard, Jean-François, and Jean-Loup Thébaud. *Just Gaming*. Trans. Wlad Godzich. Minneapolis: University of Minnesota Press, 1985.

Maiorino, Giancarlo. *The Picaresque: Tradition and Displacement*. Minneapolis: University of Minnesota Press, 1996. 296.

Malina, Debra. *Breaking the Frame: Metalepsis and the Construction of the Subject*. Columbus: Ohio State University Press, 2002.

Marable, Manning. *Living Black History: How Reimagining the African-American Past Can Remake America's Racial Future*. New York: Basic Books, 2011.

Marchetto, Marisa Acocella. *Cancer Vixen: A True Story*. New York: Knopf, 2006.

Marcus, Jane. "Sapphistry: Narration as Lesbian Seduction in *A Room of One's Own*." In *Virginia Woolf and the Language of Patriarchy*. Bloomington: Indiana University Press, 1987. 163–287.

Marx, Karl. *Capital: A Critique of Political Economy*. Vol. 1. Trans. Ben Fowkes. New York: Vintage, 1977.

———. "Estranged Labor." 1844. *Economic and Philosophic Manuscripts of 1844*. New York: Dover, 2012.

Mautner, Chris. "Graphic Lit: An Interview with James Kochalka." *Panels and Pixels*. May 3, 2007. <http://panelsandpixels.blogspot.com/2007/05/graphic-lit-Interview-with-james.html>.

McCloud, Scott. *Understanding Comics: The Invisible Art*. New York: Harper Perennial, 1994.

McDonnell, Kathleen. *Kid Culture: Children & Adults & Popular Culture*. Toronto: Second Story Press, 1994.

McGlothlin, Erin. "No Time Like the Present: Narrative and Time in Art Spiegelman's *Maus*." *Narrative* 11.2 (2003): 177–98.

———. *Second-Generation Holocaust Literature: Legacies of Survival and Perpetration*. Rochester: Camden, 2006.

Miller, Ann, and Murray Pratt. "Transgressive Bodies in the Work of Julie Doucet, Fabrice Neaud and Jean-Christophe Menu: Towards a Theory of the 'AutobioBD.'" *Belphégor: Littérature Populaire et Culture Médiatique* 4.1 (2004): unpaginated. <http://etc.dal.ca/belphegor/vol4_no1/articles/04_01_Miller_trnsgr_fr.html>.

Miller, J. Hillis. *The Medium is the Maker: Browning, Freud, Derrida and the New Telepathic Ecotechnologies*. Brighton: Sussex Academic Press, 2009.

Miodrag, Hannah. *Comics and Language: Reimagining Critical Discourse on the Form*. Jackson: University Press of Mississippi, 2013.

Mirzoeff, Nicholas. *The Right to Look: A Counterhistory of Visuality.* Durham: Duke University Press, 2011.

Moses, Wilson Jeremiah. *Black Messiahs and Uncle Toms: Social and Literary Manipulations of a Religious Myth.* University Park: Pennsylvania State University Press, 1982.

Mulvey, Laura. "Visual Pleasure and Narrative Cinema." *Screen* 16.3 (1975): 6–18.

Newell, Michael. *What is a Picture? Depiction, Realism, Abstraction.* New York: Palgrave MacMillan, 2011.

Nyberg, Amy Kiste. *Seal of Approval: The History of the Comics Code.* Jackson: University Press of Mississippi, 1998.

Orbán, Katalin. *Ethical Diversions: The Post-Holocaust Narratives of Pynchon, Abish, DeLillo, and Spiegelman.* New York: Routledge, 2005.

Orcutt, Darby. "Comics and Religion: Theoretical Connections." In *Graven Images: Religion in Comic Books and Graphic Novels,* eds. A. David Lewis and Christine Hoff Kraemer. New York: Continuum, 2010. 93–106.

Patterson, Robert J. *Exodus Politics: Civil Rights and Leadership in African American Literature and Culture.* Charlottesville: University of Virginia Press, 2013.

Pekar, Harvey, and Joyce Brabner. *Our Cancer Year.* Illus. Frank Stack. New York: Four Walls Eight Windows, 1994.

Peretz, Eyal. *Dramatic Experiments: Life According to Diderot.* Albany: State University of New York Press, 2013.

Petersen, Robert S. *Comics, Manga, and Graphic Novels: A History of Graphic Narratives.* Santa Barbara, CA: Praeger, 2010.

Phillips, Dana. *The Truth of Ecology: Nature, Culture, and Literature in America.* New York: Oxford University Press, 2003. 146.

Pizer, John D. *Imagining the Age of Goethe in German Literature, 1970–2010.* Rochester: Camden House, 2011.

Porter, James. "Is the Sublime an Aesthetic Value?" In *Aesthetic Value in Classical Antiquity,* eds. Ineke Sluiter and Ralph M. Rose. Leiden: Brill, 2012.

Pratt, Murray. "Dramatizing the Self and the Brother: Auto/biography in David B's *L'Ascension du haut mal.*" *Australian Journal of French Studies* 44.2 (2007): 132–54.

Prentiss, Craig R. *Staging Faith: Religion and African American Theater from the Harlem Renaissance to WWII.* New York: New York University Press, 2013.

Prieto, Eric. *Literature, Geography, and the Postmodern Poetics of Place.* New York: Palgrave Macmillan, 2013.

Prior, Paul. "Moving Multimodality Beyond the Binaries: A Response to Gunther Kress' 'Gains and Losses.'" *Computers and Composition* 22 (2005): 23–30.

Punday, Daniel. *Narrative Bodies: Toward A Corporeal Narratology.* New York: Palgrave MacMillan, 2003.

Rees-Jones, Deryn. *Consorting with Angels: Essays on Modern Women Poets.* Highgreen: Bloodaxe, 2005.

Reitz, Charles. *Art, Alienation, and the Humanities: A Critical Engagement with Herbert Marcuse.* Albany: State University of New York Press, 2000.

Rejaie, Azar. "Late Medieval Self-Portraiture and Patronage in Pietro da Pavia's Ambrosiana Pliny." *Authorship* 1.1 (2011): unpaginated, online.

Roach, Joseph. *Cities of the Dead: Circum-Atlantic Performance.* New York: Columbia University Press, 1996.

Robbins, Bruce. *Upward Mobility and the Common Good: Toward A Literary History of the Welfare State.* Princeton: Princeton University Press, 2007.

Rose, Jacqueline. *The Case of Peter Pan, Or, The Impossibility of Children's Fiction.* London: Macmillan, 1984.

Round, Julia. *Gothic in Comics and Graphic Novels: A Critical Approach.* Jefferson, NC: McFarland, 2014.

Rugg, Linda Haverty. *Picturing Ourselves: Photography and Autobiography.* Chicago: University of Chicago Press, 1997.

Ryan, Marie-Laure. "From Narrative Games to Playable Stories: Toward a Poetics of Interactive Narrative." *Story Worlds: A Journal of Narrative Studies* 1 (2009): 43–59.

Sandell, Laurie. *The Imposter's Daughter: A True Memoir.* New York: Little, Brown, 2009.

Satrapi, Marjane. *Persepolis I.* New York: Random House, 2003.

Saunders, Max. *Self Impression: Life-Writing, Autobiografiction, and the Forms of Modern Literature.* Oxford: Oxford University Press, 2010.

Scherr, Rebecca. "Shaking Hands with Other People's Pain: Joe Sacco's *Palestine.*" *Mosaic* 46.1 (2013): 19–36.

Sherrill, Rowland A. *Road-Book America: Contemporary Culture and the New Picaresque.* Urbana: University of Illinois Press, 2000.

Schudson, Michael. *Discovering The News: A Social History of American Newspapers.* New York: Basic Books, 1978.

Simons, Jan. "Narrative, Games, and Theory." *Games Studies* 7.1 (2007).

Singer, Marc. "Embodiments of the Real: The Counterlinguistic Turn in the Comic-Book Novel." *Critique* 49.3 (2008): 273–89.

Spillers, Hortense. "Mama's Baby, Papa's Maybe: An American Grammar Book." *diacritics* 17.2 (1987): 65–81.

Small, David. *Stitches: A Memoir.* New York: Norton, 2009.

Smith, Greg M. "The Superhero as Labor: The Corporate Secret Identity." In *The Contemporary Comic Book Superhero,* ed. Angela Ndalianis. New York: Routledge, 2009. 126–43.

Smith, Sidonie. "Identity's Body." In *Autobiography and Postmodernism,* eds. Kathleen Ashley, Leigh Gilmore, and Gerald Peters. Amherst: University of Massachusetts Press, 1994. 266–92.

———, and Julia Watson. "Introduction." In *Interfaces: Women, Autobiography, Image, Performance,* eds. Sidonie Smith and Julia Watson. Ann Arbor: University of Michigan Press, 2003. 1–46.

———, and Julia Watson. *Reading Autobiography: A Guide for Interpreting Life Narratives.* Minneapolis: University of Minnesota Press, 2001.

Smith, Valerie. "Reading the Intersection of Race and Gender in Narratives of Passing." *diacritics* 24 (1994): 43–57.

Stewart, Garrett. *Dear Reader: The Conscripted Audience in Nineteenth-Century British Fiction.* Baltimore: Johns Hopkins University Press, 1996.

Stockton, Kathryn Bond. *The Queer Child, Or Growing Sideways in the Twentieth Century.* Durham: Duke University Press, 2009.

Stowe, Harriet Beecher. *Uncle Tom's Cabin, Or Life Among the Lowly*. London: Nathaniel Cooke, 1853.

Vance, Linda. "Beyond Just-So Stories: Narrative, Animals, and Ethics." In *Animals and Women*, eds. Carol J. Adams and Josephine Donovan. Durham: Duke University Press, 1995.

Varnum, Robin, and Christina T. Gibbons. "Introduction." In *The Language of Comics: Word and Image*, eds. Robin Varnum and Christina T. Gibbons. Jackson: University Press of Mississippi, 2002. xiv–xv.

Verney, Kevern. *The Debate on Black Civil Rights in America*. Manchester: Manchester University Press, 2006.

Walker, Brian. *The Comics Before 1945*. New York: Abrams, 2004.

Wanzo, Rebecca. "Wearing Hero-Face: Black Citizens and Melancholic Patriotism in *Truth: Red, White, and Black*." *Journal of Popular Culture* 42.2 (2009): 339–62.

Ware, Chris. *Jimmy Corrigan: The Smartest Kid on Earth*. New York: Pantheon, 2000.

Watson, Julia. "Autographic Disclosures and Genealogies of Desire in Alison Bechdel's *Fun Home*." *Biography* 31.1 (2008): 27–58.

———. "Visual Diary as Prosthetic Practice in Bobby Baker's *Diary Drawings*." *Biography* 35.1 (2012): 21–44.

Waugh, Coulton. *The Comics*. New York: Macmillan, 1947.

Wertham, Fredric. *The Seduction of the Innocent*. New York: Rinehart, 1953.

Whitlock, Gillian. "Autographics: The Seeing 'I' of the Comics." *Modern Fiction Studies* 52.4 (2006): 965–79.

Whitted, Qiana. "'And the Negro Thinks in Hieroglyphics': Comics, Visual Metonymy, and the Spectacle of Blackness." *Journal of Graphic Novels and Comics* 5.1 (2014): 79–100.

Yang, Gene Luen. *American Born Chinese*. New York: First Second, 2006.

Yovanovich, Gordana. *Play and the Picaresque: Lazarillo de Tormes, Libro de Manuel, and Match Ball*. Toronto: Toronto University Press, 1999.

Žižek, Slavoj. *Looking Awry: Introduction to Jacques Lacan through Popular Culture*. Cambridge: MIT Press, 1992.

———. *The Sublime Object of Ideology*. London: Verso, 1989.

INDEX

CPSIA information can be obtained
at www.ICGtesting.com
Printed in the USA
BVOW06*1303050218
507269BV00003B/4/P